My Type of HOLINESS

Striving for Sainthood with the Temperament God Gave Me

Rose Sweet

OSV

Our Sunday Visitor
Huntington, Indiana

Nihil Obstat
Msgr. Michael Heintz, Ph.D.
Censor Librorum

Imprimatur
✠ Kevin C. Rhoades
Bishop of Fort Wayne-South Bend
December 12, 2024

The *Nihil Obstat* and *Imprimatur* are official declarations that a book is free from doctrinal or moral error. It is not implied that those who have granted the *Nihil Obstat* and *Imprimatur* agree with the contents, opinions, or statements expressed.

30 29 28 27 26 25   2 3 4 5 6 7 8 9

Our Sunday Visitor Publishing Division
Our Sunday Visitor, Inc.
200 Noll Plaza
Huntington, IN 46750
www.osv.com
1-800-348-2440

ISBN: 978-1-63966-233-3 (Inventory No. T2915)
1. RELIGION—Christianity—Saints & Sainthood.
2. RELIGION—Christian Living—Spiritual Growth.
3. RELIGION—Christianity—Catholic.

eISBN: 978-1-63966-234-0
LCCN: 2024949871

Cover design: Chelsea Alt
Cover art: *Pala Magrini* by Filippino Lippi, Wikimedia Commons/Public Domain image and AdobeStock
Interior design: Amanda Falk
Interior art: AdobeStock

Printed in the United States of America

Contents

Introduction 5

PART 1: LEARNING THE BASICS

1. Exploring the Past 10
2. Introducing the Types 19
3. Getting Up to Speed 27
4. Tempering the Theory 36
5. Learning Their Language 44
6. Shaping Things Up: Grace and Nature 55
7. Pairing the Personalities 66
8. Comparing the Opposites 77

PART 2: LIVING IT OUT

9. Taking Control 86
10. Wearing a Disguise 92
11. Celebrating Your Sex 99
12. Making Magic in Marriage 108
13. Parenting without Problems 117
14. Taking a Look at Trauma 130

PART 3: LOVING THEM ALL

15. Appreciating the Choleric 141
16. Delighting in the Sanguine 149
17. Respecting the Phlegmatic 158
18. Understanding the Melancholy 169

PART 4: LOOKING TO SAINTHOOD

19. Perfecting Your Temperament 181
20. Assessing Your Situation 191

21. Rooting Out Your Sins 198
22. Creating a Rule of Life 207
23. Making Time for Prayer 216
24. Managing the Media 232
25. Finding a Spiritual Director 241
26. Receiving the Sacraments 250
27. Setting Sights on Sainthood 260

PART 5: TAKING THE TEST
28: Uncovering the Truth 266

Appendix 289
Other Popular Personality Tests 299
Works Cited 302

Introduction

Self-knowledge is so important that, even if you were raised right up to the heavens, I should like you never to relax your cultivation of it.

— St. Teresa of Ávila, Interior Castle

"Rose, you have an eyelash on your cheek." *I do?*

"You have something in your teeth ..." *Again?*

"Come, here. Let me fix your collar." *Sigh.*

You may have a friend like my pal, Elizabeth. Whenever we are together, she is constantly checking me out — head-to-toe — to make sure I am perfectly put together. Elizabeth herself is always composed and has a porcelain complexion that underlies her flawless makeup. I mean, *flawless.*

Lizzie is not really vain; she just loves perfection. Her standards are high, her principles lofty, and her goal is excellence in all that she does. Consequently, she notices every detail that may be out of place. She is properly critical of all that is shoddy, unkempt, or poorly executed when it does not need to be.

Are her criticisms of my hair or clothes mean-spirited? No. She *loves* me!

And I love her. My friends will tell you that it's not in my nature to submit to those who point out my flaws, but Elizabeth's motherly fussing tells me she has my back. She and I also love, share, and value our Catholic Faith and, when it comes to the beauty of holiness, she's my fiercely loyal companion on my "way of perfection."

St. Teresa of Ávila (1515–1582) wants us to be perfect, too. She was (and still is) so filled with the love of God and others that she led the way to perfection for her Carmelite order. Teresa's classic *Way of Perfection* is a guide for us, too, built on the three indispensable virtues of a holy life:

1. *True humility*: This includes not only embracing your littleness but also having a grateful acceptance of how God wired you. Part of attaining perfection is to see yourself accurately — flaws and failures, but also gifts and talents. A deeper understanding and appreciation of your God-given temperament, and how God desires you to live it out, is part of humility.
2. *Detachment*: Teresa reminds us that there are times to fast and times to feast but, in the end, nothing compares to, and all should be ordered to, God's love for us. In this book you'll be reminded that the natural desires that come with your temperament are good, but they can never fully satisfy as God does.
3. *Love of others*: We must see others as God does, in a way that acknowledges and appreciates how God designed them. OK, they are not like you … so what? We'll get to that. They need you, and you need them. Understanding how God created us is crucial to living out the two greatest commandments: loving God first, and then loving ourselves and others rightly.

Self-knowledge is crucial to reaching perfection. Socrates advises us to *know thyself*. The saints of old drew upon this ancient wisdom and the best of their culture, infusing it with the love of God. All the Catholic spiritual masters emphasize the importance of self-knowledge as a first necessary step in the quest for self-perfection.

Saint Augustine prays, "Lord, let me know myself; let me know you." Some worry that focusing on the self is vanity, but we call this the "double knowledge" — knowing the Lord and knowing ourselves as reflections of him. All Christian growth is based on this duality.

The Interior Life Beckons Us

Temperaments are part of our interior lives, even though they manifest in the exterior. Life is lived from the inside out, not the other way around, and we must enter into our interior for the fullness of truth. Augustine sought to know himself honestly — past his abilities and ambitions — to uncover all his disordered desires, attachments, and sins. For all of us, this is quite a heroic undertaking!

Accurate self-knowledge is needed more than ever in a culture where there's so much confusion about the human person. This study of the classic Four Temperaments will reflect something of the mystery of your being made in the image and likeness of God. The world, including our families, friends, spouses, and others, may be quick to point out our sinfulness but slow to affirm our goodness. Sadly, we even do this to ourselves. The truth is:

We are sinners ... *and* each of us is destined to become a saint!

We are fallen ... *and* we have also been redeemed!

We are weak ... *and* in Christ we can do all things!

It can be a challenge to hold these opposing truths in proper tension; it requires our traditional Catholic approach of "both/and" rather than "either/or."

Do you naturally see the negative in yourself and struggle with believing the positive? Are you hesitant before or even fearful of the term *self-love*?

Let's reject the self-indulgent for a proper appreciation of (and gratitude for) the beauty God has imparted to each of us. We have a responsibility to care for ourselves so that we may properly care for others. Too many of us have been judged, or have judged ourselves, by ridiculously impossible standards; we see ourselves "through a glass, darkly" (1 Cor 13:12, KJV). I want this book to help you also see yourself through "rose-colored glasses." To do that, I've called upon St. Teresa of Ávila and some of our other happiest and holiest saints to encourage you throughout the book's chapters. Let them be your traveling companions.

Beyond self-knowledge, I prayerfully hope you are led to some new insight into the mystery of God. Properly understood, the love and study of the human temperaments should always be a path, not a pitfall, to holiness.

• • •

Part 1

Learning the Basics

• • •

Whenever you begin any good work you should first of all make a most pressing appeal to Christ our Lord to bring it to perfection.

— Rule of Saint Benedict

• 1 •

Exploring the Past

Remember the days of old,
consider the years of many generations;
ask your father, and he will show you;
your elders, and they will tell you.

— Deuteronomy 32:7

Sister Maria Bierer, IBVM, was our humanities teacher at the all-girls Loretto High School in Sacramento, California. She was a polished renaissance woman who was musically gifted. Prior to entering the order, she had successfully toured across the country with the popular band Fred Waring and the Pennsylvanians. Sister professionally directed our annual high school musicals and occasionally arranged for our class to take the bus into San Francisco to see world-class plays.

I admired her, but she was so perfect she scared me.

One day she introduced us to the classic teaching of the four temperaments.

"We're going to step into the past and explore a timeless teaching given to us by Hippocrates, an ancient Greek also known as the father of modern medicine."

Oh, brother, I thought. Studying the writings of an old, dead doctor didn't sound like very much fun.

"Around 350 BC Hippocrates noticed four consistent responses in his patients. Dealing honestly with him as their physician, he understood that the way they responded to life in this state was raw and real. Some were naturally gruff and bossy. Some still maintained a rosy outlook even in their illness. Others were dark and gloomy even when they got better. Others were consistently even-tempered. He began to chart and test his theories of human response patterns and gave them names. Because he believed there was an integration of the body and the soul, and that one could directly affect the other, he attributed these response patterns to a person's body fluids."

Ugh. Gross. But it got my attention.

"The label *Sanguine* comes from blood," she lectured. "Hippocrates thought one of his four types had an extra measure of red-hot blood coursing through their veins. They were full of life, excitable, energetic, upbeat, optimistic, and loved rousing humor and fun.

"The *Melancholy*, on the other hand, tended to be a bit more subdued, cautious, and suspicious. They were bright, intuitive, inquisitive, and wanted lots of information, but were naturally more pessimistic and concerned about what could go wrong. He believed they had a greater amount of black bile in their system.

"The *Choleric* was highly energetic and active, naturally took charge of things, was optimistic and quick-witted, but also loud, insistent, and prone to a quick temper. Hippocrates assumed that, like those who'd had cholera, the Choleric had lots of yellow bile in his system.

"Finally, he observed and named his fourth type, the *Phlegmatic*, from the same word we use for the phlegm in your throat."

Umm ... mucous? I hadn't expected that, but it was interesting. I wanted to hear more about the Phlegmatic, and I was beginning to think about where I might fit into these categories.

"The Phlegmatic," Sister continued, "was very even-tempered, kind, thoughtful, careful, and inoffensive. He was steady, compliant, focused, and followed directions, but also tended to shrink from any undue attention or conflict."

I don't think I'm that, I mused. Thirty minutes later, after taking sister's temperament test, the fun stopped. My highest score showed that I was primarily Sanguine. I didn't even read the strengths; I was appalled at what were apparently my many weaknesses, and my face burned with shame: brassy ... flighty ... fickle ... childish ... unorganized ... undisciplined ... untruthful ... inappropriate ... loud ... and what seemed like hundreds more criticisms.

I wanted to die.

"What types are *you*, Rosie?" my friend asked.

"I don't know, I'm still figuring it out," I lied, thereby proving one of my many character defects.

We were supposed to score a secondary temperament, since everyone has two (more on that later), but my answers were all over the place. Thinking back, I was only seventeen, trying hard to be just like my mother, get good grades, and learn how to drive a stick shift. I had very little idea of my interior self.

This is the problem with personality quizzes: We perceive them as pop psychology and afternoon entertainment. But the human person is deep, complex, and mysterious; we are made in the image of God, after all. Unless someone takes the time to guide us into a fuller understanding, taking a personality test can cause confusion and error, and sometimes do more harm than good.

Fast forward almost twenty years. It was the mid-1980s, and my girlfriends and I were passing around our favorite cassette tapes featuring conversion testimonies of popular Christian speakers and authors. One day, I stuck a cassette into my car's tape deck and began listening to a middle-aged woman named Florence Littauer. She was hilarious — and she was talking about temperaments.

Florence was a highly recognized international speaker and a giant among her Christian peers. She and her husband, Fred, had enjoyed what she thought was the perfect life, until the last two of her five children were born. Diagnosed with an incurable disease, they later died. This tragic circumstance humbled her and brought her to her knees before God. She shared in her talk: "All of my brilliant education, my charm, wit, and strength of personality could not bring my babies back. For the first time in my life, I felt powerless. I asked the Lord to change me — and he did."

She and Fred discovered the teachings of the classic four temperaments as a powerful tool to become who and what God created them to be. A gifted storyteller, Florence was excited to share how this study helped her to better understand and love her husband and children. As I listened to her story, I saw many parallels in our lives and became excited that understanding the temperaments could also help me. I gained a new perspective that helped to blow away the black clouds of my old high school humiliation.

I bought her book and took the test. This time, with more life experience and maturity under my belt, I was amazed at how accurate it was — how it not only brought clarity to why I think and act as I do, but shed real light on how I had incorrectly viewed, judged, and acted toward others. Old scales were falling, and new graces were stirring.

As I dove more deeply into the history of the teaching, I was surprised and delighted to learn that the Catholic Church had preserved this timeless study as a spiritual aid. It has been relied upon for the formation of character and the rooting out of sin, and was taught by great spiritual theologians, saints, and mystics — most notably, St. Thomas Aquinas. No wonder Sister Maria had introduced this to us in humanities class! The precious past must be preserved.

Florence and I became the dearest of friends, and we ended up writing, working, traveling, and teaching together for several decades. As I studied temperament history and other current personality theories, especially from a Catholic perspective, I was even able to enlighten her with some of our rich Catholic anthropology.

Now I'm guessing you may be eager to get into the four types, but first let's review two broad personality traits — pairs of opposites — with which you may be most familiar: introverts and extroverts, and optimists and pessimists.

Temperaments Include Introverts and Extroverts

Most people understand the hard-driving Type A (extrovert) versus the easygoing Type B (introvert). Too often, though, these designations are oversimplified and incomplete. They are also often exaggerated, which can be helpful to make a point, but harmful when it is too limiting.

Let's take a deeper look.

An *introvert* tends to first keep thoughts and feelings close to the vest, usually until trust is built or to avoid conflict. Personal safety and security are important to introverts. They default first to being receptive and then, as needed, active. Introverts will preserve their energy. When an introvert is confident and comfortable, he or she can open up and be as loud, in-charge, energetic, or extroverted as any. Introverts:

- Are shy, usually only in unfamiliar territory and until they get their bearings
- Can be touchy-feely, but only after appropriate trust

is established
- Often like to be in charge, but only after they can carefully observe and plan
- Can be energized by people, but only on their terms and amid limited numbers
- Can work steadily at whatever they find necessary or interesting
- Will speak up and love to talk when they are comfortable
- Do love center stage, but will let you go first
- Don't want to be noticed — at first — but their feelings will be hurt if you don't eventually see or appreciate them. Sometimes, they will suffer in silence, and you may not hear about it until years later!

Extroverts are the opposite; they tend to think quickly, openly express themselves, and make decisions, not immediately worrying too much about conflict or security. Clearly, that can be either freeing or extremely foolhardy. They default to being active and then, as needed, receptive. They have a seemingly endless reserve of natural energy. Extroverts:

- Are not *always* wild and crazy and do need and enjoy down time
- Don't need to take charge as long as someone else seems truly capable
- Can eventually get drained by people and need rest — they just tend to last longer in social situations
- Do know how to enjoy being alone, especially with an interesting project
- Do love the limelight but do not need it all the time
- Can get depressed and withdrawn when no one notices or appreciates them. They can also suffer in si-

lence, but not for very long — you *will* hear about it soon, and you will *not* need to guess!

How one responds to physical or psychic space can also reveal an introvert or extrovert. Those who are *introverted* tend to protect their space by keeping a safe distance physically and emotionally — at least at first. *Extroverts* often have no boundaries — intruding into your room, examining or rearranging your things, and invading physical and personal spaces. They want to touch, and their tendency will be to walk right up and give you a big hug. That urge doesn't change, but their behavior may be tempered by circumstance, boundaries, or maturity. Introverts who see jacked-up extroverts coming will want to run! If there is no escape, they will throw up an invisible force shield.

Temperaments Include Optimists and Pessimists

"Optimists versus pessimists" is another broad category we use to describe standard human responses. Do you see the glass as half full or half empty — or does it depend on your mood? Optimists don't necessarily deny the harsh or unpleasant realities, but they lead emotionally with trust and hope. They take things lightly and have a positive mindset and upbeat attitude. Optimists:

- Have the ability to make good things happen
- Can usually handle whatever life throws at them
- See problems as challenges that can be conquered
- Can see the silver linings in the dark times
- Believe troubles will be temporary, specific, or external

Pessimists are often suspicious that things will not go right or end well. Because they care so deeply, they worry for the wellbeing of others and the world. Those with a pessimistic nature:

- May have a difficult time seeing how things could improve
- Can get overwhelmed with discouragement
- Can fear problems will be insurmountable
- Often doubt that good could come from bad
- Believe troubles will often get much worse

While some may think it's better to be an optimist, don't tell that to the brain surgeon who worries until he gets every last part of the tumor. There is a suitable time to be hopeful, when we know we can do all things in Christ who strengthens us (see Phil 4:13). There is also a time to worry, when we know the devil prowls about seeking to devour us (1 Pt 5:8).

Both optimism and pessimism can be carried to an unhealthy extreme, with optimists being incredibly naïve and foolish, and pessimists falling into despair. In the world there are both good and evil, beauty and danger; we need the optimist to remind us of the hope we have and the pessimist to point out the truth of trouble around the corner. Ultimately, though, none of us should stay stuck in any extreme way of seeing the world, striving not to be an optimist or a pessimist, but a realist.

How do these general categories appear in the four temperament types? Of the four types, two are naturally introverted and the other two are extroverted. Two of the types have a more optimistic view of life, and the others tend toward pessimism.

In the next chapter we will introduce the four types in a little more detail. Do you see yourself or someone you know and love in these categories? Maybe you are someone who is both optimist and pessimist, or a little of both introvert and extrovert. It's possible.

• • •

Reflections

Who was a powerful influence or mentor in your youth? What do you remember that he or she taught you?

Who did you want to be like when you became an adult?

Was there a particular saint who inspired you?

• 2 •

Introducing the Types

I praise you, for I am wondrously made.
Wonderful are your works!

— Psalm 139:14

Introvert-extrovert. Optimist-pessimist. Quick and slow. Day and night. Summer and winter. Man and woman. It seems God loves to pair up his creation into distinctly different but complementary opposites.

Just as Adam was not meant to be alone, neither are any of the four temperaments. So, as you're reading, keep in mind that of the following four, you are a natural blend of two of them. The other two are your complementary opposites. More on that to come.

Which two best describe you?

The Peaceful PHLEGMATIC

The easygoing, careful, faithful introvert

The Phlegmatic is naturally well-rounded, even-tempered, kind, inoffensive, and thoughtful. One of the Phlegmatic's greatest strengths is adaptability, and they can easily rise to whatever the occasion may call for. Phlegmatics are sensitive, highly service-oriented, and supportive of others.

As natural introverts, they think and move carefully, slowly, and intentionally. They first watch and wait and then take decisive action, but only as necessary. Phlegmatics don't have the need to run the show, speak first, or be in charge; but don't think they can't. They reserve their energies for the right time and place, and when they are ready, they will move, shake things up, and maybe even outshine everyone. They have a good sense of humor and like a wide variety of people. When they feel safe in their environment and are comfortable and rested, they can be the life of the party or the captain of the ship. But afterward they will definitely need a nap.

While they are usually compliant, you can't force them to do anything, or they will plant their feet firmly in the ground and quietly refuse to move. They will commit when they are ready. They like things clear and simple, and if they feel there are too many choices, they can become indecisive and overwhelmed.

Phlegmatics prefer things uncomplicated and like to find and take the easy way. Not that they are inherently lazy, but they will often find the most efficient, quick, and easy way to get the job done. We could all learn from that. On the other hand, when they like what they are doing or see the necessity of it, they are dedicated, hard workers.

They thrive on peace and hate conflict, sometimes avoiding it at almost any cost. At their best, they make stable, consistent leaders; you can rely on them to be considerate, fair-minded, natural peacemakers and mediators.

They prefer to take life in bite-sized chunks. If too much comes at them at once, they can freeze, become unmotivated, or hide away as a temporary escape. Their basic desire is to maintain quiet peace.

Their optimism and pessimism are generally balanced; their particular emotional needs are respect, feelings of worth, and not being rushed or forced.

When are Phlegmatics troubled? When life, work, or relationships are too stressful, or when there is no relief or escape and they feel powerless. Sometimes they become quiet rebels just to remind themselves (and you) that they still have power.

Stress relief for them includes watching TV, reading, naps, sports, or hobbies.

How can you help them when they are overwhelmed? Leave them alone until they are ready to engage, but don't abandon them. Keep unnecessary conflict down and respect their pace and their space.

The Passionate MELANCHOLY

The deep, meaningful, creative introvert

The Melancholy is all about quality, wanting things done well and perfectly, and when they set their mind to it, they will always strive for excellence. One of the Melancholy's greatest strengths is the passion, determination, and effort they can put into their work, hobbies, art, projects, and relationships.

Like the Phlegmatic type, Melancholies are natural introverts and move with care but also precision. They observe with an eagle eye and catch all the details around them, especially anything that might be out of place or need improvement. They like to engage with others, sharing their thoughts, hearts, and talents, but they wait until just the right time, first keeping up an appropriate guard. Once they feel safe from being unfairly judged, exposed, or possibly ridiculed, they can open up with great energy, warmth, connection, and maybe even a flair for the dramatic.

They have a delightful sense of humor that can be laced with irony, creativity, and color. They like to explain, teach, and train in detail and take pride in perfection. Some are creative and inventive while some are musical and poetic. When they are passionate about something (or someone), they will go to the greatest lengths to suffer, sacrifice, or even lay down their lives for their cause. Yet, with too much self-focus, they may tend to everyday martyrdom, especially when things are not perfect.

Melancholies tend to default to a pessimistic outlook but can be happy, hopeful, and joyful when things are going well. At their core, they are highly idealistic and hold a romantic view of life. Don't constrain or label them; they want the freedom to be creative and unique. They can be suspicious and doubtful and take a longer time to trust others than the other types. Once they let you into their heart, though, no one will love you with as much enduring fidelity.

This type really wants to be understood for all their depth and complexity, but don't fawn or give them false accolades. They don't like undue attention and despise what is not genuine. Their basic desire is for perfection.

Their pessimism usually trumps their optimism, and their particular emotional needs are for meaning, understanding, sensitivity, silence, and space.

They get depressed when ideals are not met, when life, work, or relationships are not perfect, and when there seems to be no hope on the horizon. They can be dark, uncaring, and highly critical.

Stress relief for the Melancholy is alone time, time with a trusted friend, or an escape into art, music, or some distracting creativity.

How can you help when they are discouraged or depressed? Don't try to quickly lift them up. They need to process their pain. Listen to them without trying to fix it. Show understanding and warm, genuine concern. Tell them you will come back later.

The Playful SANGUINE

The affectionate, upbeat, fun extrovert

The Sanguine is all about relationships and connection. Sanguines are delighted to be part of the family, group, club, or committee, and they find people fascinating. One of their greatest strengths is being quick to see and be genuinely interested in all types of people.

They are naturally energetic and upbeat and have a knack for bringing a sunshiny outlook wherever they go. Especially when things are not going well, the Sanguine will at once look for ways to cheer others up and encourage them out of their doldrums. Even if they have no idea how to fix your problems, they will try with great enthusiasm. They want to be available to everyone and are as warm and loving with a large crowd as with a single person.

They're playful, have a light touch, and like to tease. They love to laugh and feel happy and successful when others are also laughing and happy. They love to share with and teach others and are natural coaches and cheerleaders.

They can work hard, be focused on the task at hand, and care about the details, but they can be easily discouraged when it gets too tedious. They are smart but not usually on the highly academic or genius side, which comes most naturally to the Melancholy.

Sanguines are colorful, creative, artistic, and musical, but they care less about the perfection of it and are more interested in the fun of it. Even though they are genuinely committed to you, the conversation, or their work, they can be tempted by any little distraction or excuse to go play for a while. Even though they love people, they don't mind being alone because, somehow, they will make it fun.

The Sanguine type likes to follow and conform — it's a way of belonging, they feel, so we can all get along. They trust others (sometimes too easily) because they don't want to believe in a world where people are not safe. They are quick to forgive, let go, and start again. They want you to notice and acknowledge them, and they love to give and receive verbal and physical affection. Their basic desire is to make things fun for themselves and others.

Their optimism trumps any occasional pessimism, and their particular emotional needs are connection, attention, affection, and approval.

They get sad and even feel sorry for themselves when life, work, or relationships are too difficult, or when no one is paying attention or showing affection.

Sanguines find stress relief in fun, games, movies, shopping, eating, and naps.

How can you help a sad Sanguine? They delight in their senses and love something that looks, tastes, or smells good. Bring food or gifts. Take the Sanguine out to dinner.

The Productive CHOLERIC

The take-charge, bold, practical extrovert

In the morning, the Choleric sits up in bed, surveys the day, and begins to assess the duties to be done even before his feet hit the ground. This type is extroverted, energetic, and is about getting things done — quickly and efficiently. Cholerics are naturally excited and eager to get to work and expect everyone else to also toe the line.

Cholerics genuinely enjoy people and are good at connecting. They don't need center stage, but they do enjoy it. They can be warm, friendly, and quick to laughter and fun, but their primary goal is usually production. They have a natural gift for seeing the big picture, the endless possibilities, and the roadblocks that may be ahead, and they are excellent problem solvers. They learn quickly, are capable and confident, and they make good leaders and teachers.

The Choleric can sometimes put too much on his or her plate but will see it through to the end. They do need rest and understand that balance is part of what makes a person most productive. They expect a lot from themselves and from everyone else, but they can also be extremely generous with their time, energy, and money. They like to conform and cooperate, but only when it makes sense to them; then they are happy to submit and be supportive as a non-leader.

Cholerics are a no-muss, no-fuss type. They don't like unnecessary details, steps, or words when something cleaner, simpler, and more economical would do. They bring order out of chaos and have a knack for organization. They struggle with others who don't get it, move too slowly, or are not on board. They want you to get to the point and sometimes can be too blunt and insensitive in their comments or actions. But they will fight tirelessly for what they believe and are quick to fight for you or any underdog. They are usually not afraid of much and cannot be easily manipulated by others. When things are going smoothly, they can be calm and compassionate to the introverted types, and lively and fun with everyone. Their basic desire is to get things done.

Their optimism generally outweighs any pessimism, and their particular emotional needs include appreciation for all their efforts, loyalty, obedience, and cooperation.

They get angry before they are sad or depressed, and everyone will know they are not happy. They can get impatient and easily irritated when things aren't done correctly, when life is chaotic, and when people are not listening.

Cholerics find relief in a quick, clean detachment from the problem and some time off or alone. Often just starting a new, shorter, and easier project will make them feel much better.

How can you help a frustrated or angry Choleric? Recognize his efforts. Don't ever tell a Choleric to "just calm down." Ask what you can specifically do to help. Then leave him alone because he *will* calm down shortly.

• • •

Did you see yourself in any of these? Don't worry if one or two of the descriptors in a certain type don't *quite* fit you. If we stayed at this introductory stage, we'd be stuck at a pop-quiz level of awareness. To get to a proper and fuller understanding of temperaments, we'll go further into the details and delicate nuances in later chapters.

It will have meaning for the Melancholy.

It won't be too overwhelming for the Phlegmatic.

It will provide practical steps for the Choleric.

And the Sanguine, well, he or she's already having fun, but we'll help them go deeper.

• • •

Reflections

Was there a type that seemed to best describe you? What was it, and why do you think it describes you best?

Did anything trigger doubt or concern for you? Why?

How do you feel about being labeled?

Is there a type you thought might be more conducive to personal holiness? Why?

• 3 •

Getting Up to Speed

It is not good for a man to be without knowledge,
and he who makes haste with his feet misses his way.

Proverbs 19:2

Who doesn't know about the tortoise's sheer determination in Aesop's "The Tortoise and the Hare"? The hare is fast, flippant, and full of himself. At first, we assume he will win the race against the painfully slow and awkward tortoise. But the hare is over-confident and, in typical extroverted fashion, tries to run the race and do a million other things at once.

But the seemingly dull and dimwitted tortoise is no fool! He fixes his eyes on the end goal, blocks out all distractions, and simply begins moving. Undeterred, he plods on, and on, and on … and eventually crosses the finish line to win.

Who would have thought the hare would lose? Like these two characters, we all have our own, sometimes surprising, set of temperamental strengths and weaknesses. Before we dive into that, it's important to understand that temperament, personality, and character are different things.

- *Temperament* is the hard-wired way we respond to life.
- *Personality* includes our temperament, but it is also the sum of our physical, psychological, emotional, intellectual, and social aspects — including style, dress, and mannerisms — all manifest through our behavior and actions. Some of these can be innate (like temperament), learned or developed, or even worn like a mask when needed.
- *Character* is the beliefs, moral values, and ethical qualities we hold.

Each of the three can influence the other. Some people can have a naturally charming temperament, a strong and charismatic personality, but a character that stinks; others can have a contemplative temperament, a socially awkward personality, and a beautiful and holy character.

Yes, we can acquire proper or productive behaviors, especially with parents breathing down our neck or a teacher drilling them into us. But sometimes that exterior conduct gets hung up on a hook like a worn-out coat when we come home at the end of the day. It's important to understand that your true temperament is what comes naturally to you — when required performances end, no one is looking, and the masks come off.

Temperament is the part of our personality that reacts to stimuli. Our temperaments are revealed in how we see and think about ourselves in the world, and how we *first* respond according to four modes: speed, intensity, duration, and direction.

Speed: quick or slow. Are your initial reactions mostly fast and excited, or careful and thought out? The extroverts (Choleric and Sanguine) race through the day, maintain a high speed at night, and then crash at the end. Introverts (Melancholy and Phlegmatic) can also work diligently, maintain a consistent speed, and rev up — but usually only when they consider it necessary. However, when an introvert is being pushed, or wants to get it all done and get home early so he can collapse on the couch, he may seem to be working as quickly as an extrovert. And don't be surprised if you see a balanced extrovert clock out at 5 p.m. and go home early. She may have gotten others to do her work, and she probably has a dinner party for twenty all lined up for the evening.

Intensity: strong or light. Is your first reaction mostly light and easy or more passionate and extreme? The Choleric and Melancholy are the two most driven and intense, with the Choleric intensity readily displayed and the Melancholy tending to stay concealed. The responses of their two opposites — Phlegmatic and Sanguine, respectively — are softer, lighter, and gentler.

Duration: short-lived or long-lasting. Do you tend to quickly forget and move on, or do you hold on and press in? The Choleric and Melancholy responses are the most long-lasting. They endure, and don't give up as easily or quickly as the Sanguine and Phlegmatic. But that's not always good; sometimes letting go and taking another, easier way is the most prudent response.

Direction: introvert or extrovert. Are your initial responses held inside or immediately on display? The Choleric and Sanguine default responses are extroverted, directed outward and on display. The Phlegmatic and Melancholy default responses are directed inward, where they are held for as long as is necessary but then can be directed outward.

Natural Temperament Responses	
SANGUINE	Quick, Light, Short-lived, Extroverted
CHOLERIC	Quick, Intense, Long-lasting, Extroverted

PHLEGMATIC	Slow, Light, Short-lived, Introverted
MELANCHOLY	Slow, Intense, Long-lasting, Introverted

While Hippocrates's theory about temperament sourced from body fluids (also known as the Four Humors) eventually hit a dead end, his general observations have proved accurate for more than two thousand years. We can learn controlled *responses*, such as picking things up a little more quickly or slowing down when necessary, but we never lose our innate *reactions.* When you're trying to find where you or someone else may fit in all this, remember: Extreme forces such as fear can make us all freeze up or bolt like lightning. Drugs, alcohol, exhaustion, and illness can also dull or excite our reactions.

We Are Persons, Not Temperaments

Your temperament does not trump your basic identity. Even though I may tag someone as a Melancholy, that's simply a way of describing one important dimension of an overall makeup; it's not a description of who someone is at their core. We are first creatures willed into existence by God's love. Thus, we are beloved sons or daughters of that same God, destined to share in his divine life for all eternity.

When we isolate temperament without considering the whole person before us — even if that person is ourselves — we do a form of violence against that person. In his Theology of the Body, Pope St. John Paul II says that the human body reveals the person. Similarly, temperaments are just one way that you and I are made visible in the world. They let others see and know something about how we tend to see the world and what we think about life, and therefore how best to love us.

Understanding temperaments can help counter an idea our culture currently promotes: that people are basically useful or not useful. No matter how big or small, how young or old, we must remember that people may *do* things, but they are *not* things. We come into this world with our own little nature, our own inborn preferences and built-in responses to stimuli. We may be introverts or extroverts — or a combination of both — just as we may be tall or short or somewhere in between. Regardless of our natural inclinations, all of them should be ordered to a free and full response to God's love.

Let's be aware of a few guideposts as we journey through the theory of temperaments:

Caution — hyperboles ahead: As a Sanguine, I *may* tend to exaggerate for effect. Yes, I know not every Choleric is a bone-crusher, nor is every Phlegmatic a couch potato. As you read descriptions of the four types, be careful about seeing any of them as a caricature. No one wants to be Choleric if it seems that type is mostly hard, brutish, and unsympathetic. No one wants to be Phlegmatic if it seems that type is weak, wimpy, and lazy. No one wants to be a negative, depressed Melancholy, so some might think they are a cheerful, upbeat Sanguine. But Sanguines have weaknesses, too. The bottom line? Give this study more time and thought so you don't just pick a type that appeals to you or reject one that repels you.

Warning — no cherry-picking: Try not to focus on one aspect and get stuck there. Some have said, "St. Francis De Sales went to parties, so he must have been Sanguine!" Stop and consider: He was wealthy, and the wealthy all had parties; he became a bishop, and everyone invites the bishop to the grand events. So, yes, he went to parties. But to hinge a person's entire makeup on that one fact — especially when we've never really met him — may dangerously derail us from discovering who that person really is.

Go slowly with assigning labels: Don't readily handpick desirable traits for yourself or assign them to others. This will only lead to an incorrect assessment. If we don't want labels quickly slapped on us, we must be careful about doing it to others. Everyone gets depressed at different times and for different reasons. Everyone can work hard when they enjoy it and when the rewards are worthwhile. And everyone likes to have fun. Some have fun in groups; some like solitary fun. Each of the temperaments has an idea of "fun," and that doesn't make them all Sanguine. There is a clear distinction between capacity (I can be *all* these traits) versus inborn tendency (I most naturally *lean toward* these specific traits).

Watch for the different outlooks: Temperamental responses are rooted in the way we first see the world and ourselves in it. You could say:

- Cholerics are like *telescopes*: They are quick to see the big picture.
- Phlegmatics are like *periscopes*: They come up to look around only when necessary.
- Melancholies are like *microscopes*: They see and care about the minutiae.
- Sanguines are like *kaleidoscopes*: They see the sparkle even in the broken pieces.

To use the temperament tool well requires honest and even rigorous self-reflection. And it must be understood properly, as a reflection of man being made in the image of God and not apart from God.

Let's take a quick peek at the four temperamental outlooks:

The Four Temperaments — Quick Overview	
EXTROVERTS	
PLAYFUL Affectionate • Upbeat • Colorful SANGUINE	***POWERFUL*** Take-charge • Bold • Practical CHOLERIC
Relationship-oriented, fun, and sparkling — but easily distracted, often childish	***Results***-oriented, confident, and bold — but sometimes demanding and insensitive
Basic desire: Make things fun	**Basic desire:** Get things done
Emotional needs: • Attention • Affection • Approval	**Emotional needs:** • Loyalty • Achievement • Appreciation
Causes of depression: • Life/work/relationships no longer fun • No affection • No change	**Causes of depression:** • Life/work/relationships are chaotic • No plan • No cooperation
Stress relief: • Fun, games, movies, shopping, naps	**Stress relief:** • Detach from problem; start new project
How to help: • Visit and bring gifts • Take him or her out to eat	**How to help:** • Recognize his or her efforts • Let him or her take charge

INTROVERTS	
PEACEFUL Easygoing • Careful • Faithful PHLEGMATIC	*PASSIONATE* Deep • Meaningful • Creative MELANCHOLY
Service-oriented, adaptable, and kind — but sometimes indecisive and unmotivated	***Quality***-oriented, sacrificing, and dramatic — but sometimes negative and critical
Basic desire: Maintain quiet peace	**Basic desire:** Strive for perfection
Emotional needs: • Respect • Feeling of worth • Peace and quiet	**Emotional needs:** • Meaning and perfection • Sensitivity • Silence and space
Causes of depression: • Life/work/relationships stressful • No rest • No escape	**Causes of depression:** • Life/work/relationships not perfect • No hope • No improvement
Stress relief: • Watching TV, reading, naps, hobbies	**Stress relief:** • Time alone, time with trusted friend
How to help: • Keep conflict down • Respect his or her space	**How to help:** • Listen to his or her problems • Show warm (genuine) concern

Do you see yourself in this chart? Or someone you know? It is tempting to find yourself here now, but hold that thought. There is still so much more to learn! You can refer back to this chart throughout the book, but we will wait until the end of the book (Part 5) to take the temperament test.

• • •

Reflections

When someone offends you, are you quick or slow to let it go?

Can you think of a specific example from your own life? What happened?

Does it come naturally to you to stop and think before you speak or act?

Why do you think self-reflection is crucial to growth in holiness?

• 4 •

Tempering the Theory

Do not judge by appearances, but
judge with right judgement.

— *John 7:24*

I respect the skeptics who are reading this with lips pursed or arms crossed. You are still questioning, may not yet be convinced, and are reserving judgment until the last chapter. Good! I used to think, *What's wrong with you guys?* But now I know the wisdom of being careful and not making quick assumptions or rash judgments. Temperament theory needs to be tempered with a balance between trust and healthy skepticism.

Temperaments are only part of our complex nature. In addition, we can have various physical, social, and cultural characteristics, learning or leadership styles, spiritual gifts, and even love languages. In temperament theory, as with all true things, we are sometimes beset by three temptations:

1. To *simplify* it to the point where we force all these interesting indicators into the same package and move on. (Sorry, don't try to fit Gary Chapman's "five love languages" into the four temperaments. It doesn't work.)

2. To *amplify* it to the degree that we make it so complex and pleasingly precise that it becomes a creation of its own. This only invites the possibility of error and loss of the purity of truth.
3. To *modify* it to suit our prejudices. Some early authors on temperaments mixed in truth with some error and obvious personal bias for the powerful Choleric and perfect Melancholy, and against the poor Sanguine and Phlegmatic. Although these books are still in some Catholic libraries, consider more recent works for the most up-to-date analyses.

Where other avenues address this subject, look for these common misconceptions and remember: Body types do not determine our temperament. Birth order does not determine our temperament. We are only two types each; one cannot be three or all four temperaments. If one scores as three types, one of them is usually a "mask" or wished-for personality. We can mask or hide ourselves — presenting, or choosing to present, as a type we are not (in response to work, pressure, fear, and more), but it is a dishonest presentment. Temperaments do not change, but they can, and should, mature.

The Temperament Test

Some people get nervous about the word *test*, but rather than being a cold, impersonal, "pass/fail" device, psychological assessments can be helpful in pointing us to the truth of both *who* we are and *where* we are.

Who we are, made in God's image, does not change; where we are in our development and maturity can (and usually should) change. Understood this way, temperament tests can be mirrors and maps.

Temperament tests also need validation. Licensed therapists

and other formally trained experts have years of coaching, experience, and scientific methodology to validate many of their assessment tools. They rightly warn against unvalidated, superficial testing mechanisms. However, there still can be truth found in these simple "tests."

Pick one: Are you more like a dog or a cat?

Pick one: Are you more like a cloud or a thunder bolt?

It is true — and sometimes pretty amusing — that some people share similar characteristics to cats and others to dogs. Clearly, these superficial "tests" can never plumb the depths of the human person, but they can quickly identify some truths about us. Sadly, the reverse is also true. Even highly complex testing mechanisms can be wrong. It's important to bear in mind that temperament test results aren't always accurate. Some personality tests can be misunderstood and manipulated. They can also be erroneous or even heretical. Others have become popular in our churches and workplaces. Each is rooted in the classic four temperaments — some loosely based, some watered down, and some so convoluted it would drive even a Melancholy mad. Over the years I've taken and tested most of them and have found that sticking to the basics is best. Refer to the Appendix if you're interested in a brief summary of some other current or popular testing models.

The teaching of the classic four temperaments has matured over the eras. It stands above other models and has been validated by centuries of use by wise — even brilliant — and holy saints and scientists.

As we explore these temperaments, we will also be introduced to many saints who embodied aspects of them. Sir Isaac Newton claimed, "If I have seen further than others, it is by standing upon the shoulders of giants." Pope St. Clement is credited with saying, "Follow the saints, because those who follow them will become saints." The spiritual life is an adventure, and the saints show us the best way to enter in and live it to the full, not in spite of, but because of the temperament God gave us.

In our Catholic saints we have some real titans of the spiritual life, and we can draw from their wisdom and lived example in our study of temperaments. St. Hildegard of Bingen studied Hippocrates's four temperaments and noted other interrelated "patterns of four" in the world: the four elements (air, water, earth, and fire); the four zones of the earth (North, South, East, and West); the four major winds; and the four seasons. Some of her conclusions about the created world could benefit from our modern scientific discoveries, but she was a true pioneer.

In some cases, we can presume much about a saint's natural temperaments, but we can also get it wrong. Here are some important truths to remember about assessing our own or others' temperaments:

- *Maturity can soften the differences*: The natural effects of maturity and sanctity are the wearing down of a person's rough edges. The emotionally and spiritually seasoned man or woman is no longer extreme in most responses and, as such, may be difficult to accurately assess. As my own heart has been pulled more deeply into the things that matter, my Sanguine silliness has not gone away, but it has also made welcome room for seriousness. Maturity has not changed my temperament, but my attitude.
- *Proper assessment often requires careful observation and time*: We may think we know someone's temperament, but if we give it time, we may be surprised. I wanted my outgoing little stepson to be just like me and so prematurely assigned him a Sanguine nature. We were both extroverted Cholerics, but as he grew, I could not ignore the Melancholy

signs: he lined up his toy cars by color, and he went into depression when he could not get his hair part perfectly straight. A Sanguine would have said *the heck with it* and run out to play.

- *Situations can minimize or emphasize one's traits*: For decades in my real estate career, I wrote voluminous reports of great Melancholy depth and detail, including discounted cash flows analyses, internal rates of return, and issues of functional obsolescence. I was driven mostly by my high-achieving Choleric side, so you'd never know there was a silly Sanguine sitting at my desk.

Of our oldest Catholic saints, we know only what has been written by or about them. It would thus be foolish to try to identify with a great degree of accuracy the natural temperament blends of each saint. It's also not necessary. Whatever temperament they were, they showed us a wide range of human responses that may have at first been sinful but in the end were tempered and virtuous. With God's grace, they ordered their natural thoughts and desires to the good, true, and beautiful.

Scripture reminds us that "there is nothing new under the sun" (Eccl 1:9). Those of us who love and teach the temperaments have simply picked up the baton that has been passed along for centuries by others who knew the value of understanding human behavior.

Temperaments Should Point Us to God

"What do you observe, Rosie?"

My dad had just given me an exquisite kaleidoscope for my twenty-fifth birthday, and I was holding it up to the light. I turned the lens, mesmerized by its sparkling patterns.

Dad always encouraged us to take the time to look further

and deeper than what we simply saw on life's surface.

"I see endless possibilities of color and design," I answered.

"What else?"

"Hm-m-m. Well, the little colored pieces are broken and dull in themselves. It's their ability to reflect the light that makes them beautiful."

"And … ?"

"The designs change but the colors do not. There are limited bits and pieces inside, and those do not change."

Then, hoping to win his approval, I posited: "So we are like glass in kaleidoscopes — chips off the Old Block; God has endowed each of us with limited gifts but by allowing his light to shine through us, and going where life turns us, we can bring endless possibilities of beauty into the world."

That was quite an insightful observation, if I do say so myself! And it illustrates some truths about the temperaments: Our temperament makes up a sizable part of our limited "bits and pieces." We are never brilliant on our own, but if we allow God's love to shine through us, even in our brokenness and irregularities, we have unlimited ways of expressing goodness, truth, and beauty in the world. And by looking at ourselves in the right light, we can learn about the God whom we image.

God lovingly poured a part of himself into each of us, and this study clearly credits God as the author and creator, with the four temperaments as sharers in and reflections of his nature. As we come to understand the temperaments more deeply, we'll be better able to cooperate with Our Lord in the purification and perfection of our temperament so we can:

- *Gain more insight into his beauty*: When we experience something good in our or another's temperaments, it points us to see the Source of that goodness.

- *Understand more deeply the beauty of how God made us, and specifically you*: The more we discover about our mysterious complexity, the more we can appreciate — and be thankful for — his handiwork.
- *Identify natural strengths, so as to celebrate and work within them*: Knowing where God has super-equipped us can help free us from trying so hard in other areas so we can begin to polish and hone our temperament's natural skills.
- *Be freed from false guilt or shame about who we are*: The world will frequently tell us to have unrealistic expectations, or shame us for our natural bent. Instead, seeing ourselves as God sees us is liberating.
- *Get off any unhealthy, performance-based treadmills*: When we understand the delights of our temperament and the goodness of how God made us, we can stop trying to be what others expect.
- *Expose and begin to eliminate some of our weaknesses and sinful tendencies*: Understanding our temperament can help us pinpoint specific fears, anxieties, and sin habits that keep us stuck.
- *Develop deeper humility*: Looking down at and judging those who are different from us is something many of us struggle with. This study opens our eyes to the strengths of others and exposes our own weaknesses.
- *See and appreciate the goodness and giftedness of others*: It's one thing to think of others in general terms as "good," but seeing their delightful temperament traits laid out in detail can deepen our appreciation for them.
- *Better understand what others most desire so we can "speak their language"*: When we learn each temper-

ament type's preferences, we can speed it up, slow it down, soften it, or otherwise more specifically meet someone else's particular needs.

- *Learn to love others in the way they want to be loved*: If a temperament type needs affection rather than a pep talk, we can give it to them. If they need silence and solitude, we can learn to give them that, too.
- *Allow Christ to perfect and conform our characters to his*: Once aware of our own temperament's weaknesses, we can work with the Lord to get to the root of them and bring about specific healing and growth.

• • •

Reflections

Do you like or dislike personality tests? Why?

How do you think such testing can be useful in your quest for holiness?

Can you think of a way in which your own maturity has tempered you?

What is your understanding of a healthy humility?

• 5 •

Learning Their Language

And how is it that we hear, each of us
in his own native language?

— Acts 2:8

Each of the temperaments has its own "language." Listen for the fun clues! Some typical words you will hear the four use:

SANGUINE:	Yay! This is fun! That's hilarious! Come on, let's do this!
CHOLERIC:	Move! NOW! Let's nail it down. Get to the point. Wrap it up.
MELANCHOLY:	I'm not sure. But what if? Wait a minute. Not looking good.
PHLEGMATIC:	Maybe. Whatever. I don't know. You pick. I guess. I'll try.

It's been said that when you speak to a man in a language he understands, it goes to his head. But speak to him in his native language, and it goes to his heart. This is certainly true of the temperaments.

In addition to knowing *how* the temperaments respond, we should be curious as to *why* they do. What in the world is driving each of them? In a word: desires. Regardless of our temperament, everything we do or say in some way reveals our desire for happiness. But each of the four temperaments defines "happiness" differently. If we don't understand our temperament, we may not be aware of why we consistently seek attention or compliments, avoid conflict, or try to take charge. Understanding the primary, foundational needs of our temperaments, as well as those of the people around us, makes harmony and productivity possible.

Of the universal hungers for security, value, understanding, and love that we all share, each temperament has a stronger emotional appetite for some of them. This quick review will give you some insights into what is often more important to each of the four temperaments:

Sanguines: "Please love me." Sanguines are naturally warm, loving, affectionate, tender, and forgiving. They truly care for you even if they seem to occasionally forget you. What they give to you they also need from you. They need and thrive on open attention and affection, both vocal and physical.

Cholerics: "Please appreciate me." Cholerics work tirelessly and confidently to look out for their family or team and take care of things for the people in their lives, sacrificing personal needs for the greater good. Since they will lead everyone to safety or success, they need your loyalty and appreciation for all their efforts.

Melancholics: "Please understand me." Melancholics can burrow deep into the mysteries of life — not afraid of the "dark" — searching for that which has profound meaning and value. They want to bring the world the highest and the best, and they long for your understanding and even (when appropriate) your awe.

Phlegmatics: "Please respect me." Phlegmatics work hard, too, but may sometimes be more easily overwhelmed or hesitant. They are the stabilizing backbone of families and companies, and they are supportive, present, calming, and balanced. They want peace and for you to value and respect them.

Now let's look at some other assorted truths about temperaments.

Temperaments Are Driven by Fear or Love

No matter what our unique temperament might be, either fear or love will mold our desires. Healthy fear is necessary as it helps us avoid danger. But when inordinate self-love competes with authentic love, the tension between them feeds inordinate fear. When we're far too attached to something and afraid of losing it, that attachment can make us stressed, obsessed, and lead to us clinging too tightly. That's when fear has replaced trust. Such fear is part of our broken nature, and it is always quietly lurking in the shadows to catch us off guard.

When we have unmet needs, we fear emotional starvation, and some kind of acting out is bound to happen. When children are physically hungry, they begin to cry, scream, wilt, whine, wail, or worry. Perhaps our own childhood needs, long unsatisfied, have us behaving like adult versions of a first grader. No matter our age, the empty interior space created by our unmet needs will manifest in extreme external behaviors. It's fear — and its gang of negative emotions — that drives us into sin.

Sanguines fear no one will see, love, or affectionately embrace them.

Cholerics fear they will fail, and no one will ever follow them.

Melancholies fear no one will ever truly love or understand them.

Phlegmatics fear others will dominate them, and no one will respect them.

But Scripture is clear: *"Perfect love casts out fear"* (1 Jn 4:18). Fear is what lures each temperament off the balanced path and into the black, tangled forest of sin and weakness. Love is what brings it back and sets its feet on the golden path to heaven.

Love — and its posse of positive emotions — rides to the rescue and leads us away from fear and into the direction of holiness and true happiness. Everyone wants to be loved, understood, appreciated, and respected, and that's as it should be. And in the end, when we stand alone before God, he will not quiz us on the four temperaments or any other knowledge, as important as it may be for us now. God will simply inquire of us whether we were willing and able to give and receive love.

Temperaments Are Unequally Distributed

Everyone's blood is red, but not everyone's blood is the same type. The Stanford School of Medicine Blood Center estimates the percentage of people in the world who have the four basic blood types:

TYPE	PERCENTAGE
AB	4%
B	10%
A	42%
O	44%

You can see an unequal division of types. Now, blood types do not determine your temperament, but like them the temperaments are also unevenly distributed. No consistent scientific studies on temperament distribution are available, and those I've found make no important distinction between behaviors that are learned or natural.

In my work and study of temperaments over the last thirty years, I've consistently found far fewer true extroverts than introverts. Think about your own experience in a school classroom, a grocery store, or a church filled at Mass. If something surprising, shocking, or unusual were to happen, how many would remain in their seats and wait, watch, and assess? How many would quickly react, speak out, jump to their feet, or take immediate action? Not a majority. Our culture values extroversion, though, and unless the quiet strength and real power of introverts is understood and honored, they can feel unjust (and damaging) shame for their introversion.

Remember that with human behaviors, all four temperaments can behave similarly in different situations for different motives and reasons. But only two of the four types are most naturally "extroverted": the Choleric and the Sanguine. Everyone can function as a take-charge, hard-working, bossy Choleric — especially in home or work leadership roles — but there are fewer Cholerics than the others. Everyone can be silly, upbeat, and light like the Sanguine — especially when life is rosy — but there are fewer Sanguines than the others.

I'm going to go out on a generous limb here and surmise that God knew we needed more of the kind, careful, methodical, deep, introspective, stable, steady, and thoughtful types to keep the extroverts from blowing the world off its axis.

Temperaments Express with Style

I have a thing for red shoes. My introverted mother, on the other hand, would never even think of calling such attention to herself. Mom had been a brilliant chemist and was both an intellectual Melancholy and an understated Phlegmatic. No sparkle, shine, fluff, or frou-frou for her!

Once, when I was seven, Mom took us kids to the Groth

Shoe Store. She was also an overwhelmed parent watching a tight budget, and with six children to outfit, shoe-shopping was not her idea of fun. After measuring me, Mr. Groth brought out two pairs of shoes for me to try, even though Mom had directed him to bring only sturdy white Oxfords. He opened the second box, pulled back the tissue, and revealed a pair of bright red Mary Janes with little flower cut-outs in the toe. For me, they were gorgeous!

"Do you like these, Rosie?" Mr. Groth asked. Like? I wanted to dance in them forever.

But being the obedient firstborn, I first looked up at Mom for her approval and was dismayed to see a silent but firm scowl on her face. I knew what I had to do. "No, thank you, Mr. Groth. I like the white ones."

"Are you sure?"

I was quiet, but he knew, and tried one more time to convince me — and Mom — to get the red ones.

"They're the same price," he added.

"We'll take the white ones, Frank," Mom stated kindly but flatly.

It was a sad day for me, and in a way, I have been making up for those shoes all my life. As a young girl, I admired my mother and tried to dress as she did: tastefully and simply (Phlegmatic) but also, in her Sunday best and evening clothes, very high quality and elegant (Melancholy). Dad would often take her to San Francisco, to the high-end department stores to buy the latest fashion, but in my little life there was no room for red, or anything with glitter or gold lamé.

Once I moved out on my own and started to gain a little self-confidence, I bought my first pair of bright red shoes — *so* cute! Then I bought another pair, and then in other bright colors, and then shoes with polka dots, bows, and bling. That was many years ago, and I finally got my fill. Today, opting for comfort, I wear mostly slip-ons, but I do still have one stunning pair of red heels.

You may be able to spot a certain temperament type by the way they dress but not always. Dress can function as an art form, a magnet, a social requirement, or even a façade. A taste for the colorful is usually indicative of Sanguine or Melancholy, as both can be the more artistic, showy, and dramatic. If a Phlegmatic woman feels too reticent to call attention to herself, her Sanguine or Melancholy side may convince her to don something daring and allow her exterior to gain attention.

Rumpled and thrown-together can be any of the four if they are late, depressed, or simply don't care. We mustn't isolate dress, however, as the final indicator of one's type because all four can easily adopt a look they like. Still, you can sometimes tell a type by the details. Perfect hair and dress will (usually) signal a Melancholy. Others can come close, but no one is more put-together than they are — except for the Melancholies who prefer to be nerds and geeks (who usually are also part relaxed Phlegmatic). Do you know someone who must get their look just right or they will have a meltdown?

Clothing aside, what is the person's overall look? What are their mannerisms and facial expressions? Phlegmatics can be ultra-relaxed; some adult Phlegmatics still watch TV slouched, lying down, or on the floor. Big, bright eyes and quick, toothy smiles usually belie a Sanguine. Focused, alert, and ready to spring into action? You just may have a Choleric there. Deadpan, serious, or guarded are often Melancholy looks. And yet, all four can be skinny, pudgy, short, tall, big-boned, muscular, or delicate. Others have tried to make a physical correlation here, but there is no credible evidence that body types determine or influence temperaments. Just look at your own family.

You may also see a hint of one's temperament in how he or she speaks and moves. Cholerics and Sanguines tend to be louder and more intense when speaking with others. Some people think they are always yelling when they are not — or at least *they* don't think so. They are fast with words and retorts and are quick to laugh, sometimes at others rather than with them. They often like to call attention to themselves as if to reminds others, "See me? I'm funny!" or "I am in charge here. Don't you forget it."

When it comes to tone of voice, these two extroverts usually need to dial it down, and the introverted Melancholies and Phlegmatics sometimes need to crank it up. On the other hand, a soft, gentle, and even soothing response comes naturally to the introvert. My friend Sherry is a Melancholy-Phlegmatic, and her soothing "FM deejay" voice would calm a raging bull. The Sanguines must work on that. All forms of eloquent speech are usually Melancholy and something the others envy or must work harder to achieve.

Temperaments Move Differently

It only happened once, but I actually saw my Phlegmatic husband run. He was slowly ambling across the street when a car came zipping around the corner. Suddenly, his long legs kicked into high gear! Bob typically saunters and moseys; I usually zip, whip, dart, and dash. He thinks our home is like a dangerous pinball machine where I shoot myself from room to room like a silver ball. Extroverts are fast; introverts are slower — unless there is a fire.

However, I know one Phlegmatic man who sprints through his day, speeding here and there, getting a lot done. He appears Choleric, but he's not. He heads a large organization and feels the pressure of what he must get done, and he hopes that, if he moves faster, he will get to go home and plop into his easy chair sooner.

"Move!" only makes the introvert go even more slowly. Extroverts must remember the introverts will get there in their own time, and others must adjust their own responses accordingly. Perfect Melancholies like to be early or on time, but if anyone you know is slow, tardy, hesitant, or reluctant, don't yell and scream. Do what I do with them: lie about when the movie starts, and they will get there on time.

Melancholies are reserved. Like the Phlegmatic, their handshakes are usually gentle, unless they have learned otherwise. The extroverts are squeezing and pumping your whole arm like a farmhouse water faucet.

Temperaments Have Power

I met my husband again at our fortieth high school reunion. He'd been my senior-year sweetheart and, once I got past how handsome he still looked, I immediately recognized that he was a Melancholy-Phlegmatic. I recalled that Bob played guitar, wrote songs, made homemade movies, and was in all the school plays. He was definitely a creative Melancholy. He was also gentle and slow and an easygoing Phlegmatic. He didn't know the temperaments, but I did, and I knew I had him pegged.

As the night wore on, we reconnected in a warmly reminiscent way. He mentioned several times that he was a "free thinker," and I just smiled knowingly. Creative Melancholies like to think outside the conventional box. He told me that he worked as a professional voice artist on radio commercials. More creativity. I listened attentively to the details of his last forty years and hardly talked about myself all night. Instead of countering or commenting as part of me would naturally do, I had learned to lean in and listen more. He was surprised when I told him that I understood him.

"You do?" he asked. (Melancholies suspect that no one really understands them.)

"Yes, Bob, I know you have such depth that there is no way I could know all about you, but here is what I do know: You are the sensitive, creative type."

I then began to list the Melancholy-Phlegmatic strengths, one by one. I was careful not to be glib and to remember that no one can really know another person after not seeing them for decades. And from the study of the temperaments, I've learned that beneath all our exteriors beat sensitive hearts.

He was astounded. And then, because I know he felt years-long affection from me and was safe in our conversation, he opened up. "Wow, you've just now touched me at my core." He was being funny but sincere at the same time when he said, "You crunched right through the hard, cherry candy and got right into that chocolaty, soft, chewy center of my Tootsie Roll Pop. How did you do that?"

• • •

Reflections

What type of response from others makes you feel most loved?

How do you respond when you feel unloved?

What specific words would you love to hear from others?

What is one way you show love to others through your temperament?

• St. Thomas Aquinas (1225–1274) •

St. Thomas Aquinas was a quiet and studious boy who entered the Dominicans at age fourteen and became a scholastic theologian and Doctor of the Church. Because of his love for and magnificent works on the holy angels, Aquinas is called the Angelic Doctor. He's arguably the most eminent philosophical theologian ever to have lived.

What do we know about his temperament?
He is a good example of the quiet power of the Phlegmatic. G. K. Chesterton said this about him: "St. Thomas was a huge heavy bull of a man, fat and slow and quiet; very mild and magnanimous but not very sociable; shy, even apart from the humility of holiness." We see, too, his incredible Melancholy depth in his methodical and brilliant *Summa Theologica*.

What can we learn from Saint Thomas?
You don't have to be Choleric to be powerful. Stay the steady course, you beautiful introverts! A few months before he died, Thomas received a revelation that so affected him that he stopped all his writing, leaving his dense *Summa Theologica* unfinished. He told his secretary, "The end of my labors has come. All that I have written appears to be as so much straw after the things that have been revealed to me." We can presume Our Lord showed him something of his dazzling glory that put all works on earth into their proper place. Thomas tells us that no matter how magnificent our works, they are nothing compared to the splendor of God. Nothing.

St. Thomas Aquinas, pray for us.

• 6 •

Shaping Things Up: Grace and Nature

Behold, like the clay in the potter's hand, so are you in my hand, O house of Israel.

— Jeremiah 18:6

Michelangelo, the artistic genius and Renaissance master, was part Melancholy. It's sometimes said that he once stood gazing intently at a huge block of Italian marble and remarked, "There is an angel in there, and I must set her free!" He then patiently and skillfully chipped away at the stone until he found her.

In a similar way, God allows life to chip away at us with the promise that his grace will shape and smooth our edges. This is important when it comes to temperaments, because while they do not change, they *can* be shaped.

Some critics take little stock in temperament theory because they believe temperaments can and do change. They'll say, "People are not limited to labels!" or "I don't like it when someone says, 'You are a (fill in the blank)'!" These people are usually defending the effects of God's grace and the power of the human will to choose. And, in that regard, they are correct that people can and do change. But as regards the temperaments, they do change in some ways … and they do not in others.

For example: When we ask a man to get in touch with his "feminine side," we are not asking him to change into a woman. We are asking him to be open to and consider things in a way that may come more naturally to a female. We can ask a Choleric to tone it down, sit back, and be patient, and allow others to go first. We're not asking him to change his nature but his attitude. There's a reason God created him with Choleric gifts — that label is not limiting and certainly no barrier to grace or maturity.

I am *not* the same person I was at age eight, but I *am* the same person *who has matured*. Thus, temperaments do not define everything about us, but certainly part of us. Our temperamental natures will be shaped by how we have been nurtured in life. But just as the color and quality of Michelangelo's marble remained in the newly revealed angel, our raw temperaments will also remain "in radix" (at the root) of who we are.

Another important thing to understand, especially as we explore the temperaments as part of our path to sainthood: Virtue doesn't make our temperament disappear. Virtue makes *vice* disappear. St. Thomas Aquinas taught that grace does not remove or destroy nature but fulfills and perfects it. Grace eliminates fear and shame, sinking roots that run deep into our soul. It enlivens and strengthens us, and it empowers us to receive God's love and then bear it to others.

Sadly, though, as grace builds on nature, so does evil. Our character can be drawn up into the virtues or down into the vices; our temperament, then, will be manifest either in our strengths or weaknesses:

Can inspire us to virtue	Can lead us to vice
Healthy family upbringing	Dysfunctional family up-bringing
Affirmation and love	Criticism and shaming
Attention and support	Neglect and (all forms of) abuse
Discipline and training	Laxity and indulgence
Education	Lack of education
Strong faith practice	Weak or no faith practice
Positive social and cultural influences	Negative social and cultural influences
Maturity	Immaturity
Grace	Sin habits

Time, too, is no guarantor of proper growth and maturity. It takes a willing spirit and continued cooperation with God over the long haul. But don't be discouraged; God will help you take your temperament to the top!

We Can Change Our Behavior, But Not Our Temperament

You can put on a wig or wear new makeup, but you have not made a permanent change. Put in some blue contacts and no one will know your eyes are brown. Outside influences like social environment, family dynamics, age, maturity level, or even birth order may have shaped your temperament — making a "brown" personality appear "blue" — but they do not determine or change your true temperament.

Many other factors can influence or shape our behaviors, including:

Customs and manners of speech: Quiet, refined parents tend to require quiet, refined children around the house. But observing those kids on the playground or at someone else's house, one might not know how quiet and well-behaved they are at home.

Birth order: Where you fit in the family system can shape you, but it does not permanently define or change you. The oldest child is usually placed in an in-charge Choleric role, working, helping, teaching, and even disciplining the younger ones for mother. The true Choleric will thrive on this; the Phlegmatic first-born can dutifully take on these traits but be exhausted and need more naps or alone time. Oldest Sanguines will take charge quickly but forget important details and melt down when it's not fun anymore. First-born Melancholies will be diligent in their role but may slip into imbalanced perfectionism. Middle children can "get lost" in family chaos, but that does not mean they are introverts. Look for obvious high levels of frustration in the extroverts (Cholerics and Sanguines), who can be quick to anger and argumentativeness, pushing and pulling, loud crying, and even manipulation. Look for more subtle signs such as withdrawal in the introverts (Melancholies and Phlegmatics). They can go quiet, disengage, or even disappear. Because these two types do not like to call direct attention to themselves or cause conflict, they might hope you see, love, and value them if they are quiet and obedient. The youngest child may typically be the family clown, but that can come from what is expected or a reaction to other family dysfunction (alcoholism, abuse, and more). Parental exhaustion and even neglect can negatively affect how the younger children are raised, but it can also be a needed and even favorable loosening of too-tight reins. The youngest can certainly be coddled and perhaps become the family "pet," or become an irresponsible risk-taker or a rule-breaker, but these are more issues of virtue, not just temperament. Good parenting happens when Mom and Dad know each child's temperamental needs and preferences and work to meet them as best they can.

Parenting: Most of us learn to pick up some of the traits of our parents — hopefully only the best ones. My intelligent, introverted, Melancholy-Phlegmatic niece, Elisa, knows her temperament but often functions as a take-charge, roll-with-the-punches Choleric: "I know it's my fast-moving, ever-changing Choleric mom's influence. Growing up, we were so often on-the-go that I always had a little overnight bag ready at any moment!"

Peer pressure and social expectations: When we give too much weight to others' opinions, we can get trapped trying to be whatever everyone else and the world think we should be. How draining! Constant comparisons between people lead us into a special sort of hell on earth. There are saints who were vocal, high-energy Cholerics as well as the opposite soft-spoken, low-key Phlegmatics; saints who were lively and charming Sanguines, and those who were deep and even sometimes brooding Melancholies. If you know who you are and strive for virtue, God will give you the grace to perfect your temperament, not shape it to gain the attention and approval of others.

National heritage: We can put on a colorful costume, and it can change our mood or behaviors, but it does not change who we are. Whatever our culture or the customs we have been raised with — quiet, laid-back, loud, or dramatic — depend upon it, they have contributed to the shape and formation of our social behaviors, for better or worse. Remember that the next time you find yourself sounding like your grandparents.

Drugs and alcohol: When we are stuck in an extreme of our

behaviors — over-excited and spinning or lethargic and almost lifeless — we may turn to alcohol or drugs to temper our temperaments. When a revved-up extrovert (Sanguine or Choleric) throws back a shot of whiskey, he will soon settle down into the mellower, all-is-well world attitude of the introverted Melancholy or Phlegmatic. But he is still an extrovert. When the shy Melancholy or Phlegmatic has a few margaritas, she may begin singing and dancing on the tabletops. But she is still an introvert. Occasional alcohol and appropriately prescribed drugs may temporarily help take off an edge, but we should never depend on them to achieve balance. They can cause as much trouble as not. Episodes of exhaustion, injuries, and illness will tend to subdue or shut all temperament types down; chemical imbalances have powerful effects on behavior, regardless of type. For example, low blood sugar might bring out anger and aggression in even the sweetest and most stable of us.

Mental, emotional, or spiritual illness: It's not likely aliens have taken over your spouse or child, but some days it may seem like it. Serious struggles within our relationships with people we love — like mental illness, addictions, and spiritual warfare — can also affect our behaviors. Unless there has been extreme brain damage, the temperaments remain, and you will see them play out in disordered ways.

Serious life disappointments: A priest observed to me that otherwise gentle women seem to get angrier and more demanding as they get older and can "become Choleric." I explained that being angry does not mean one has changed into a Choleric. When we age, our filters thin; some may reach the point where the suffering endured for decades in a career, marriage, or with children is finally too much. They are overwhelmed, done, and angry; time has flown, youth is gone, and do-overs are unavailable. They are disappointed with life, hurting, and, yes, angry. And now they are speaking up, which may make them seem suddenly Choleric.

Age, wisdom, and grace: The closer one approaches to God, the simpler one becomes; we learn to better *listen* to God, to let him *love* us and to love him in return — to allow him to lead us away from all that we cling to so tightly. Part of practicing rightly ordered detachment is to "let go." That's when the Spirit rushes in with torrents of grace. With that grace (and over time), the extroverted Cholerics and Sanguines settle down and become even more docile. Introverted Phlegmatics and Melancholies become fearless and bold. Optimistic Sanguines take greater heed and no longer shame the pessimistic Melancholies, and the Melancholy pessimists begin to lighten up.

If we have responded to God's grace throughout our lives, we will have gained immense wisdom. Our younger natural responses will be led more by our intellect and less by emotions, but when we are older, our temperament will be much more beautifully balanced. We encounter both joyful triumph and sorrowful disaster and, as Rudyard Kipling wrote, "treat those two imposters just the same."

God is our builder (see Heb 3:4), and we are his works of art; he will lovingly and carefully work all things together for our good because he has the perfected vision of each of us always in his mind. His grace is sufficient for us (see 2 Cor 12:9). Trust in God's sometimes painful chisel, and he will give you release from the boulders of fear, shame, anxiety, and worry.

Your Temperament Has No Weaknesses

It may be surprising, but it's true: Our temperaments have no "natural" weaknesses. As Catholics, we believe that everything God made is good. And as Saint Augustine reminds us, God's good creation cannot be destroyed, only weakened or augmented. Our temperaments are part of our human nature, which has been wounded (infected, as it were) by sin, which attempts to move us away from virtue and toward vice. Fortunately, God's super-nature (and the supernatural graces he showers forth) will lead our human natures back to virtue. So, we do not need to overcome our temperaments, only our sinful natures.

With God's help, we can master our thoughts and behaviors and order them to the good. Worried about the devil? Old Scratch cannot create anything new, but he can and does attack our human nature. His seductive voice, the cultural lies, and our own innate brokenness distort our perceptions so that our strengths get carried to the extreme and become weaknesses.

But don't confuse virtue and vice with temperament traits. Sin doesn't begin with our temperament but is rather directed by it. Sin begins in our disordered and darkened thoughts and desires. Our temperamental inclinations are morally neutral, but by an act of the will can be caught up into the virtues or dragged down into the vices. For example: A Phlegmatic's tendency to find the easy route and take it is, in a sense, morally neutral. That trait, moved by grace, will become a virtue, helping a clever Phlegmatic discover the easiest way to cross a raging river, fix a stubborn problem, or even save a life. Fueled by fear and pride, however, taking the easy way becomes a vice.

In the physical world, warm showers and crackling fires are wonderful, but anything too hot will kill you. Chilled drinks and soft snowfall are delightful, but anything too cold will also kill you. So it is in the inner life: Virtue is in the center and, whatever our temperament, any extreme disposition must be eliminated. For example, if fueled by fear and pride, the virtue of *discernment* will move to the extremes of either foolishness or judgmentalism; *love* will be pushed into the two extremes of selfishness or enabling; and *courage* will be moved to the extremes of cowardice or foolhardiness.

What does it look like when fear and pride attack the strengths of the four temperaments? It's not pretty: The playful Sanguine becomes an obnoxious attention-seeker, while the peaceful Phlegmatic becomes a weak, quiet coward. The powerful Choleric intimidates and steamrolls over everyone else, and the perfect Melancholy crushes others with cruel criticism.

Despite negative influences, our goodness is still there. As one might tenderly wash away the heavy rouge of the repentant harlot, God's grace wipes away our fears and our prideful sins to reveal the original rosy face made in his image. As St. Catherine of Genoa reminds us, "I see clearly with the interior eye, that the sweet God loves with a pure love the creature that He has created, and has a hatred for nothing but sin, which is more opposed to Him than can be thought or imagined."

No One Temperament Is Superior

Some think Cholerics or Sanguines must be superior because they tend to produce more than others, or because they are so outgoing and entertaining. However, some Melancholies and Phlegmatics might think *they* are more intelligent and deeply complex. Without grace, none of us is immune from pride. No one likes to feel inferior or ashamed. On the other hand, we can sink into self-pity and unhappiness when we gaze upon the beauty and strength of the others — but stop that. Just stop! Competition can be appropriate, but when disordered, it disregards the importance and value that all four temperaments bring to the human family.

In the Book of Job, God points out how he has made the ostrich:

> The wings of the ostrich wave proudly;
>   but are they the pinions and plumage of love?
> For she leaves her eggs to the earth,
>   and lets them be warmed on the ground,
> forgetting that a foot may crush them,
>   and that the wild beast may trample them.

> She deals cruelly with her young, as if they were not hers;
> though her labor be in vain, yet she has no fear;
> because God has made her forget wisdom,
> and given her no share in understanding.
> When she rouses herself to flee,
> she laughs at the horse and his rider. (39:13–18)

The gorgeous feathers of the ostrich are magnificent, true, but she's not the most tender of mothers. Still, she is strong, fearless, and stands taller and runs faster than even a man on his mighty steed. Like all of us, the ostrich naturally excels in some areas and not so much in others.

When it comes to your temperament, you have gifts that the others don't because God made you as he wished you to be. Thank him for it.

• • •

Reflections

Name some things in your life that you know have shaped your personality.

How did your family of origin or birth order affect you?

Do any of your natural strengths ever get carried to an extreme? How?

How do you think the saints overcame their extremes? Can you think of any examples?

• Saints Mary and Martha •

Saints Mary and Martha were sisters who were close friends with Jesus. We know from Scripture that he often stayed with them and their brother, Lazarus, at their home in Bethany, about an hour's walk away from Jerusalem.

What do we know about their temperaments?

They were complementary opposites. In Luke 10:38–42, we see that Jesus is at their home, and Martha is furiously scrambling around trying to prepare food, serve everyone, and make things perfect. We know she (Choleric) was disturbed and maybe even a little angry at her sister Mary, who seemed to be avoiding work by happily sitting (Phlegmatic) and listening to the Lord.

However, we can also see that Martha was part Melancholy, the type that frets, stresses, and worries more than the others. Most people think Jesus came down on Martha for working and not resting at his feet like Mary. But in the Gospels, Jesus is not calling Martha to put down her work — only her worry: "Martha, Martha, you are anxious and troubled about many things" (v. 41). Martha's busyness was the manifestation of her inner worry; the worry was a result of her thinking how important her tasks were. Work is good, but it must be properly ordered with prayer (and sometimes people) first.

What can we learn from them?

The sisters' story illustrates two different ways to follow Jesus. Both are good, but any way we try to follow or serve him that causes us worry or anxiety must be reexamined.

Saints Mary and Martha, pray for us.

• 7 •

Pairing the Personalities

While the earth remains, seedtime and harvest, cold and heat, summer and winter, day and night, shall not cease.

— Genesis 8:22 (God's promise to Noah)

Temperaments come in twos. By this I mean that everyone is a natural blend of two of the four temperament types. As you consider your two temperaments, you might think of the disciples whom Jesus sent out two-by-two (see Mk 6:7–13 and Lk 9:1–6). Your temperament has a built-in buddy system where each one tempers the other. For instance, on her own my flighty Sanguine would tend to lack the gravity that's required by many of life's situations, but thankfully she is often grounded by my clearheaded Choleric nature. In turn, my light-hearted Sanguine helps my workaholic Choleric turn off the light, leave the office, and go connect with loved ones. Your two temperament types are helpmates; God knew what he was doing when he paired us up.

The other two temperaments are your opposites, meant not to oppress or compete with you, but to enhance and complement you — and sometimes to hold you accountable and balance you. There is some truth in the saying that "opposites attract." Opposites are drawn to one another because they are, in a sense, deliciously "other," completing what is lacking in us. But when understanding and appreciation are missing, sometimes opposites repel.

Here's the thing about personality pairs: no one is all four. Yes, we can experience all four types of responses, but some will be learned, developed, or even forced upon us. Only two will come most naturally to us. "But Rose," I hear you saying, "Saint Paul said to be all things to all people!" (see 1 Cor 9:19–23). So he did, and so we can be all things without changing who we are. I can be kinder and softer with the Melancholies. I can step it up and get to the point with the Sanguines. I can be silly if that is what someone needs, and I can be serious when the situation calls for it. That adaptability is virtuous (and, by the way, it's one of the strengths of the flexible Phlegmatic). As we begin to dig in and discover our types, let's take a look at some ground rules:

1) *Each of us is a blend.* No person is just one temperament, although one can be dominant over the other, to varying degrees. I've often seen my two temperament parts as siblings; one may certainly dominate at times, but there is always room for the other, and I love them both. Circumstances such as parenting, work, socializing, or vacation will set the stage for one of our parts to lead and one to take a back seat.

2) *You may not be an exact 50-50 blend.* This is very common. My sister Barb is primarily Melancholy with some Choleric; in most situations her Melancholy dominates, but in roles where she is a leader, employer, or parent, her Choleric nature quickly steps up. My sister Malia is super Choleric with some Melancholy. Most of the time you'd better listen to her (or, better yet, get out of her way), but you can always count on her sweet, self-sacrificing Melancholy heart.

3) *Different situations (and different relationships) can call for*

us to function primarily in one temperament over the other. You may say that the two sometimes take turns as needed. My third sister, Serena, is a pretty even blend of Phlegmatic and Melancholy. She's smart, kind, easygoing, and careful, but when she is in a familiar or safe place or role, or functioning as a leader or parent, she can (temporarily) be as decisive, bold, or bossy as the rest of us! Sadly, some people mislabel Phlegmatics as weak, hesitant pushovers or lazy couch potatoes, and so there may be a natural resistance to being labeled a Phlegmatic.

4) *You can't be your opposite.* You can head Northeast or Northwest, but not North-South, since those two are directly opposite. So it is with the four temperaments. Sanguines and Melancholies are opposites; you cannot be both of these. Cholerics and Phlegmatics are opposites; you cannot be both of these.

Even if, under certain circumstances, you function as an opposite, you weren't born that way. Sanguines can be serious like the opposite Melancholy, but it's not their default, and they don't stay there very long. As a Sanguine, I used to play mermaid in the swimming pool and later realized what a fun little analogy that was for me: We Sanguines can deftly dive down into the depths and realities of life, but we can't stay there too long without coming up for some air and sunshine. As a Sanguine, I definitely have my "melancholy moments," but they pass.

Melancholies, when relaxed and confident, can often have a joy and a lightness that make them seem as if they are a Sanguine temperament. But their beautiful nature to care most deeply about creation, the state of the world, and their loved ones comes back as a familiar burden of worry.

Cholerics can slow down, step back, let others lead, and be at peace — responses that come naturally to the opposite Phlegmatic. But they must work at this and keep their inner lion on a leash. When he has had enough down time, the Choleric will be readily roused to action once more.

Phlegmatics can be outspoken and bold like the opposite Choleric, but usually only when they feel safe and comfortable in their surroundings where the possibility of causing friction is reduced.

The demands of home, society, or work can move us into functioning in an area that does not come quite as naturally to us. But we thrive best — and are less stressed — living and working out of our true temperament.

5) *You can be both an extrovert and an introvert.* While you can't be your opposite, you can be both an extrovert and an introvert. Or you can be either a double-extrovert or a double-introvert. If either of these gets too out of control, the double-extrovert will explode into the atmosphere and the double-introvert will disappear into the woodwork. Some of you have an extrovert-introvert combination. Lucky you! That combination can help you stay more balanced.

Let's look at the four natural combinations. Don't worry too much about which one is dominant or not. Why? Determining your temperament combination can help clarify your understanding of yourself and others, but a quest for exactitude can also become too limiting. The measure of each part of a person's natural temperament blend can fluctuate from person to person and vary with circumstances, and we must hold a tension between precision and personhood: You are unique and can never be perfectly pinned down here.

Additionally, there may be layers of still unhealed emotional wounds that block some of our natural strengths or make us afraid to be who we are. If you had an overly dominant or otherwise unpleasant parent for example, you may not want to see yourself as that type. We'll address that in later chapters.

SANGUINE and CHOLERIC: The Double-Extrovert

They both have the highest energy levels and a generally cheerful, optimistic outlook.

Playful Sanguine responses are quick, light, and short-lived. Productive Choleric responses are quick, intense, and long-lasting.

The Sanguine-Choleric (double-extrovert) combination says, "We'll all have fun as long as you do it my way!" They might not have the most class, but Sanguine-Cholerics brighten and lighten everyone's load. They do well as leaders if they function within their strengths. They love to be the up-front chairman, with opportunities to boss people around and make them laugh. They both have high energy, but the Choleric side has an intensity the Sanguine lacks.

Both are quick and optimistic. Both temperaments are eager to jump into situations and to quickly engage with others. As to their natural optimism, Sanguines don't really want to think about possible negatives (that's no fun!), and Cholerics are unafraid of problems. Both will say "hello" first to the stranger without any hesitation or reservation. Both will run up to the front of the room and take over — the Sanguine so we can all have fun, and the Choleric so we can all get things done. But in all that eagerness (and self-focus), both can forget, push aside, and even roll right over everyone else.

Both are encouragers. This double-extrovert type is drawn to those who may be hesitant, stuck, fearful, or overwhelmed. Cholerics like to solve problems and like to help others face and tackle tough issues. The Choleric wins when everyone wins! The Sanguine is a great cheerleader, expressing affection by words of encouragement, hope, lightness, and laughter. Both are generous with pats, hugs, slaps, and other physical engagement, but both get easily frustrated when people don't respond quickly enough for them, so they must develop sensitivity.

Both like change and to try new things. There's a big world out there, and both types want to see and taste it all. So do the Melancholies and Phlegmatics — after sufficient consideration and analysis — but while they are counting the cost, the Sanguine-Cholerics have already packed their bags and flown away. They are leaders in changing it up, blowing away the clouds, getting rid of boredom, and spicing up life, but they may risk losing sight of the beauty, value, and security of those things that need to remain steady, stable, and of enduring value.

If all this accurately describes you, you may not always be sensitive, but you will work hard and bring joy to many.

CHOLERIC and MELANCHOLY: An Extroverted Introvert

Those who possess this combination are idealistic, driven, and passionate.

Productive Choleric responses are quick, intense, and long-lasting. Passionate Melancholy responses are slow, intense, and long-lasting.

The Choleric-Melancholy combination says, "I'll be in charge, and you'd all better do it perfectly!" This person may seem the most demanding, but she'll take the whole team to the finish line and buy everyone dinner afterward. Often people with this combination become the CEO and impress others with their flashes of brilliance and generosity. These two are the most intense of the four types.

Both sides of the Choleric-Melancholy are drawn to lofty ideals and principles. They carry the standards of high ideals and fight to preserve timeless principles. One Choleric-Melancholy girlfriend reported to me: "If I were a hired assassin I could patiently hide in a pile of dung for fifteen hundred years, but when I finally emerge, I will quickly and deftly slit your throat." Yikes! In this case, her Melancholy was exaggerating to entertain me, but she was describing this combination well: It wants to go *to* war when necessary but doesn't want to be *at* war. The world needs this powerful combination, but these two types combined can also scare others away. So, they need to occasionally show their heart, with the deeply loving Melancholy shining in this area.

Both are highly ordered. Order makes things move more quickly and with less trouble later. Efficiency increases what the Cholerics love: production! Melancholies may not have memorized the train schedules, but they love the order of both the sciences and the arts. They have complex and structured ways of thinking and a million little drawers in their minds, each filled with treasures. Only they know where everything is, and they usually fret when something is out of place.

Both are driven, but the tenderness of the Melancholy will soften the drive. Of the four combinations, Choleric-Melancholy is the most fueled by high ideals and natural intensity. Those who are mostly Melancholy will drag themselves through many a Via Dolorosa, while the practical mostly Cholerics may question the necessity, yet both comprehend the act of true love behind it. Thus, the Choleric-Melancholy will save the world we're all in.

Both are critical and judgmental. We desperately need that when quality and accuracy lead to truth, or improve (or save) lives, but we don't always need it at home, so they must stifle the urge to correct every little thing. People love, admire, and depend on those with this combination, which, like the hired assassin, might crush them with a look but can also go to the cross for them.

If this natural combination rings true, you may be too intense for some, but you will lead them well.

MELANCHOLY and PHLEGMATIC: A Double-Introvert

Those who possess this combination can readily function as extroverts, but they will *not* be pushed into it before their time.

The Peaceful Phlegmatic responses are slow, light, and short-lived. The Passionate Melancholy responses are slow, intense, and long-lasting.

The Melancholy-Phlegmatic (double-introvert) combination says, "I will sail the seven seas seeking perfection, but not if it makes any big waves." It takes time to earn their trust, but once you do, they'll go to the ends of the earth for you. These are serious, thoughtful people who like to mediate problems or broker office spats and world peace talks.

Both respond slowly and carefully. Slow is different from dull and dim-witted. This combination is both prudent and appropriately cautious when others are too rash or getting ridiculous. These types are drawn to energy and optimism, but they understand the hazards and exhaustion that come from rushing about without caution.

Both are rich in kindness. They're slow to connect, but when they do, the Melancholy-Phlegmatics are all-in. Their patience and persistence make them faithful, staunch, and loyal friends, even though they don't need a lot of relationships; the ones they have are deep and enduring and never surrendered. This combination is naturally kind, gentle, compassionate, generous, and understanding. Phlegmatics will forgive offenses more easily than Melancholies, who may struggle longer with letting go of resentment — although, ultimately, they will.

Both are focused. When something is important to them, people possessing this combination will press in and hold strong and steady, persistently and patiently going far, wide, deep, and high into whatever matter needs attending to. Melancholies will almost kill themselves to seek the ultimate in perfection, knowledge, mystery, or art. The Phlegmatics will keep a steady focus on the important issues they're dealing with, unwilling to let them go, but they may need to take a few more naps in between.

They will quietly surprise the world with solid achievements and brilliant mastery over their interests but must be careful not to hide forever in the library, laboratory, or living room to avoid the busy extroverts who love and need them.

If this combination fits, you may not be in the limelight, but you bring a steady, rich, warm glow to the world.

PHLEGMATIC and SANGUINE: An Introverted Extrovert

Such people are loyal, supportive, and bring a light touch to life's heaviness.

The Peaceful Phlegmatic responses are slow, light, and short-lived. The Playful Sanguine responses are quick, light, and short-lived.

The Phlegmatic-Sanguine (introvert-extrovert) combination says, "I really do like you just the way you are, and I only want to have fun!" These people are not the most productive, but they can be the most lovable. They see humor in everything, enjoy a nice nap, avoid problems, and have no enemies.

Both sides of this temperament blend have responses that are light and short-lived. Neither of these types naturally responds with the intensity of the Choleric or the Melancholy. They *can* be "intense," of course, when cornered or pushed, super excited, or overwhelmed and ready to crash or blow. As a rule, though, Phlegmatic-Sanguines are generally easy to be around. Sanguines respond much more quickly; Phlegmatics move more slowly, after careful observation. Sanguines have higher energy; Phlegmatics are more laid-back. So, this combination is both light and easy — and sometimes a teensy bit too lazy.

They can hold tight but also be the quickest to let go of fears, worries, resentments, and grudges. The Phlegmatic just wants peace again, and the Sanguine just wants to be loved again. Sadly, if the Sanguine is too focused on the fun, and the Phlegmatic on life being easy, both may "let go" too quickly; they'll forget, drop the ball, not follow through, or flake out.

Both are open to being led. Because they trust most easily, Phlegmatic-Sanguines generally comply with rules so that people will love and approve of them and there will be peace.

Both tend to be naïve, too trusting, and avoidant. They want the world and everyone in it to be loving, affectionate, and peaceful. They tend to trust too quickly, but some people should not be trusted, and some conflicts cannot (and maybe even should not) be avoided. The Phlegmatic-Sanguine sighs, "Why can't we all just get along?" and really doesn't get why it's not possible. They can get discouraged and feel overwhelmed by the darkness and intensity of life, just wanting to escape. The Phlegmatic will just disappear, and the Sanguine will laugh it off or go shopping.

If this natural combination is you, you may not get much done perfectly, but (most) everyone adores you!

• • •

Reflections

What two temperaments seem to fit you best most of the time, based on these descriptions?

Can you readily identify the temperaments of someone close to you?

If you have children, how do you see these temperaments in them?

How has God blessed you in your temperament combination? Name at least one way.

• St. Philip Neri (1515–1595) •

St. Philip Neri lived in Rome during a time when there were grave abuses within the Church, and humanism and skepticism were replacing Christian ideals and thinking. Indifference, luxury, and corruption were rife among the clergy. To evangelize the people of Rome became Philip Neri's life work.

What do we know about his temperament?

It's said that from infancy Philip had a docile (Phlegmatic), merry (Sanguine) disposition. He began his lay missionary work on the street corners, making friends and engaging in personal conversations. He didn't believe that piety meant that life was somber — just the opposite. He was amusing and charming and would arrange talks or excursions for others, sometimes with music and a fun picnic on the way. Even given to wine-drinking contests and practical joking, his goal was to establish warm, personal bonds with others. When he eventually became a priest, he could see through people's pretenses yet gracefully get through to them with his warmth and humor. He's called the "laughing saint" who never took himself too seriously and was always ready with an entertaining witticism or joke.

One of his biographers said he was so adaptable he could be all things to all people — a Phlegmatic strength. His days were Sanguine, wholly given up to others, but towards evening it was his habit to retire into solitude, as a Phlegmatic must do, to gather strength for another day's work.

What can we learn from him?

You can be holy and even pious, and still be able to take yourself and others lightly and have fun.

St. Philip Neri, pray for us.

• 8 •

Comparing the Opposites

But when they measure themselves by one another, and compare themselves with one another, they are without understanding.

— 2 Corinthians 10:12

Are you ready to explore some more uncharted territory? *Even opposites can have similarities!* North and South are opposite, but they are both the coldest places on earth.

While one cannot naturally be a light-hearted Sanguine and a deep, weighty Melancholy, the two do have some common ground. Outer responses may be similar, but the inward motives, speeds, and intensities will necessarily differ.

As a teen, I loved sewing my own clothes. Using our allowance for Butterick or Simplicity patterns, my sisters and I would pin, cut, and sew shorts, shirts, and summer shifts. I loved being creative and colorful and congratulated myself on being able to sew in a zipper. That's as far as I got. In later years I could easily hem pants or whip up some simple curtains and was happy with my limited skill.

But my Melancholy sister, Serena, stuck with it and went

above and beyond. She took lessons and became an expert, surpassing me with her top-stitching and perfect buttonholes — all on a basic, old-fashioned Singer sewing machine. As a mother, she went on to sew her children's clothes and school costumes. So, both of us were creative and colorful in our work, but I, Miss Sanguine, was satisfied with "good enough" while my Melancholy sister was driven to become a master needlewoman.

The distracted Sanguine and focused Melancholy are opposites, but — of the four — these two are the more naturally flamboyant, artistic, musical, creative, exotic, erotic, and romantic. The main difference is that the Sanguine responses will be light, quick, and short-lived, while the Melancholy responses will be intense, slow, and enduring. As a Sanguine, I do have my "melancholy moments" of genuine depth, intellectual insight, and heart-wrenching compassion — but I don't linger there for as long as a Melancholy would.

One of the pitfalls of temperament testing is that it can bring out a dangerous human weakness: *constantly comparing ourselves with others.* We can end up thinking far too greatly of ourselves while we sit in judgment of our opposites. *Those Melancholies need to lighten up! Those Sanguines are airheads!*

Or we can fall into discouragement, shame, or even self-pity because we do not have the temperament of someone we admire. Comparison can breed all manner of sinful responses, each rooted in some sort of pride.

But let's consider some healthy comparison in this chapter. Instead of looking at our opposites with criticism or envy, we can celebrate those areas where we are alike, even as opposite.

Sanguines and Melancholies

If you've read this far, you already know that Sanguines and Melancholies are opposites in many of their basic responses to life. The Melancholy naturally leans toward pessimism, the Sanguine toward optimism. Melancholies are careful, sensitive introverts, and Sanguines are attention-loving extroverts. But looking past any extreme behaviors and attitudes that might trigger the other, these two are the most colorful of the four.

Both are musical and artistic: These opposite types both have a natural gift for singing, dancing, painting, decorating, playing instruments, designing, writing, waxing poetic, and other forms of creativity, and both like to confidently push the proverbial envelope in these areas. Both are drawn to other realms, both high and low, and have vivid imaginations. The Sanguine, though, tends to be much more easily distracted (or, like the Phlegmatic, overwhelmed if it gets too complex or deep), unlike the driven, disciplined, and more dedicated Melancholy. Sanguine art will tend to be sweet, upbeat, and a little wild; the Melancholy's may also be quirky (think Dr. Suess), or rich, romantic, exotic, and sometimes dark. Their other temperaments will provide extra drive (Choleric) or a softer, calmer, or steadier dimension to their efforts (Phlegmatic).

Both love deeply and passionately: Sanguines and Melancholies are the sentimental and sometimes maudlin temperaments. When it comes to love, affection, and attachment to others, they are both the most sincere, passionate, and romantic. But (as in other areas) the Sanguine will probably forget her lover's birthday and laugh it off. The lover who forgets the Sanguine's birthday will be treated to some pouting but quickly forgiven. The Sanguine can be as snotty and aloof as the Melancholy, but her smile will come back quickly, accompanied by a hug. The Melancholy will plan the perfect gift for a lover, making sure it is extra special, and will be quietly but deeply wounded if the thing is not a hit. There might be forgiveness, but not forgetting.

Both are the most sensuous: The Sanguine and Melancholy are the most quickly seized and utterly captivated by all that is physically beautiful: art, color, music, taste, touch, romance, love-making — all that is "erotic." The true (and quite Catholic) meaning of *eros* is the upward impulse of the heart toward all that is good, true, and beautiful. It's the fundamental ache of the heart to be completely possessed by beauty in all its forms. It is a noble desire that is meant to lead us to God, who is the unimaginable fulfillment of all our passions. When *eros* is infused with *agape* (love of and for God), it will shoot us to the stars and beyond.

Sadly, we can get too attached to the world's beauty and pleasures. The beauty and pleasures of this world should be enjoyed in a way that leads us higher. When we make beauty and pleasure into a kind of "god," we are not possessed by God's beauty, but obsessed with something less. When that happens, *eros*, not infused with *agape*, can become dark and hedonistic.

Sanguines can get pegged as being the most sexually impure temperament, but that's over-simplified reductionism. Some of the earlier writings on the four types suggest this, and I have, unfortunately, seen it get handed down as fact. But I disagree. Yes, Sanguines are the most quickly, visibly, and physically demonstrative, but that does not always lead to impurity. At a party, the Sanguine can be outwardly (maybe even shamelessly) flirtatious and touchy — so busy laughing and caught up in the fun as to be oblivious to how it looks. That does not immediately mean there is a predisposition to sinful behavior. The thing to remember is that we are all sexual by nature, and *everyone* can be sexually tempted or sinful. Others just hide it better than the Sanguine, who does (admittedly) tend to rush into relationships without taking the time to discern. For Sanguines, it's not the sex that is the big draw as much as the connection and hoped-for affection.

Sanguines and Melancholies bring *eros* to whatever they do. They make the world's greatest sinners and greatest lovers, which — as many of the saints have shown us — are not that far apart. The saint directs those deepest yearnings of the heart upward and is caught up in heavenly love; the sinner turns those desires inward and becomes imprisoned by lust.

Both are dramatic and engaging: Both types may tend to see things in exaggerated ways — who doesn't love a more colorful story — but both are better off when they tamp down that impulse and avoid any habit of useless chatter.

Both can be engaging, highly expressive, and emotionally dramatic but the Sanguine will be quick to laughter or tears, and the Melancholy slower, with a reaction that's deeper and more enduring. Both can be highly theatrical. The Sanguine rushes into the limelight, while the Melancholy saunters slowly to center stage. Like the extroverted Sanguine, the Melancholy introvert has something to say and may also want to be the center of attention, but will wait for just the right time and place to ensure against ridicule. Sanguines don't like ridicule, either, but they will not think about it at first, risking it for attention.

Both Sanguines and Melancholies are comedians. Making others laugh — another art form — is also a way of gaining control and assuring approval. My husband is a double-introvert. But when he is around a small group of people he knows and loves — and where he feels safe to be himself — he launches into silly body movements, cartoon voices, and one-liners. He loves to talk and muse on sometimes-endless details. He is not Sanguine, but he may look like one to those who don't understand the nuances of the temperaments.

Being the clown can also be a learned survival role in dysfunctional families or situations, or a disguise one uses to keep the real self from being exposed.

Cholerics and Phlegmatics

A common label we may hear for these two opposites is the assertive Type A (Choleric) and more passive Type B (Phlegmatic). May I amplify it a little? Cholerics are fast and furious, far-seeing and fearless extroverts. Phlegmatics are measured and careful, single-focused and cautious introverts. Of course, the culture tends to value the Choleric in business and sports, but whom do we value in art, science, or medicine? Trust me, we do not want fast-and-furious structural engineers, dentists, or doctors. Despite being polarized in many aspects, these two have much in common.

Both are uncomplicated: While the Sanguine and Melancholy (opposites) are like complex ice cream flavors (nutty and chock full of swirls, berries, or candies), the Cholerics and Phlegmatics are more like vanilla and chocolate. They're not boring at all, just simpler and with less fuss and flamboyance. Where Sanguines and Melancholies tend to catastrophize, Cholerics and Phlegmatics minimize. "No problem!" says the Choleric. "What, me worry?" asks the Phlegmatic.

Both are focused on the task at hand: With their natural simplicity, the Choleric and Phlegmatic will both stay on the direct path, while the Sanguine will quickly jerk a head around at anything that flies by, and the Melancholy may drift off into the weeds of worry or wistfulness. Phlegmatics can be just as bossy as Cholerics — gentle dictators — but if they run into too much resistance, they'll get tired of trying to manage an opponent and withdraw. Cholerics will likely do more than expected — sometimes that is desirable but sometimes not — but Phlegmatics will do exactly what they are told, no more and no less. Then, they will wait for the boss to issue more orders.

Both are the most easily detached: In relationships, Phlegmatics tend to be satisfied with the status quo, not because they don't care, but because change may be too much effort, or because — not needing much — they are quite content with whatever they have. And they think everyone else should be as well. Push a Phlegmatic or make too many demands in the relationship and he'll cry, "intense," "controlling," or worse, and then will keep his distance.

The Choleric, too, is often more about the work that needs to be done and finds that too much emotional relationship "stuff" gets in the way. Both can seem like they don't care or are cold and cut off. We all need healthy detachment in our lives and relationships, but when Cholerics and Phlegmatics carry this natural ability to be detached too far, it does begin to seem unloving.

The Sanguine and Melancholy souls are the ones who dream, imagine, worry, pursue, romance, and long for deep and meaningful connections. If they get too badly hurt, they, too, can become detached, but that may be tinged with hopelessness or bitterness. If a Sanguine is furiously begging for attention or a Melancholy is fretting over a lack of deep intimacy, it is the more easily detached Choleric or Phlegmatic who will urge a step back and a few deep breaths, restoring calm and balance.

Rightly ordered detachment — sometimes called "holy indifference" — is helpful in understanding the interior life. It seems a contradiction because we think pulling back is unloving, but that is not always the case. Sometimes creating a bit of space may be the most prudent and loving thing we can do. When we hold on too tightly to things (or to others), we have less room for God, or none at all. With grace, proper detachment is achievable for everyone, but Cholerics and Phlegmatics may have a natural head start over the others.

• • •

Reflections

Where do you see yourself in this discussion of opposites? What are some of your own strengths that you recognized from this chapter?

What responses do you have when you recognize some of your weaknesses?

Why do you think God made people with opposite temperaments?

• St. Clare of Assisi (1194–1253) •

As a teen, Saint Clare heard Saint Francis preach and was deeply inspired. Reluctant to marry, she asked Francis to guide her in living a holy and austere life. She renounced worldly living, had Francis cut off her long, beautiful hair, and exchanged her fine clothes for a coarse, brown robe. Francis helped her start a Franciscan religious order for women (first called the Order of Poor Ladies), which today we call the Poor Clares.

What do we know about her temperament?

In the convent, Clare led a quiet life, praying and helping the poor. She and her nuns did no public preaching or teaching, but Clare wrote letters to those who were important to her. For a short period, the order was directed by Francis, but in 1216 Clare, not caring for titles or positions of power within the order, reluctantly accepted the role of abbess at his instruction.

Clare referred to herself by such terms as *mother*, *handmaid*, or *servant* rather than abbess. She was very shy and did not like giving orders. When necessary, she would do so meekly, and with great humility.

Wait! She was reluctant to be in charge? Too shy for the limelight? Quiet, slow-paced, servant-hearted, and always caring for others? While grace, time, and effort can help us all to become more like Clare, these are the beautiful marks of a peaceful Phlegmatic.

What can we learn from her?

As are most Phlegmatics, Clare was most comfortable dealing with others one-on-one. Read some of her letters available on Franciscan websites.

St. Clare of Assisi, pray for us.

Part 2

Living It Out

Therefore, since we are surrounded by so great a cloud of witnesses, let us also lay aside every weight, and sin which clings so closely, and let us run with perseverance the race that is set before us, looking to Jesus the pioneer and perfecter of our faith.

— Hebrews 12:1–2

• 9 •

Taking Control

The way of a fool is right in his own eyes,
but a wise man listens to advice.

— Proverbs 12:15

"You all stay right here and don't move. Rosie, you're in charge."

Mom usually went to the grocery store after she had picked us up from our schools. There was no way she would drag all her children up and down the aisles, so she left my younger siblings in my care for the hour. Imagine it! All nine of us were trapped in the family van with no food, water, or bathroom. The natives always became restless, and I knew chaos would soon ensue. What could I do to distract and entertain them?

Even though I was only fourteen years old, I decided to climb into Mom's driver's seat and put my hands on the wheels. Ready to take them all on an imaginary adventure, I hollered above the din, "Okay, everyone! Where do you want to go?" On cue, they stopped their bickering and rang out in unison, "DISNEYLAND!"

For children in our generation, that truly seemed like the happiest place on earth. Our family had spent three magical days there and often dreamed of returning. The point here is that Cholerics control by driving the bus; Sanguines control by promising fun; but everyone, regardless of their temperament, likes to be in control.

It's part of our human nature to do what we must to get what we need or want so that we can survive and thrive. There are lots of reasons — some good, some bad — why we try to control our environment, but when we do, we are not always at our best.

Have you ever observed that people tend to exercise control in different ways, according to their temperament? Some will take over to be in control ("Do this now!"); others run away or procrastinate to stay in control ("You can't make me!").

Extroverts (Choleric and Sanguine) control actively, while introverts (Melancholy and Phlegmatic) control passively. So, when we hear someone say, "That person is so controlling!" they are usually talking about the bossy Choleric, because of the obvious, loud, pushy behavior. But in truth they *can* be talking about any of the four temperaments.

Sanguines can control with charm or childish acting out; they think humor is like a magic wand that will make troubles simply disappear. Sometimes it works; sometimes it only makes things worse. Sanguines can be sweetly free of fear or manipulation but fall into self-protective methods of self-reassurance, resulting in negative acts of last resort. They will begin by seeing only the positive and dismissing the negative, or making light of things, cheering people up, but sometimes trivializing people's pain. They'll try laughing, disarming, charming, flirting, offering prizes, or bribing, then resort to demonstrative begging, pleading, pouting, or tantrums — even descending into hitting, slapping, whining, crying, or appearing helpless. They're not above pretending, seducing, lying, cheating, or stealing.

Cholerics can control with conviction or conquest. Cholerics believe everyone should be smart enough to listen to them. They don't always embrace the power of listening or offer a kind ear. As with the Sanguines, when the positives fail, the negatives rise; Cholerics start out feeling effective and productive but can fall back on negative actions when things don't go as they planned. Cholerics will try to convince, presenting logic, setting goals, and keeping order. They will delegate, asking clearly for what they need, making quick decisions, and working hard. Frustration, however, brings manipulation, glowering, demanding, and a hot temper that can involve yelling, screaming, barking orders, hitting, grabbing, name-calling, cussing, threats, punishment, or penalties.

Melancholies can control with management or moods. It's good to be critical, but it can go too far. Melancholies think everyone should be perfect and will often let us know if we aren't. That's fine when we want training; it's bad when we want love. Melancholies try to control their environment or relationships by keeping things where (and how) they should be. They research all the details and stay within the budget, striving for perfection. They'll give selflessly to worthy causes. When they feel like things aren't moving toward perfection, they'll become moody, issuing melodramatic sighs and well-planned silent treatments; they'll withdraw and withhold, descending into silence, secrets, lying or snide remarks, name-calling, contempt, and quiet revenge.

Phlegmatics, who think everyone needs to calm down, can control with passivity or procrastination. They have a hard time speaking up. To control their environments or relationships, Phlegmatics will try being flexible, staying reasonably detached, and avoiding high drama. They'll do what they are told, attending to others' needs to keep them happy and avoiding problems by finding the easier ways, while being friendly and helpful.

These attempts keep Phlegmatics fairly peaceful … until they don't work. Then they will resort to nondisclosure, quiet refusal, procrastination, appearing helpless, and hiding. They'll ghost the group, withdrawing and retreating into silence, secretiveness, and lying. They will withhold, speaking quietly and giving only the very minimum required. They will answer with, "Fine," "Sure," "Nothing," "I don't care," or "Whatever" to every question.

The Extroverts might get in your face

Playful Sanguine	**Productive Choleric**
Controls by: Charm, Humor, Begging	*Controls by*: Arguing, Anger, Force

The Introverts might block you out

Peaceful Phlegmatic	**Passionate Melancholy**
Controls by: Delay, Avoidance, Silence	*Controls by*: Moods, Criticism, Shaming

We shouldn't be quick to judge when we see any of the four types in control mode. Control behaviors can come from old, unthinking habits, laziness, selfishness, or fear. Recognize that and remember that most of the time, we do not need to criticize or correct someone who is trying to control a situation. We are all fragile. We all struggle with trust. We are all afraid of losing what we need or want.

The goal of the spiritual life is to redirect our desires away from things, people, and outcomes — even good ones — to God alone. When we realize God is all we need and that he is already present to us, we can begin to let go of the things we try so hard to control. St. Teresa of Ávila says it so succinctly in her Bookmark Prayer: "Let nothing disturb you. Let nothing frighten you. All things are passing away. God never changes. Patience obtains all things. Whoever has God lacks nothing; God alone suffices."

When we trust God more, we will surrender to him; when we surrender, we will unclasp our firm and sometimes fearful grip on our life's steering wheel. And when we permit God to drive, we don't have to wait for heaven for true joy. At every moment, even at this moment, Our Lord wants to take us unto himself, truly the "happiest place on earth."

• • •

Reflections

What control responses did you recognize in yourself?

Can you think of a time when you felt controlled by someone else? How did you react?

When do you think control is necessary?

How might a need to control hinder our advancement in holiness?

• St. Genesius of Rome (d. c. 303) •

According to legend, Saint Genesius was a renowned actor and comedian who led a theatrical troupe during the reign of the Roman Emperor Diocletian in the third century. Before his conversion, he wrote numerous popular plays mocking the secret rites of the Christians.

What do we know about his temperament?
We can't be sure, of course, but Sanguine and Melancholy are the first to take to the stage. Most of the great thespians, playwrights, and even comedians who excel in satire and sarcasm are part Melancholy. To win the emperor's favor, Genesius took on a role ridiculing Christian baptism. During the play he hoped for lots of laughs, but when the other actor poured water on his head, Genesius had a vision of God's hand touching him and an angel who showed him that his sins had been washed away. While reciting the act of faith during his performance, Genesius was seized by the truth of what he was saying. He converted, there and then, to Christianity.

The emperor was infuriated, demanding that the actor recant his faith. When he declined, the outraged ruler ordered him to be tortured. When Genesius still refused to worship pagan idols, Diocletian had him beheaded.

The details of the Genesius story can't be verified, but he has been revered throughout the centuries in many countries.

What can we learn from his story?
Even if the truth is obscured by a role we play or a mask we wear, God can reach through to draw us to himself.

St. Genesius of Rome, pray for us

• 10 •

Wearing a Disguise

For though I am free from all men, I have made myself a slave to all, that I might win the more. To the Jews I became as a Jew, in order to win Jews.

— 1 Corinthians 9:19–20

"Do you wear glasses?"

"Um, no."

"Do you have smaller earrings, maybe simple pearls?"

"Well, I could get some."

"Pull your hair back. Let's see how that works."

The custom stylist was helping me with my first day appearing in court for a multi-million-dollar real estate case. I'd been hired to appraise the property and would be appearing as the expert witness before the judge, jury, and opposing counsel's team of expensive lawyers. Their goal was to make me look incompetent. Even though I was an authority in my field, I also had to look and act it.

Fair or not, people judge us on appearances. My job was to convince those in the court of the facts and my professional expertise, reliability, and integrity. I was only thirty years old and single, and only now learning that sexy hair, sparkly earrings, and funny retorts might be assets at a cocktail party, but not in the courtroom. I had to leave my silly Sanguine side at home.

Before leaving the office for the big trial, I asked Dad how I looked.

"Very professional, honey."

"I'm still a little nervous, Dad."

He looked me right in the eye and said something I will never forget: "Rosie, who inspected that property inside and out? Who did weeks of intensive research? Who interviewed the buyers and sellers? Who knows more about that subject property than anyone else in the room? More than the judge, the jury, or the highly paid lawyers?"

"Um … me?"

"*You* are the expert," he reminded me. "Don't worry as much about how you look. Remember who you are."

Certain situations — especially at work, at school, or in public — call for certain behaviors. We may need to "veil" part of our natural responses and present ourselves in ways that look like the other temperaments. In court, I had to present as a serious Melancholy not to deceive, but to help others to trust me. Sanguines can genuinely feel and act "Melancholy" because they do go into the deep, and they do care about the details. As explored earlier, the difference is that they don't go there as quickly, nor do they stay there as long.

Modification or even temporary repression of your nature for a greater good is virtuous. This begins in childhood when little Sanguines learn how to settle down like the Phlegmatics in church, or Melancholies learn to stop moping, and Cholerics step back to let others have a turn. It continues throughout adulthood as we see what others need and expect of us, and we freely choose to respond accordingly.

When we modify or hide part of our true nature out of fear

or deceit, however, our disguise is less like a veil and more like a mask. In psychological terms, "masking" is considered a defensive behavior in response to fear of rejection or some social pressure. For what we may think is a good reason, we don't want our true self to be seen, and so we hide behind outward dress or behavior. Any of the four types might suppress or adjust their natural responses when there is a risk of others withholding approval, affection, or attention. Being human, all four are susceptible to the threat of others heaping criticism, shame, or contempt on them, pressuring them into being what they are not. Masking in that sense is perfectly normal.

Hiding ourselves behind a mask is not always done deliberately or with malice. It's most often a typical response to the trauma of being exposed, feeling unsafe, and lacking the skills to navigate the situation or the relationship. One Phlegmatic man admitted to me, "My real estate sales boss was a high-powered Choleric — so much so that he really was a bully. He expected me and everyone else in the office to be like him, so I tried to act and talk like him. I even started to talk louder and swagger until my wife told me I was being a jerk. Ha! She was right: I was being an imposter because I didn't want to get fired. One day I had the courage to tell him, *'I'm not you, I will never be like you, and I don't* want *to be like you. I'm an easygoing guy but I get the job done. You need to respect that.'* Do you know what he said after that? 'Good; now let's get to work.' Can you believe it? I had been so afraid to be my Phlegmatic self for no reason."

Why We Try to Hide Our True Selves

We must all work to change our sinful or broken habits, but we should not be forced by fear to deny and suppress our God-given natures. Sadly, we can lose sight of our true temperament and assume a different persona, even for a lifetime. Cultures, families, and societies can make us feel that, if we are not who they want us to be, we are worthless.

Introverted Phlegmatics will put on an energetic, high-power face that suits for a while — the imposture will seem to give protection against being rushed, revealed, or rejected and can provide a sense of authority where conflict skills are lacking. The action will finally be exhausting, though.

Extroverted Sanguines will wilt while trying to be Perfect Peter or Polly. Still, they'd rather say "No" to the shiny new shoes mother clearly disapproves of, opting instead for maternal approval and acceptance.

Extroverted Cholerics will pretend passivity when seeing they cannot wrestle control in their closest relationships, but they'll find someone else to dominate, like talking down to the waiter or salesclerk.

Introverted Melancholies, who like to entertain, will act like the cheerful clown or life of the party, but there is likely to be a touch of sarcasm or a bitter edge. Inside they may be dying.

Sadly, the longer we hide behind a behavior, especially for approval, the more we may end up believing this is really who we are and losing track of ourselves. Self-pity and resentments may build and show up in biting sarcasm, anger that seems to come out of nowhere, or overindulging in eating, drinking, shopping, or sleeping. Over time, sustained pretenses may also invite deep depression and lead to mental illness. Ask the Lord to help show you if you have been wearing a disguise and if it is time to take it off.

Bl. Carlo Acutis has something to say about this. A young, self-professed computer geek, he observed: "We are all born originals, but many of us die as photocopies." Pope Francis praised him: "Carlo did not fall into a trap. He saw that many young people, if they seem to be different, end up, in reality, looking like each other, by running behind what powerful people impose on them via mechanisms of consumption and stupor. In this way, they do not let the gifts that the Lord has made for them flow into them. They do not offer the world these personal and unique gifts that the Lord has sown in each one of them."

All of us may be similar to someone of the same temperament, but as we grow in our understanding of types and temperaments, we will learn to love our own temperament and to let it shine, so we will never be photocopies.

Some people try on the traits of another temperament because they desire to be something other than what they are. Who isn't attracted to a beautiful, vivacious Sanguine with a bright, sunny smile — or an elegant, cultured, and sophisticated Melancholy beauty brimming with confidence? Who doesn't admire the strong, fearless Choleric who walks into a room and dominates, or a gentle, loving Phlegmatic whose warmth draws everyone near?

I would like to be all of these! But only two come most naturally to me, and even then, I must work to keep them balanced. I will try to develop strengths that do not come as naturally to me but not at the expense of rejecting the truth of who I am.

God Made Us to Be Saints

It is good to see and be drawn to the unique beauty in the other temperaments, but our attractions do not define us. When we feel like an ugly duckling — trapped in a temperament not of our choosing — we reject the beautiful swans that we are.

Each of the four temperaments has something wonderful and unique to offer the world. If we wrongly label Phlegmatics as always lazy, or if being Melancholy sounds too depressing, no one will want to be either one. If all we ever do is tout the bright, sunny nature of the Sanguine or the capable, super-human virtues of the Choleric, everyone will want to be them! That's not fair to any of the four.

Let us not worry too much about how we look to others.

Let's instead remember what Dad told me and *remember who we are!*

• • •

Reflections

Think of a time when you "veiled" your natural responses out of necessity to respect the needs of others. What was the situation? What came of it?

Think of a time when you wore a "mask" out of some sort of fear of rejection. What was the situation? What was the outcome?

Is there a false personality you're still wearing that you'd like to remove? What is it? How do you think you could start to take it off? Ask the Lord for his help in this.

Why do you think the saints were unafraid to be just who they were?

• St. Augustine of Hippo (354–430) •

St. Augustine of Hippo was a theologian, philosopher, and bishop. His writings influenced the development of Western philosophy and Western Christianity, and he's a Doctor of the Church (known as the Doctor of Grace). His many important works include *The City of God*, *On Christian Doctrine*, and his *Confessions*.

What do we know about his temperament?

By his own admission, even as a youth Augustine was daring and unafraid to push boundaries (Choleric). By age seventeen he was living a hedonistic lifestyle; he took in a woman as his lover, had a son by her, and stayed with her for fifteen years. But while studying at the university, he had also fallen in love with wisdom and truth, and eventually (at age thirty-one) he fell in love with God and became a priest.

He was a deeply expressive and romantic Melancholy. He wrote that when he gave up his mistress, his heart was "racked, and wounded, and bleeding." Once he directed his heart away from lust and toward God, however, his perfected and poetic passions remained, reflected in his beautiful prayers and poems. He had a powerful intellect and was a stirring orator; his writings are deep and rich in philosophy and theology, and he preached thousands of long and creative sermons.

What can we learn from him?

No matter how old we are — or what sinful past we have — we must keep moving away from all the exciting and sexy distractions of the world and into the heart of God. As he wrote in his *Confessions*: "Late have I loved thee, O Beauty ever ancient, ever new, late have I loved thee!"

St. Augustine of Hippo, pray for us

• 11 •

Celebrating Your Sex

We've been deceived by the thought that we would be more pleasing to God in our own way than in the way God has given us.

— *St. Catherine of Siena,* Dialogue

Vicki was my roommate for seven years. In our early twenties, we met at work, moved in together, and set up a cute and comfortable apartment. Both single, and with no marriage prospects, we were alike in so many ways but complete opposites in our temperaments. We were perfect for each other!

We both loved Mexican food, driving to faraway places on the weekends, and listening to Carole King on the stereo. Vicki was creative, sensitive, a good cook, and she made me laugh with her droll Melancholy humor. Prone to occasional mild depression, she'd take to her bed and let me know it was her (overwhelmed Phlegmatic) "escape sleep." I learned to give her space but then would lure her out by suggesting a fun shopping spree or a wild-and-crazy road trip. She was neat, methodical, and never in a rush. I learned to slow down a bit and be less of a Sanguine slob around her.

I loved Vicki dearly. And I was shocked when someone asked if we were lesbians. Back then, deep, enduring friendships were not so quickly romanticized or sexualized. It's tragic when the purity of being pals is soiled by the "masters of suspicion" who are constantly looking to be titillated. Yet I suppose from the outside, I could have appeared to be the "husband" in the relationship, while Vicki seemed to be the "wife." But that language is both limiting and misleading. Those labels are less about the sexes than an attempt to identify universal *roles* that are both opposite and complementary. They are the two halves that make a complete whole. This relationship reality — dualism — is everywhere in creation!

Male and female are the biological versions of the much bigger, cosmic "masculinity" and "femininity." *Masculine* and *feminine* are descriptive words not limited to persons but are universal principles. The universal "feminine" is that which responds, opens, and receives — like your wall socket. The universal "masculine" initiates, penetrates, and donates — like the electrical plug. The "feminine" flower opens to receive; the "masculine" bee enters and deposits. The "masculine" heavens surround, envelop, and overshadow the "feminine" earth, which opens to receive the sun, the wind, and the rain. Her seeds are germinated and together, in this cooperative "embrace," they produce new life. Thus, properly and cosmically understood, "masculine" and "feminine" are both (a) unchangeable universal realities and (b) changing roles in and out of which both sexes can move according to temperament or roles.

In God's relation to everything — from angels to humans to matter — he is the initiating Masculine. We love him only "because he first loved us" (1 Jn 4:19). All of humanity (male and female) is "feminine" in this analogy, opening our hearts to be tenderly and powerfully possessed and penetrated by God's love, our hearts to be "impregnated" with divine life, and to bear that divine life and love to the world.

Pope St. John Paul II said of this spousal analogy found in Scripture:

> It is obvious that the analogy of earthly human love of the husband for his wife, of human spousal love, cannot provide an adequate and complete understanding of that absolutely transcendent Reality which is the divine mystery, both as hidden for ages in God, and in its historical fulfillment in time, when "Christ so loved the Church and gave himself up for her" (Eph 5:25). The mystery remains transcendent in regard to this analogy as in regard to any other analogy, whereby we seek to express it in human language.
>
> At the same time, however, this analogy offers the possibility of a certain cognoscitive penetration into the essence of the mystery.

For our purposes in this book, the important thing to understand is that temperament does not define one's sex. Biology defines one's sex. As humans, we exist as a single entity composed of body and soul, and that unity is so profound that it forms a single nature (see *Catechsim of the Catholic Church*, Nos. 364–365). Who has a female body, has a female soul. Who has a male body, has a male soul.

A woman *can* have natural feelings, preferences, and responses that are considered globally "masculine" — most often because of her temperament. That still doesn't make her a man. Even when and if she assumes a traditionally masculine role in her work or any relationship, she is still a woman. There is an obvious corollary with men, as well.

The topic of body and biology is complex and important, and excellent Catholic resources are available for study and understanding. It's the Church who has always taught that — hard-driving or gentle — a woman is still a woman, and that — commanding or compliant — a man is still a man. And *vive la difference!*

Our attractions also don't define our sex. Let's admit it: Women like to look at other women, and for a variety of reasons. Most of the time we can be comparing or judging. As a Choleric, I appreciate the beauty, softness, gentleness, and elegance I find in Phlegmatic women, and sometimes think I would like to be more like them. They naturally have graces I do not, and I love to be in their presence. While I am attracted to them, I do not need or want to reduce or characterize that admiration into expressions of sexual desire.

The admiration for or intimate friendship we have with our same-sex friends is an affirming gift. We should thank God for the relationship, revel in the joy it brings, and remember to celebrate all womanly beauty.

The same is true for men. If a gentle, creative, introverted man admires his Choleric brother's take-charge machismo, let him admire! Such admiration is perfectly natural and moral, as it is run through the intellect, rather than genitalia.

Sex Does Not Determine Temperament

Just as our temperament does not determine our sex, so our sex does not determine our temperament. I hear some generalize, saying: *Men like to go into the store, get what they want, and get out. Women like to browse up and down the aisles.* This, of course, is not always true. Some men love going up and down all the aisles and seeing what's there, whether in the hardware store, auto parts shop, cigar emporium, hobby shop, or even the grocery store. It depends on their mood or temperament, not their sex.

One time, Bob suggested we get ice cream. When we parked

the car along a quaint street lined with shops, I headed straight for the ice cream vendor and went inside. Bob was nowhere to be found. I went back outside and saw him a few blocks behind me, looking in all the windows.

"Where were you?" I impatiently demanded. We were supposed to be going for a jamocha almond fudge, not inspecting the entire city! My husband is a curious Melancholy and free-and-easy Phlegmatic who used the ice cream to build a long, lingering, and creative outing. He has said of Choleric me: "You're too literal. *I'm* liberal!"

Another common generalization holds that women talk too much, and men do not. Ha! Melancholies and their details and interesting side topics can use 1,000 words to another's 10. Choleric women get to the point and hope you will, too.

Historically, men have typically been expected to be leaders: bold, fierce, commanding. That's terrific if he's an extrovert, but where do the kind, gentle, easygoing men fit in? Is your quiet, laid-back son or spouse "effeminate," or is he just a healthy, content, introverted male who is unlike his rowdy father or brothers? If he likes drama, costumes, fantasy, cooking, gardening, or any art interest traditionally viewed as feminine, quite possibly he is simply a deep, creative Melancholy.

Conversely, women have historically been expected to be sweet, quiet, supportive, and docile. That's fine for the introverts, but where do we loud, confident, extroverted women fit? A tom-boy daughter who hates pink and perfume is most likely a no-nonsense temperament who doesn't have time for what she considers fluff. Think about it; the division between masculine and feminine can be seen most clearly in the contrasting Choleric ("masculine") and Phlegmatic ("feminine") traits:

Choleric Strengths	Phlegmatic Strengths
Bold	Gentle
Adventurous	Adaptable
Self-reliant	Submissive
Outspoken	Obliging
Forceful	Diplomatic
Animated	Reserved
Decisive	Friendly
Mover	Patient
Leader	Supportive
Chief	Contented
Productive	Consistent
Promoter	Pleasant

A common form of assuming a false persona happens when men resist being labeled the *peaceful* Phlegmatic because they, their wives, and even the culture expect them to be a *powerful* Choleric. No "feminine" men allowed! (Note: With the other two types, the quick cultural caricatures tend to be that Sanguines are "childish" versus the Melancholies who are deep, wise, and more "mature.")

In more recent times, the feminist movement started in the late 1800s and exploded in the 1960s. As the culture became more aware of the need for women's full range of social and legal rights, "women's lib" also appeared. A distorted view of true feminism, it claimed that to be truly liberated women must compete with and act like men: loud, in charge, and running the show. They must reject anything that looks like feminine stereotypes and even the social graces that men had been willing to offer them, such as opening doors, paying for meals, and helping them to handle difficult tasks. Helen Reddy sang what became a familiar cry: "I am woman, hear me roar."

Then some men, fed up with the angry, bossy female, decided to embrace their "feminine side," and we saw the rise of the swishy, fashion-conscious beta male. For crying out loud. What a gender-confused mess we have been in for so long!

Society has served all of us poorly by glorifying the extrovert and not appropriately honoring the introvert. Too often "real men" are conditioned to be brute sports enthusiasts or insensitive louts, with beefy biceps and bulging egos. As a result, the sensitive, creative, or genius Melancholy-Phlegmatic men may find themselves trying to walk with a swagger, talking louder than they must, or expressing anger as a means of self-assertion. And we've seen naturally gentle women trying to take on what seem to be masculine behaviors.

In other words, men are still men, and women are still women, but they can share temperaments, just as the two sexes can have the same blood type or hair color.

When we don't fit in, we search for some explanation to avoid feeling ashamed. Just as the Ugly Duckling discovered, though, there *is* a reason for the confusion, and it's not that we are trapped in the wrong body or were born with some unusual sexuality. It may simply be the temperament we were born with.

We limit ourselves and others when we don't understand the role that temperament plays in all that we are. Taken to a horrible extreme, some may even try to surgically or chemically change their biological sex, thinking their "masculine" or "feminine" temperamental preferences are a primary indicator of their truest selves. Gender dysphoria or confusion is a complex topic and worthy of much more study if you or someone you love is dealing with this. But understanding how temperament impacts the way we inhabit the world can help all of us embrace our natural tendencies while also embracing the fullness of our masculinity or femininity. Today more than ever, we must help others to understand and embrace their natural temperament.

• • •

Reflections

What do you think of the relationship between one's sex and one's temperament? How does understanding the role of temperament help you to accept and celebrate the unique woman or man God made you to be?

How would you explain this concept to someone who is struggling to embrace their God-given personality?

Can you name a strong, handsome, heterosexual male who is also easygoing, kind, and gentle? Or a kind, beautiful, heterosexual female who is also bold, forthright, and a strong leader?

Can you think of a modern male saint known for his gentle, quiet demeanor?

• Pope St. John Paul II (1920-2005) •

Pope St. John Paul II reigned as the head of the Catholic Church for twenty-seven years, from 1978 to 2005. He was and still is a beloved saint who left us not only his prolific writings but also the Luminous Mysteries of the Rosary.

What do we know about his temperament?
He was deep, passionate, and creative (Melancholy), and he loved the theater; in his younger days, he was a playwright. He was a brilliant philosopher and a polyglot who learned fifteen languages. He was also a strong, steady, even-tempered leader of the Church (Phlegmatic) who excelled in being a diplomat. We can see the Phlegmatic strengths in his humility and simplicity; he was known to accept suffering quietly, and he was patient and met challenges with gentle humor and in an unruffled manner. Another hallmark of the strong Phlegmatic is his stubborn and uncompromising defense of the truth. This unyielding Phlegmatic strength infuriated some of his critics.

His Theology of the Body — a series of 129 short talks given at his Wednesday audiences from 1979 to 1984 — reveals his deep Melancholy nature. In it he develops a rich and beautiful study of Scripture's "spousal analogy" (which earthly marriage is modeled on and draws from), and the tender and divine love of the Bridegroom for his bride, the Church. His understanding of what it means to be a man or a woman is magnificent.

What can we learn from him?
Just as man and woman are different but equal in dignity, so, too, are the temperaments.

Pope St. John Paul II, pray for us.

• 12 •

Making Magic in Marriage

You got to find somebody who likes the same stuff. Like if you like sports, she should like it that you like sports, and she should keep the chips and dip coming.

— Alan (age 10)

When people ask me, "Which temperament should I marry?" I reply, "The one who knows how to love you rightly."

The previous pages explored what to expect with each of the temperaments — good or bad — in any relationship. But more important than temperament (especially in marriage) is our wisdom, maturity, and ability to love others as Christ loves us. The good news? All four temperaments, cooperating with God's grace, have that ability.

In my book on romance, I share Pope St. John Paul II's four marks of the marriage bond drawn from how Christ loves his Bride. The right spouse for you is one who both intends to and can love you:

- *Freely* — with no grave fears, pressures, force, or selfish agendas

- *Fully* — with nothing held back and unimpeded by serious attachments or addictions
- *Faithfully* — with you first in his heart and with your greater good as a primary goal
- *Fruitfully* — with an openness to life, both human and divine

With maturity and grace, each of the four temperaments has the natural capacity to love a spouse as Christ loves his Church. As we've seen, relationship troubles do not stem *from* the temperaments but show up *through* them. In this chapter let's consider some truths about how different temperaments may be drawn to one another.

There Is No Perfect Marriage

No matter her temperament, every woman is wired to have a soft, surrendered part of her soul toward her husband. That tender vulnerability allows him to enter and implant himself into her heart. But when we have been violated and are then afraid, we will naturally shut down at least parts of ourselves for protection. We must ask God for the courage to forgive and the wisdom to develop healthy relationship skills.

No marriage is perfect — the struggle is real! So, please seek out any good resources that will help you to prepare, discern, or live within the challenges of matrimony. In addition to all I've shared thus far, consider the following when it comes to the temperaments and marriage:

There is no perfect temperament: They all have strengths and weaknesses. Marry only after enough prayer, time, and deep and honest discussion. Seek input from those you trust, and without any serious pressure or agendas of your own. We are most properly disposed for choosing marriage when we already have purpose, contentment, and joy without it. Even though in many ways it is the most important relationship we can have, marriage must add to our life, not become the center of it. That place is reserved only for God.

There is no perfect spouse: Only God can meet your deepest needs; no human can bear the weight of those desires. Never tolerate abuse from another, of course, but also consider when good enough may be good enough.

We are attracted by the strengths and repelled by the weaknesses: We are drawn together by our differing strengths, but it's our weaknesses that can drive us apart. When faced with a character defect in oneself or the other, remember the underlying strength that has just been distorted by fear or sin. But in remembering the good, don't overlook the negative, especially if it is serious. Before marriage, discern carefully with magnifying glasses. After marriage? Get rid of the microscopic lenses and keep those rose-colored glasses within reach.

Sidebar: Some people incorrectly believe it is merciful to tolerate habitual neglect, disrespect, or abuse from another — even a spouse or child. Allowing oneself to be put in physical or emotional danger to keep the peace is a grave offense to one's own dignity, and it allows the offender to remain in his or her sinfulness. Beyond tolerating the occasional offense, we must never cooperate in another's sin in that way. Rose-colored glasses can assist us in mercy and forgiveness, as long as they do not blind us to real threats.

Warning: If you are functioning in an extreme in either of your temperaments, you may be likely to attract another who is operating in an extreme. Regardless of sex, dominant, bullying types attract the meek little mice. Overly powerful women (natural or masking) usually attract excessively passive men, and overly powerful men most often attract excessively passive women. Passivity and submission are not always virtues. Anyone who is operating in extremes is likely carrying unhealed wounds that are fueling these responses. If you find yourself here, I encourage you to seek wise and holy counseling to help restore balance.

Same is comfortable; different is exciting: When someone is like you, you feel safe, familiar, and comfortable. It's easy; there are no communication gaps to close and little effort to be made. But someone who is different can be interesting, mysterious, and even exciting. Both of those desires — for someone who is the same and for someone who is different — are good. The problems start when we see *same* as boring or *different* as threatening. There are a lot of psychological factors at play here and they are mostly rooted in some fear that drives a normal desire to an extreme. Temperament extremes are usually the tip of a psychological iceberg that signals a need for counseling. Don't be afraid to dive below the surface with a good guide and find out what is really going on. Jesus told us that if we would abide in his word, we would know the truth and it would set us free (see Jn 8:31–32). We forget that the process is sometimes longer and more painful than we would want. But it's worth it.

Opposites Don't Always Attract

It's human nature to boil complicated truths down to bite-sized nuggets to save time or space. I've often done that throughout this book and my dear, sweet, Melancholy editors were all over me. *Explain. Give us more. Why did you say that? Is that really true all the time?* Argh! But I appreciate them because keeping things too short and simple often hides the deeper truth. Such is the case with the popular maxim "opposites attract."

The truth is that sometimes opposites do attract and sometimes they do not for reasons we've discussed. Let's take a closer look at whom the temperaments may be drawn to, and why, when it comes to romance and marriage.

Cholerics are naturally drawn to Phlegmatics: Whether in marriage or friendship, the brave, outgoing leader and the strong, loyal supporter are drawn to and need each other. The overworked and stressed Choleric needs the Phlegmatic's stable, quiet peace. The sometimes stuck or overwhelmed Phlegmatic needs the clearheaded Choleric to lead the way. Both play their heroic part in any adventure, and thus Cholerics and Phlegmatics can be beautifully suited to one another.

In my decades of doing this work, I have not seen a true Choleric marry another Choleric. Why might that be? Well, there are fewer Cholerics in the world than Phlegmatics, to start with. Moreover, Phlegmatics who are capable heads of household or workplace bosses can mistakenly think (and act like) they are Choleric. Wives who *want* their husbands to be the take-charge type will define them as such. Phlegmatics who have some high-energy Sanguine can think they are Choleric. And finally, Phlegmatics who do not want to be labeled as couch potatoes will identify as Choleric.

If you think you know two wedded Cholerics, I'll bet one is a naturally adaptable and capable Phlegmatic. I suspect the marriage of two Cholerics would be more common if both were to reach a point of a mature, healthy, and holy integration. At marrying age, most of us are surely not there.

Choleric men don't usually show long-term, romantic interest in Choleric women. They have wonderful fun with and deeply respect us, but when it comes to romance or a life partner, they prefer the soft, sweet gentleness of the Phlegmatic. It's the same for the Choleric woman who is attracted to the Choleric in men, but usually marries the kind, easygoing Phlegmatic — not necessarily so she can dominate him, but because she is attracted to and needs the calm, steady quiet that he can bring.

After the honeymoon, though, the Choleric will be irritated by the Phlegmatic's slow stubbornness, procrastination, or indecision. The Phlegmatic will have been attracted by the Choleric's strong, firm, take-charge disposition, but may end up feeling dominated, controlled, and disrespected. The Phlegmatic may be constantly running from reality while the Choleric wants to shove people's faces in it. The Choleric must back off, and the Phlegmatic must step up. Cholerics and Phlegmatics can have a happy and mutually supportive marriage, but they both must understand and appreciate their differences.

Phlegmatics may be drawn to another Phlegmatic: Despite the magnetic draw of opposites, some Phlegmatics will marry another Phlegmatic. If they have been dominated by Cholerics, and have no confidence in their ability to deal with or are exhausted by them, they will marry someone more like them — someone seemingly safer and more comfortably familiar.

Do you recall Jane Bennett and Charles Bingley in Jane Austen's *Pride and Prejudice*? They are described throughout as being similar in nature with a simple kindness; they are good-natured, friendly, and gentle. They avoid conflict, resist seeing the bad in others, and have a steadfast love. No dramatic ups and downs, no hot-headed prejudice or cold, arrogant pride as with Elizabeth and Darcy. In contrast, Jane and Mr. Bingley's love is shown to be mildly dull. I suspect those of us who are older and wiser would welcome a little "dull," which really is another name for peace.

Who will be the leader in this pair? Usually, the one with more intense Melancholy or the one with high-energy Sanguine. There are other reasons Phlegmatics may marry each other, though. As there are fewer natural Cholerics, there are more natural Phlegmatics. Also, Phlegmatic men conditioned to function as leaders at work can be quite capable as heads of the family. Two Phlegmatics can have a long, peaceful, and contented marriage. They must be on guard, however, not to have a marriage where disappointments are quietly and bitterly endured, buried, and never discussed.

Melancholies tend to be drawn to Sanguines: Sanguines are a cool drink of water to the Melancholy, who is thirsty for lightness, laughter, and sparkle. Melancholies are mysterious and romantic to the Sanguine; their richness and depth feel intoxicating. But since both types are also the most passionate and dramatic, they can exhaust each other with their ultra-highs and lows.

The Melancholy may soon tire of the Sanguine's disregard for detail and apparent lack of deep concern and, with aloof criticism and nasty barbs, may crush their spirit. After too many years and tears, the Sanguine will simply stop caring and skip off to seek attention elsewhere — if not in an affair (emotional or otherwise), in fun trips and other forms of entertainment and play. Some Melancholies who find the Sanguines too coarse, loud, flighty, or fickle will flirt with them but not marry them. Sanguines, being less fussy and more (naively) optimistic might — sad to say — just marry anyone who says, "I love you."

If you are Melancholy or Sanguine, don't worry: With maturity and grace, these two can learn to lean into and love each other with both tenderness and ferocity.

The Trouble Is Not the Temperament

If you are having trouble in your marriage, seek help. Don't spin wheels focusing on he-does-this and she-does-that. "Communication" is not the real issue, but a symptom of something much deeper. Look past the emotional behaviors to find the root of the disordered thinking that will be slightly different for each temperament.

Oh, how I pray that everyone who reads this will discover the truth: Each of us is burdened with self-importance, something I know we do not want to bring with us when meeting our heavenly Spouse. The cross of learning to live with and genuinely love another for his or her own sake will help smooth the edges of our egos. In God's amazing, crazy, and brilliant economy, earthly marriage will help to prepare the soul for the sweetest marriage of all. As St. John Vianney encourages us, "You must accept your cross; if you bear it courageously it will carry you to Heaven."

• • •

Reflections

What "type" have you always dated? Why do you think that is?

If you are married, what "type" did you marry?

What particular challenges have you encountered between your temperament and that of your spouse? How do you complement one another?

How do you think understanding your spouse's temperament can help you grow in holiness?

• St. Thérèse of Lisieux (1873–1897) •

Saint Thérèse was a Carmelite nun whom Pope St. Pius X called "the greatest saint of modern times." You may know her affectionately as "The Little Flower," who, from heaven, delights in showering roses on those on earth.

What do we know about her temperament?
Thérèse's mother described her as generally happy but also sometimes easily frustrated and overwhelmed (Phlegmatic). She also said that Thérèse was very intelligent and remembered everything (Melancholies never forget). She didn't want to be the center of attention and preferred the safe intimacy of her family, where she could be herself. Her sister, Celine, said Thérèse developed a fondness for hiding.

At school, she was bullied. Thérèse suffered very much because of her sensitivity, and she cried in silence. Furthermore, she avoided the boisterous games at recess, preferring to tell stories or look after the younger students. When she entered the Carmelites at age fifteen, she wanted only to lead a hidden life, to pray and offer her suffering for priests, to forget herself, and to increase her discreet acts of charity.

What can we learn from her?
Thérèse believed that it was not necessary to accomplish great, impressive acts of heroism. She wrote, "The only way I can prove my love is by scattering flowers, and these flowers are every little sacrifice, every glance and word, and the doing of the least actions for love." Her Melancholy high ideals coupled with her Phlegmatic simplicity gave us her famous "Little Way" to holiness. May we all begin by doing small acts with great love.

St. Thérèse of Lisieux, pray for us

• 13 •

Parenting without Problems

Train up a child in the way he should go, and when he is old he will not depart from it.

— Proverbs 22:6

Rose: "Well, you four, what should we say about parenting in this chapter?"

Melancholy: "Be very careful. You can never adequately address all the important issues about being a good parent in one chapter. After all, there are thousands of books, courses, videos, and more on parenting. What makes you think you have anything different to add to the many who have come before you?"

Phlegmatic: "Melancholy is right. It's a *huge* responsibility. We have already put in a lot of helpful charts. Can we just skip parenting and be done?"

Choleric: "No, that's ridiculous. Just give them a few tips — bullet points. If they want more, they can get it elsewhere."

Sanguine: "I like that! Short and sweet. Let's tell the funny story about Mikey!"

Different Kids Need Different Parenting

My stepson, Mikey, and my sister Barb's little Phlegmatic son, Joe, were close in age and grew up like brothers. Choleric Mikey would usually boss Joe around, but Joe was generally happy to go along. One day they had been particularly and willfully disobedient, and even though I was sure Mikey had been the ringleader, they both needed correction. I called them in from play and announced, "That's it! I've had it. Have I been talking to myself all this time? You two will be doing chores for the rest of the afternoon!"

I assigned Joe the Windex duty for every glass window, door, and tabletop in every room and sent Mikey to clean the bathrooms.

A few minutes later I noticed Joe. He was slumped over the glass coffee table, despondent and depressed, pushing the paper towels around on the table slowly and dramatically as if the whole world needed to see how miserable he was. His little body language seemed to say, "Why did I ever listen to Mikey?"

This satisfied me. But from down the hall I was surprised to hear Mikey cheerfully whistling the Pink Panther theme. When I walked in the bathroom, he was working away, scrubbing the toilet, wiping the counter, and cleaning the mirrors. The little Choleric was productive, so he was much too happy. *This will not do as discipline*, I decided.

Recalling that Cholerics hate to do nothing, I sent Mikey to his room, told him to sit on the bed, and forbade him to even touch any toy, read any book, or rearrange the bedcovers. He had to just sit there. For an hour.

He hated it.

And Phlegmatic Joe? Well, I let him continue to polish every glass surface in the house until he was exhausted.

The boys were both perfect angels after that.

A whole separate book could be written to help you more

deeply understand the dynamics between parent and child and each of their various temperament combinations. This chapter will give you some insight into how your own temperament might affect your parenting style. While it's vital to know your children's temperaments, it's equally important to first know your own. As a parent, your call to holiness will play out in these four ways: (1) being aware of your own temperamental strengths and weaknesses and how they affect your family; (2) understanding how you may be drawn to or triggered by certain temperament traits in your children; (3) seeing, loving, and guiding your children according to the particular needs of their temperament; and (4) teaching them how they are called to love others in and through *their* temperaments.

Growing up with eight siblings — and many more neighborhood kids who were often at our house — I had an early education in the temperaments. I just didn't know it at the time. As a Choleric, I loved doing dishes after dinner. Some of my Phlegmatic siblings, though, ran away and hid in the bathroom. I loved to be in charge and make things fun! Why did they keep calling me bossy? In school, I got an A in art but a bad checkmark for my desk being messy and for losing my papers. My Melancholy sister Barb never lost her papers. She did things perfectly, but I felt bad for how she would work herself into a tizzy over it. My Phlegmatic sister Serena was so quiet! Also with some Melancholy, she was often worried and didn't want to try new things. My Choleric brother Charlie protected us from stray dogs, but he could also bully us. I only had one Sanguine sibling: John was an outgoing, energetic, and silly middle child, but he could melt into tears and whine incessantly when he felt pressed between his Melancholy brothers.

My Phlegmatic mother — who never referenced the temperaments — would instinctively parent us according to our types. Unless I was overstepping my bounds, she put me in charge and allowed me to be a junior mother. She soothed Melancholy Barb, spent quiet one-on-one-time with the Phlegmatic and the Melancholy introverts (who were most like her), and called all of us to be virtuous.

I was glad to have rediscovered the four temperaments by the time I had a family. It gave me a jump-start in seeing my children (and others' children) as God made them, in knowing their particular emotional needs, and in catching my own temperamental biases in the parenting process. Thankfully it has made all the difference in the world!

The Hand That Rocks the Cradle Rules the World

"What is the matter with you?" "Why are you so difficult?" "Why can't you be like your sister?" These are common questions some hear while growing up. Children who think they are a disappointment to their parents may spend their life looking for someone who will like them as they are. And if they don't find a place where their personality is appreciated, they may experience problems.

It doesn't take long for a parent to realize that not all children act alike, but seldom do we know what to do with each one — the peaceful, easygoing one; the moody, tearful one; the bubbly, into-everything one; and the one who is issuing presidential proclamations from his or her crib. If you parent all children the same way, some will flourish, some will rebel, and some will give up trying to please you. As Catholic parents, we'd be aghast at the thought of trying to change the sex of our children surgically or chemically, but we may be doing something similar when we try to form them into a different temperament. This attacks the deepest core of who they are as persons made in God's image.

Recognizing each child's type and particular emotional needs, and making efforts to meet them, will give parents an immensely positive power and will help them successfully launch children into the world. If you are a parent, don't be afraid to:

- *Gaze upon their loveliness*: Studies reveal that a child's sense of self, value, security, and wellbeing is largely formed first through the gaze of his mother's eyes. Of course, throughout life, a father's love is equally vital. Just as we see and love our child's smiles, or their chubby little cheeks, we can and should see and love their different temperaments, too. For those children whose temperaments may be different than yours, let them see in your eyes and hear in your voice that you value them just as they are.
- *Be aware of your own disposition*: Our own temperamental desires can get in the way without us realizing it. One Melancholy mother, who holds lofty ideals and high hopes for humanity, believed she should be able to sit down calmly and discuss behaviors with her two tiny tyrants. No matter her children's temperaments, she didn't want to lower herself to *any* distasteful discipline. Why couldn't just a calm discussion do the trick? It was her Melancholy ideals that stood in the way of her taking appropriate disciplinary action. In the ideal world her ideal children should understand and immediately behave. Because she was unwilling to let go of her high hopes, she — and everyone else around — suffered from the disrespect and disobedience of her children.

All four types can bring a bias into our parenting styles. Unaware of their own temperamental bent, Choleric parents can push, push, push all their children into exhaustion. Fun Sanguine parents can deprive children of the disciplined structure necessary for thriving. Phlegmatic parents can avoid or put off addressing some of the important family issues that keep causing conflict.

Thankfully, with a little understanding, a lot of grace, and plenty of time and practice, everyone can become a good or even better parent.

Good Parenting Usually Takes Planning

Every good effort requires some type of planning. You can incorporate some of these tips in planning how to perfect your parenting.

Never be too quick to assess: Our egos and particular desires can get in the way of properly discerning our child's natural type. My Sanguine niece, Kristin, really understands this. Her son, Matthew, can be silly and attention-seeking, but Kristin has observed him carefully through a temperamental lens. "He's not Sanguine. I know because I *am* one. Matthew is a clever, creative, crazy, and dramatic Melancholy who was born for the theater. To get what he wants, he might try his melodramatic performances on us, but we have his number. I admit, though, some days he could win an Oscar."

Be a detective: Invite your children to share not just what they did or learned that day, but what they saw, heard, or found interesting. Then, *listen closely*. Watch how they dress, walk, talk, and play with others. There will be plenty of clues to tell you who they are, or to signal a problem that may need your attention.

Give it time: If you're not 100 percent sure, don't push a personality on your child. You'll only end up contributing to the creation of a falsehood that may block his gifts and burden him for life.

Follow the tips in Chapter 3's chart: Appropriately adapt the "How to Help" tips to the child's age. Two-year-old introverts (Melancholy or Phlegmatic) need time and space just as much as tweens do. If you have a tomboy daughter, there is nothing wrong with that. She may simply be a rough-house Choleric, a no-fuss Phlegmatic, or a little Melancholy who has gone far past frills into the mysteries of much deeper things. She may be modeling after her dad or an older brother with whom she shares a similar temperament. She might be distancing herself from an over-the-top glamorous sister. Introduce her to feminine fluff, but don't force her to like it. Likewise, there's nothing wrong if you have a tender and soft-hearted son. He may simply be a people-loving Sanguine, a low-key Phlegmatic, or a creative Melancholy. Introduce him to Tonka trucks but don't force them upon him.

Make colorful charts: Hang them in the hallway and ask each child to consider what they are. Are they hoping to be something you know they are not? Help them to understand your temperaments, too, and to value their own. Allow input from the rest of the family. No criticism or shame allowed, just fun and affirmations.

Indulge them once in a while: If your little Melancholy asks if his shirt needs ironing — and, really, it looks just fine — tell him yes and show him how to iron. Let the Melancholies hang on to some of their old possessions that you may think need discarding and teach them to let go of unforgiveness and resentments instead. Hug and kiss and fawn a little bit over the attention-seeking Sanguine. Let the Phlegmatic stay in her room for a while if she really doesn't want to come out just yet. If the Choleric wants to cook dinner for the whole family, buy him a cookbook and let him make crepes flambeau for dessert!

Look for the underlying fears: When kids (and adults!) are overwhelmed, overstimulated, criticized, or neglected, we will see outward behaviors of hyperactivity, anger, withdrawal, disinterest, or depression. Remember "the trouble is not the temperament" and rush to remedy their underlying fears.

Your own underlying fears might play into this as well. Keep these in mind.

Every parent wants the children to obey quickly and get it right the first time. But the Choleric, most of all, can expect it immediately and be afraid that they will have to stop everything and drag everyone along. Quicker to anger than the rest, they may bark (and even "bite") at their own children. If you're a parent who is part Choleric, don't be triggered by the slow Phlegmatic, the hesitant or worried Melancholy, or the distracted Sanguine. Be patient, get creative, and find ways to motivate or encourage the kids. Adjust any overly rigid schedules and allow time for them to come along.

Parents who constantly want to make their child happy run the risk of creating an entitled brat. Being overly eager to please our children keeps them from developing virtues and forming good character. Let's admit it: A child's warm affection is heady and even intoxicating, in a sense, and no parent wants to lose that. No one wants pushback from their kids, but the parent who is part peace-loving Phlegmatic is the most likely to fear children will argue, resist, and go into full-steam arguing or drama. They want to avoid any conflict and hope everyone will just *please* get along. Instead of being triggered by their demanding Choleric child, the overly inquisitive Melancholy child, or the whiny Sanguine child, these parents can be proactive instead of avoidant.

And it's not just the Phlegmatics; all parents can fall into this and must learn to draw on their God-given authority to say "No" or "Yes, but not just yet." They must learn to face their fear of conflict or rejection and set and enforce healthy boundaries with less talk, pushback, and drama.

A parent who is part Sanguine often doesn't mind arguments or drama because it's a way to connect and can even be a springboard for bringing in humor to lighten things up. But Sanguine parents who are too quick to make things light and fun can deprive their children of much-needed grounding and gravity. The kids might withdraw, sulk, or argue, and Sanguine parents must avoid the temptation to simply cheer them up by promising treats. Encourage your Phlegmatic to get out of bed, your Melancholy to see the silver linings, and your Choleric to let others take a turn. You're naturally good at that.

All parents want their children to be perfect, but the Melancholy, more than most, will be keeping an eagle eye out to correct, fix, and straighten out the children. They won't always do it as directly or harshly as the Choleric might and instead will throw out critical comments or give long lectures. Melancholies can be inordinately afraid of failure, and because they feel at peace when things are perfect, they expect it of their children. God expects our perfection, too, but he gives us a lot more grace than some Melancholy parents give their children. Don't withhold affection and avoid shaming the Sanguine who will not be perfect very often. Instead, try to find fun ways to help her improve. Don't use criticism to control your headstrong Choleric child, or he will find ways to fight you; appeal to his love of production and find ways to reward him when he improves. Never crush your Phlegmatic child with overwhelming demands. Help him or her learn to work for perfection in small, manageable steps. Even when they are not perfect, don't withhold your affection from any of them.

Look for the unmet needs: Some kids will develop food or other sensory (noise, touch) oversensitivity. Other childhood diagnoses will label lack of focus, hyperactivity, or sensory issues as being a chemical or biological problem. While there is truth to that in some cases, we may also not want to admit that our child has had insufficient attention, structure, order, security, or discipline. Sometimes these behaviors are quiet screams from a child who is stressed and hurting.

Encourage them according to their dispositions: Rather than trying to repress or rid a child of his temperament, help direct it upward to the ultimate Good, not inward to selfishness:

- "You are wonderfully wired for keeping and making

peace, my little Phlegmatic. Thank you for being so calm when things got rough with your siblings today. That was helpful."

- "Sally Sanguine, I saw how you encouraged your siblings today when I said we didn't have money to go on vacation this year. You have a real gift for helping to blow away the black clouds."
- "Thank you, my little Melancholy. Leave it to you to worry about getting sunburned. I forgot all about bringing sunscreen to the beach. Your gift of worrying about problems is sometimes a big blessing to us all."
- "I'm so thankful for all your hard work, my Choleric son. I know I can leave you in charge any day and any time, and things will get done."

Allow teenagers to be confused: They are still growing, learning, testing, and wondering who they are and where they fit in the world. This is the time that some of them will mimic and model others' dress, speech, attitudes, and behaviors in a search for their own identity. Don't tolerate selfishness or sin, but do reassure them of their natural strengths and give them as much appropriate freedom as possible, especially in expressing themselves. Don't use shame or force when it comes to college or careers.

Encourage all your little temperaments to be saints: Pope St. John Paul II described the family as the "school of love." Loving God first, and then others, is the universal path to holiness for all of us.

Just one final word of parenting advice to each of the four types:

- *Cholerics*, don't push and pull your kids along —

you may be exhausting them. They do need the simple, clear structure and accountability you give them, but each of them may have a non-Choleric side that is hurt or discouraged. Don't tolerate the dawdlers but be patient with them. You're good at teaching; slow down and give each child a hand in the area where they can learn order and necessary life skills. Then celebrate their successes.

- *Sanguines,* don't trade necessary character development for your kids' affection — they need to grow up. Childlike silliness and fun are good in small doses, but don't let your children get away with sloppiness and lack of self-discipline. They may not like you temporarily, but don't let that keep you from being their parent, not their pal. You are good at giving that spoonful of Sanguine sugar to help their medicine go down.
- *Melancholies,* stop shaming and criticizing every little thing; you may be crushing their spirit. Your children need you to hold up those high and lofty ideals so that someday they can reach them, but your non-Melancholy types will be deeply discouraged if you don't give them some room to fail. See the positive in them as equally as you see the negative and replace your fear of their failure with trust in God. Never withhold or reserve physical or verbal affection as a prize.
- *Phlegmatics,* take calm, loving authority over your children — otherwise, you'll have disrespectful and disobedient children. They need you to have the courage and skills to set and enforce necessary boundaries even when they cause you conflict. Remember, your goal as a parent is not to be nice, keep

the peace, or make them happy; it's to prepare and equip them for virtue and holiness. It's a tough world out there, as they will find out soon enough. They need your calm, tender, loving reassurance that if they take the high path, everything will be OK.

• • •

Reflections

If you have children, do you know their temperaments?

Which aspects of their temperaments do you enjoy most? Which aspects do you find most challenging and why?

Whether in parenting, teaching, or caretaking, what have you done right in responding to any child's temperament?

What's one thing you wish you had done better?

• St. Josephine Bakhita (1869–1947) •

Born in the Western Sudan, Saint Bakhita was seized by Arab slave traders when she was seven or eight years old and forced to walk barefoot about 600 miles. She suffered atrocious cruelties and was sold and bought twice before she arrived at her destination. Over the course of twelve years, she was sold three more times. Her traumatic life of cruel slavery eventually ended and, when she was twenty-four, she became a Canossian religious sister.

What do we know about her temperament?
For the next forty-two years, Bakhita served as her sisters' cook, sacristan, and portress (doorkeeper), and was in frequent contact with the local community. We know at least part of her was Phlegmatic, as she was known for her gentleness, calming voice, and ever-present smile. Since we have no evidence of a high-energy, outgoing Sanguine, we can presume her other temperament was a sweet and pious Melancholy. This seems especially apt because, in the first publication of her story, she was described as having a special charisma and reputation for sanctity.

Pain and sickness marked her last years. In a wheelchair she still retained her positive attitude and, when asked how she was doing, she would always smile and answer, "As the Master desires." Upon her deathbed, the traumatic memories of slavery returned, and she cried out, "The chains are too tight, loosen them a little, please."

What can we learn from her?
Some people have suffered terrible traumas, the effects of which can stay with them until death. But with God's grace, our temperament can remain steady, calm, peaceful, and "as the Master desires."

St. Josephine Bakhita, pray for us.

• 14 •

Taking a Look at Trauma

Therefore do not be anxious about tomorrow, for tomorrow will be anxious for itself. Let the day's own trouble be sufficient for the day.

— Matthew 6:34

"I was only twelve years old," Jim shared. "An older neighborhood teen sexually molested me. I was devastated, confused, scared."

My heart went out to Jim, whom I knew to be a peaceful Phlegmatic and a deeply sensitive Melancholy.

"I'm so sorry, Jim." I paused. "What did you do afterward?"

"Well, I went to my dad hoping he would stand up for me, protect me, and give that kid a lesson he would not forget. Instead, my dad shamed me and beat me to a pulp."

While his name is changed, this is a true and (sadly) not that uncommon story. Years later, naturally introverted Jim experienced typical relationship trauma, enduring rejection from peers, being dumped by girlfriends, and being bullied at work. He was eventually diagnosed with adjustment disorder — also called stress response syndrome — where a person has excessive reactions to stress and impaired social functioning.

"What did you think about that diagnosis?" I asked.

"That caused me even more shame. 'Impaired social functioning?' I thought, *Something is really wrong with me!* But then I learned about my temperament." He continued, "As a Phlegmatic, I was born not liking conflict. God made me a natural peacekeeper and peacemaker. I process things more slowly and carefully than extroverts and need time for that. I tend to focus very well on what is in front of me and don't always pick up clues from others. So, of course, I may seem a little slow on the uptake, but I am not stupid."

"No, you are *not* stupid, Jim," I agreed.

"I was utterly traumatized by the molestation. I think I was even more traumatized when my dad beat me, and that's when a part of me made up its mind that I am not really safe in the world. No one is here to protect me. That part has held that belief all my life. There are other parts of me that love life and hope for the best but, when I feel unsafe in a situation, that little part gets triggered and can go nuts. Then, I admit, I can freeze, or get too indecisive, too hesitant, and too passive."

"What about your Melancholy side?" I asked.

"That part of me is naturally suspicious so, yeah, I really have trouble trusting. I admit that as much as I love God, and I know in my head he loves me, a part of me sometimes doesn't trust that he has my back."

"Jim, that is so sad and so understandable. Your dad *didn't* have your back."

Jim was quiet so I asked, "What's next for you?"

"I'm working with a Catholic therapist using Internal Family Systems.* We're going back and exposing all the hidden beliefs and protective pacts I made with myself after each trauma and allow-

*Internal Family Systems (IFS) is a sound model for understanding the inner self where psychological, emotional, and spiritual healing can take place. I encourage you to check it out at https://transfigurationcounseling.com or https://soulsandhearts.com.

ing the truth to take its place. It's working!"

"So, you don't have some terrible disorder; you have unaddressed and unhealed trauma that shows up in exaggerated temperament traits. Right?"

He laughed. "I couldn't have said it better myself!"

We All Carry Some Unhealed Trauma Wounds

We've all experienced some sort of trauma, starting in childhood. It's had a lasting effect on us, even if we don't recall or are not aware of it. Trauma can be catastrophic, moderate, mild, one-time, sustained, or tied to a person, place, or event. It can be as violent as rape or as devastating as suffering through years of a parent's shaming and belittling. We need to take an honest look at how unhealed wounds are affecting our human interactions and responses — and how our temperaments play a role in our responses.

Examples of Trauma

Catastrophic	Less Catastrophic
Natural disaster	Being rejected
Sexual/physical abuse	Neglect (physical and emotional)
Car/plane crashes	Verbal and emotional abuse
War	Bullying
Kidnapping	Stonewalling
Accidents	Being used by others
Being the victim of/witnessing a crime	Losing, failing

The emotional effects of trauma are almost endless: shame, insecurity, neediness, anxiety, fear, terror, overwhelm, hopelessness, depression, despair, and all manner of psychological and emotional disorders. The wounding and negative effects of trauma will manifest through the temperaments. When a part of us is still holding the hurts of past trauma:

- Phlegmatics will be more timid, fearful, and avoidant than normal.
- Melancholies will be more suspicious, worried, and depressed than normal.
- Sanguines will be more flighty, fawning, and forgetful than normal.
- Cholerics will be more demanding, impatient, and brash than normal.

Sustained trauma wounds are never an excuse for functioning in our temperament's extremes, but they help us understand what is behind the behavior and point to the areas where the Lord can continue to heal, purify, and perfect us.

Our trauma experiences can range from little "t" trauma, like being called a nasty name by a parent or peer, to more devastating forms (big "T" trauma), such as natural disasters, witnessing a gruesome crime, or being sexually violated. Double trauma happens when, like little Jimmy, one is additionally rejected, shamed, attacked, or abandoned because of the first trauma. When any hurtful or harmful thing happens, a traumatized person will first seek two things: *safety* and *soothing*. One's temperament combination will affect the way in which one seeks these things.

Seeking safety is also seeking some sense of control over your environment or the situation. Remember that temperament defines the four particular ways in which a person most naturally responds to any stimuli: 1) slowly or quickly, 2) lightly or intensely, 3) long-lasting or short-lived, and 4) extroverted or introverted. Consider this in relation to the classic trauma responses: fight, flight, freeze, or fawn:

- *Fight*: This is a direct and active response. Tackle the threat head-on: push back, push down, argue, criticize, shame, blame, threaten, yell, scream, hurt, crush. Fighting can happen with words as well as weapons.
- *Flight*: This is an avoidant and passive response. Ignore, withdraw, distance, ghost, isolate, avoid conflict, deny, procrastinate, seek distractions, numb with substances, "hide" in excessive work, activity, or ministry.
- *Freeze*: This is an avoidant and passive response. Inability to think, speak, or move. Complete overwhelm, shut down, chronic uncertainty and indecision, daydreaming, brain fog, disassociation.
- *Fawn*: This is a direct and active response. Charming deflection, humor, excessive complimenting, begging, pleading, bargaining, caretaking, over-the-top "guest services," bending over backward, or inappropriate accommodation.

Most of us don't experience huge catastrophes or natural disasters, but we still have some trauma. Most trauma comes from our relationships. When feeling threatened or unsafe, introverted types (Phlegmatic and Melancholy) will first freeze or take flight; disengaging gives them the extra time and space they need to process. But they are not pushovers and, when they can get their wits about them, they can *fawn* and *fight* just as fiercely as the extroverts.

The Phlegmatic may be more likely to fawn to keep the peace, but he can also fight tooth and nail. The Melancholy can also quietly crush the opponent into dust — usually with words.

Extroverted types (Choleric and Sanguine) will first fight

or fawn; they stay readily engaged to gain control by arguing, convincing, joking, barking, or threatening. But when it is all too much (and it can be for anyone), they also can become overwhelmed and *freeze* or take *flight.* The Sanguine will plop down and burst into tears, and the Choleric will be smoking a cigar on the last train out of town.

Undiagnosed and Unhealed Trauma Can Show Up in Temperamental Extremes

Exaggerated temperament responses are a symptom, not a condition. They can present us with the loud, brutish Choleric; the brassy, attention-seeking Sanguine; the passive, withdrawn Phlegmatic; and the bitter or anxious Melancholy.

Each of these exaggerated types is holding some belief about themselves, others, the world, and even God which is rooted in trauma and fueling outrageous, harmful, and sinful behavior. It's not an excuse, but resolution will only come by exposing the roots and unencumbering their wounded parts from the lies, fears, and habits.

When a part of us holds fear of being used, hurt, betrayed, ignored, crushed, tricked, or worse, we may always have some low-level anxiety humming in the background — no matter our temperament. When anyone has been conditioned to expect trauma, he or she may be hypervigilant; even the slower-reacting introverts will have quick(er) defenses or avoidant responses. If we have any part of ourselves that feels we cannot safely attach and feel secure in the world or in our relationships (at home, work, school, or anywhere), there is healing to be done.

What are some other signs that we are trying to control our environment, seeking safety, and still suffering from disintegration of our parts? Here are some common ones and the temperaments most likely to struggle with them:

- People-pleasing (mostly Phlegmatics and Sanguines)
- Self-neglect (all four)
- Perfectionism (mostly Melancholies)
- Anxiety (all four)
- Addictions (all four)
- Compulsions (all four)
- Having to stay busy (Cholerics and Phlegmatics, both to avoid other things)
- Lack of energy (mostly Melancholies and Phlegmatics)
- Overthinking (mostly Melancholies and Cholerics)
- Trouble saying "no" (mostly Sanguines and Phlegmatics)
- Fear of failure (mostly Cholerics and Melancholies)
- Fear of missing out (mostly Sanguines and Phlegmatics)
- Depression (most often Melancholies, but all four when they reach a limit)
- Anger issues (mostly Cholerics outwardly, interiorly for the Melancholies)
- Overcommitting (mostly Sanguines and Phlegmatics)
- Not speaking up at mistreatment (mostly Phlegmatics and Melancholies)
- Making excuses for another's bad behavior (mostly Phlegmatics and Sanguines)
- Not scheduling rest, prayer, or enjoying alone time (all four)

This list is far from complete. Do you recognize yourself or someone else in it? Don't be disheartened by fears of "going crazy" or worries that someone else is headed to an asylum. Don't accept being accused of oversensitivity or told to get over it. Don't let others get away with saying "just pray."

Indeed, we should always pray, but we should also ask God to reveal our own unaddressed and unhealed trauma, and to give us the courage and energy needed to make and keep a plan for our perfection. Let us thank him for our temperaments and commit to doing what it takes — for as long as it takes — for the Lord to lead us to perfection. And if you need healing of any kind, get help, even if your temperament type resists.

"Get help? I already know it all," says the Choleric.

"OK, if it's fun, but *no* self-denial," says the Sanguine.

"Can't I just pray about it?" asks the Phlegmatic.

"I don't trust others to understand me," says the Melancholy.

"Just do it!" says Rose. I'm praying that everyone who reads this book will find a mentor, therapist, spiritual director, or coach (or all of the above!) who can provide accompaniment and help speed healing on the journey toward the way of perfection.

In Alcoholics Anonymous and other twelve-step programs, the first step to recovery and healing is admitting you have a problem and that, without God, you are powerless to change it — a difficult but necessary admission for all temperament types. The truth is, we are all fragmented. We are all broken, but we all have access to God's powerful graces — especially in the sacramental life.

How did we get this way? It's always been understood in the Church that we are each an integrated composite of mind (the intellectual life), body (the physical life), heart (the emotional life), and soul (the spiritual life). Original sin caused the disruption and disintegration of these four dimensions of the human person. God can and does love the fragmented soul, but no matter how much we love and seek God, we must still do the work of integration.

Do you recall the little shoulder angels and devils we watched in cartoons, as kids? We actually all have parts that can be in conflict, and that's not due to a pathological fracturing, but is because there are distinct parts of our inmost self that carry valuable qualities of who we are: memories, desires, hopes, beliefs, fears, and unhealed wounds. Even the saints recognized this:

Saint Paul speaks of the inner conflict and the inmost self. One part of him kept doing what another part of him truly did not want to do (see Rom 7:15–20). St. Augustine of Hippo describes how we have "split hearts" in his *Confessions.* St. Thomas Aquinas talks about "parts" of the soul, writing in his *Summa Theologica* (q. 78, a. 1) that the "powers of the soul are called its parts." St. Teresa of Ávila even assigns rooms to our parts in her book *The Interior Castle.*

One part of us can truly desire God above all else, while another is still too attached to some earthly good. One part can still hold the memory of a hurt and make a vow to stay on guard, self-protect, and not forgive, only to conflict with another part of us that wants to forgive and be merciful. Our unhealed and needy parts can push to the front of our interior life with their cries, objections, or demands — almost like children in our internal "family." When these parts of ourselves begin to clamor for our attention, a stronger part of us needs to be attentive and loving, but in charge.

If we desire deep union with God — and at least a part of us truly does — our perfection will go beyond temperament to an interior integration of all our parts, centered on God.

• • •

Reflections

Do you have some past trauma that you know still affects you? How has it done so?

Are you aware of different parts of you that are in conflict? How does this impact your life?

Which of the four standard trauma responses most fits you?

Is there any specific past trauma you'd like God to help you overcome?

Part 3
Loving Them All

Let both grow together until the harvest; and at harvest time I will tell the reapers, Gather the weeds first and bind them in bundles to be burned, but gather the wheat into my barn.

— Matthew 13:30

• Bl. Pier Giorgio Frassati (1901–1925) •

Bl. Pier Giorgio Frassati — a handsome, young, Italian activist — was also a Third Order Dominican and dedicated to Catholic social justice. Born into a wealthy family, he put his Catholic faith into practice by giving practical aid to whomever needed it most. He died young, at only twenty-four, from poliomyelitis.

What do we know about his temperament?
His talents were limitless; he was an avid mountaineer and athlete who could swim well and could even recite entire passages of Dante with relative ease. He had boundless energy, attended the theater, visited museums, helped establish a newspaper, worked for social reform, studied to be a mining engineer, and loved Tuscan cigars. He was also known as the "Terror" due to his fondness for practical jokes. (While Sanguines are also quick to make jokes, they earn labels like "clown," not usually "terror"!) He often said, "Charity is not enough; we need social reform." Clearly, he was a take-action Choleric.

He also had a beautiful "bleeding heart" for others, typical of the Melancholy. Once, his father refused to help a man who came to their door because he was drunk; the sobbing Frassati told his mother, and she instructed him to find the man and bring him to the home for something to eat.

What can we learn from him?
From this highly action-oriented saint, we have this encouragement: "If you have God at the center of all your action, then you will reach your goal."

Bl. Pier Giorgio Frassati, pray for us.

• 15 •

Appreciating the Choleric

She rises while it is yet night
and provides food for her household
and tasks for her maidens.
She considers a field and buys it;
with the fruit of her hands she plants a vineyard.
She clothes her loins with strength
and makes her arms strong.

— Proverbs 31:15–17

I once asked my dad if he could recall what I was like when I was a baby.

"I remember it well, honey, since you were my firstborn. You were so small I could hold you in one hand."

"But could you tell my personality back then?"

He thought back. "I do recall when you were only a few months old, and your mother was ready to get out and go somewhere again. So, we packed you up in our station wagon and drove over to see the Hoover Dam."

Then Dad's detail-obsessed, Melancholy side drifted off into the enigmatic world of engineering and began to share that the

Hoover Dam was built between 1931 and 1936 during the Great Depression. "It's a concrete arch-gravity dam in the Black Canyon of the Colorado River …"

Blah, blah, blah … my Sanguine side grew restless. "But do you recall anything about *me*, Dad?"

We both laughed.

"Well, Rosie, you normally were a very happy little baby who liked to sleep. But when we were taking the tour of the dam, I remember you being bright and awake, holding your head up, and about ready to jump right out of my arms. Your eyes were wide open, and you were clearly scanning the huge horizon!" My elderly Dad imitated me, sitting up straight, craning his neck, and making his eyes as big as saucers. We both laughed again.

I was a baby Choleric, already alert and ready to go.

So far, we've explored all the temperaments together. In this and the next three chapters, let's look at each one separately. What do we know about Cholerics?

A Choleric is an extrovert: Our responses to life tend to be quick and enduring. We are expressive, demonstrative, and open with our thoughts and feelings. We have a positive outlook, tend not to get too emotional, and are admired by others for being strong, courageous, and hard-working.

Cholerics are born looking up and out to the world around them: Others can see the big picture, too, but most are slower to take it all in as quickly as Cholerics do. Some will keep getting distracted by the smaller details and may miss the horizon altogether.

Cholerics are optimistic: Believing that everything will turn out right in the end, we rarely get discouraged. We're confident in our problem-solving skills, because we know that problems are only challenges to be overcome. If no one else can produce an agenda, we will create one!

Cholerics are unafraid: Others may skydive, mountain-climb, or swim with sharks, but we will face dangers in other ways. Unafraid to make waves, we'll call the president of the company, challenge the bully, or think far outside the box to solve a problem. We can take calculated risks, and if those don't work, we'll keep trying.

Cholerics love to work: Everyone likes to work when it is interesting, meaningful, easy, and rewarding. But Cholerics go a step further: The more we do, the happier we are! We're the ones whistling through the daily doldrums, deadlines, and disasters. Be warned, though: Hustle is good, but heart is better; don't fall in love with production and forget the people!

Cholerics thrive on challenges and problem-solving: Men aren't the only problem-solvers; all Cholerics see challenges as rousing adventures. Problem-solving is a combination of other things at which we excel: seeing solutions, taking charge, thinking clearly, and daring to reach for new and different solutions.

Cholerics are strong, quick, and decisive: We move quickly and don't waste time "dilly-dallying" as my mother used to say. When a job needs to be done, a relationship needs healing, or a friend needs our help, we are first in! Our energy and drive usually exceed that of others. We usually recognize the point at which it's time to stop talking and start acting.

Cholerics are suited to being in charge: Everyone likes to be in control, but not everyone likes to be in charge; it's a big responsibility. Cholerics almost thrive on the hard work and problems that may arise in positions of leadership. We trust in our ability to see with clarity and to remain emotionally balanced.

Cholerics are natural delegators: Cholerics easily see the big picture, and we find delegation easy because we know it is efficient; we're not afraid to exercise authority. With maturity, we learn not to do it all by ourselves but to allow others to grow up, man up, or shine. Some call us bossy. So be it. To avoid being *too* bossy, though, Cholerics need to stay out of everyone's business and doublecheck where our responsibility lies and where it does not.

Cholerics are self-reliant: We can spend hours alone working, cleaning, planning, fixing, learning, changing, remodeling, and more. "There is so much to do," we think. "Who needs other people?" Well, *we* do.

Cholerics do need others: Being in charge all the time is exhausting and even lonely for any of the temperaments. As self-sufficient as they can be, Cholerics need the balance of having others whom they trust and love, and upon whom they can depend. In romantic relationships, a balanced Choleric woman really does hope the dominant man will choose her, so she doesn't always need to be leading. Sadly, she may struggle with trusting others and will have a difficult time vacating the throne so other rightful rulers can sit in it.

Cholerics are rescuers: When my little Choleric brother Charlie was four, we went to Old MacDonald's farm to see the animals. Who knew pigs could be so huge and scary? When one large porker came running toward my two little sisters and me, Charlie — smaller than any of us — instinctively stepped before us and tried to hold back the pig, crying, "I'll save you!"

Thank God for the fence.

So, yes, Cholerics can be bullies, but they can also be brave!

Cholerics think and speak clearly and logically: Cholerics quickly get to the point and expect others to do so, too — no time to waste yapping about things. Small talk is boring! But this risks overfocusing on the task at hand and forgetting about the others. Ignore the attention needs of others, and alienation — or worse, rebellion — may result.

Cholerics are not easily offended: What others think about us is far less important than our being able to do the right thing. We *do* expect others to appreciate all our hard work and follow our lead. If they do not, we will feel hurt and will lick our wounds, but we won't wallow in self-pity. Onward and upward!

Cholerics are forceful: Force inappropriately applied is assault, but Cholerics have the natural boldness to be a force for good. With our clear thinking — aided by years of wisdom, grace, and virtue — we can provide the strength that others need but can't find. Jesus was often a "force to be reckoned with." Cholerics are called to be that kind of force.

Cholerics do things right: It might not need to be Melancholy-perfect, but Cholerics will not settle for shoddy work. Growing up, our housekeeper, Celestine, was a second mother to us all. She was warm and loving, and tough and terrifying. Celestine had three small children, whose father had abandoned them, and she was desperately in need of work. With no car, she took the bus to the unemployment agency where she sat patiently opposite a clerk who rifled through a 3 x 5 index card file for open positions.

"Well, here's one. But I'm not sure you would want this."

"I'll take anything," Celestine replied quickly.

"It's a family with … eight children. They're looking for full-time help."

Eight children! But without hesitating, Celestine replied, "I'll take it."

It was the late 1950s, and my Phlegmatic mother felt completely overwhelmed with diapers, bottles, and doctor appointments. She'd placed an ad for household help in the *Sacramento Bee*. Celestine arrived on our doorstep that afternoon and — after taking one look at my mother's tired face — stepped resolutely into our home and simply and efficiently took over.

"Where are the aprons?" she asked and quickly tied one on. She and my mom hit it off right away, and after that she and her children were, and are to this day, a permanent part of our family.

Celestine was Choleric — upbeat and optimistic, but she took no prisoners when it came to keeping an orderly house. With Mom and Dad's permission (he loved her, too!) she held and enforced high standards. She never hesitated to call us out on our bad behavior or send us to our rooms without lunch. But she also picked up and soothed the crying babies, laughed at our jokes, and made us feel seen and heard. Her sensitive Melancholy side prayed ceaselessly, loved us as though we were her own, and sacrificed long hours whenever my parents needed her. We adored her.

Because Mom was mostly occupied with the babies, Celestine taught me to cook. She was a Melancholy master in the kitchen, an artist of Southern fried chicken and homemade peach cobbler (tapioca, not flour, a tad more butter, and a little extra dash of nutmeg were her secrets). She also taught me to iron Dad's shirts and keep house. And she was tough.

"Come back here, Rosie."

I had just cleaned the entire kitchen and mopped the floor — just like she showed me. It was spotless.

She didn't waste words. "When you clean the counters, pull out all the cannisters and wipe behind them."

Gulp. I did, and of course there were lots of breadcrumbs and a few dead flies, just as she knew there would be. It was a Sanguine's lesson in humility and in the value of doing a job well — even if no one else will see.

What's Wrong with Cholerics?

Nothing that grace, wisdom, and experience can't fix. Our weaknesses are our strengths carried to extremes — and this is true for everyone. Pride and fear are usually at the heart of our sinfulness. Our innate desires are to work hard, and for everyone to see and appreciate all we have done for them. Those desires, and the fear of their going unfulfilled, may move us into bad behaviors.

We can be too sure of ourselves, and then we may act too quickly and overlook some important detail. We can be too bossy, lording over others when that's not our right or responsibility. We are often too task-oriented, forgetting the hearts of the precious people around us. We tend to be too self-reliant, cutting ourselves off from the support of others. And we can be too loud, opinionated, arrogant, bold, and harsh.

Take heart, Cholerics! We are powerfully and beautifully

made in the image and likeness of God. Like the Hoover Dam, we serve to be both strong and beautiful, holding back the flood waters that would otherwise destroy the world. In that, we share in the saving, protecting power of God, who will work alongside us and perfect us — if we will get out of his way and let him be the Boss.

Do you think you are a Choleric but are not quite sure? Depending on the specific reasons, time, place, and circumstances, anyone can take quick action, be tireless in doing easy things they love, take charge when necessary, and solve problems. But the Choleric is blessed with these virtues and strengths in abundance and is naturally and effortlessly predisposed to them.

And remember — every Choleric also has another temperament, either Sanguine or Melancholy. A Choleric with a Sanguine side will bring a light touch, avoiding being too heavy-handed or working too hard. Cholerics with a Melancholy side may worry a bit more about important realities but will also bring a high level of perfection to all they do. The Choleric side will not permit the Melancholy side to get too bogged down in any unnecessary details.

• • •

Reflections

If you are Choleric, what do you like most about having this temperament?

If you are not Choleric, what do you value most in them?

What can you say to or do for a Choleric to make him or her feel more appreciated?

What is a natural Choleric trait that can help lead them to sainthood?

• Saint Peter (d. c. 64–68) •

Saint Peter is the Apostle to whom Jesus gave the keys of the kingdom and was our first pope. He was martyred in Rome, and Catholics believe his bones are buried under St. Peter's Basilica in Rome.

What do we know about his temperament?
Part of Peter was clearly Choleric, and Jesus put him in charge. When Jesus asked a question, Peter was first to respond: "You are the Christ" (Mt 16:16), and "Lord … you have the words of eternal life" (Jn 6:68). Peter witnessed the Transfiguration and immediately wanted to build on it: "Lord … I will make three booths here" (Mt 17:4).

But Peter was also a sometimes impulsive Sanguine, who jumped off a boat and then started to sink, and who rushed in to fight when Jesus was arrested, cutting off someone's ear. Sanguines are known for well-meaning grand gestures that they may soon regret. Recall Peter's bold claim, "I will not deny you" (Mt 26:35), followed by his bitter weeping after his third cowardly denial of Jesus only a few hours later. But even in his rash, impulsive bravado, Peter had a heartfelt love for the Lord. God worked with that, giving him the graces to become a great saint and martyr.

What can we learn from him?
There is hope for the unpolished extrovert (Choleric or Sanguine). A consoling scene for us all is Jesus and Peter around the fire after the Resurrection. As a healing balm to Peter's "triple treason," Our Lord gave Peter three chances to declare his love and fidelity once again.

Saint Peter, pray for us.

• 16 •

Delighting in the Sanguine

Strength and dignity are her clothing,
and she laughs at the time to come.
She opens her mouth with wisdom,
and the teaching of kindness is on her tongue.

— Proverbs 31:25–26

After Dad told me about that day at the Hoover Dam, I wanted to know more.

"Let's see now … well, when you were a little girl, you were quite the hambone."

Hambone? Back then the term described a performer who does a lot of silly jumping around, stomping, slapping, and patting of the arms, legs, chest, and cheeks. *Thanks, Dad,* I thought. *You just called me a clown.*

After I had studied the temperaments, though, I was not so put off by the description anymore. Sanguines are naturally silly and prone to physical antics. It's one way we connect — by entertaining others and infusing lightness and humor into a situation. We are the sunny personality who loves to make others laugh and smile. Just as the Phlegmatic feels good when everyone is peaceful, the Sanguine feels good when everyone is laughing.

But that can backfire. If the Sanguine hams it up, not to cheer others but to get attention, or goes too far at inappropriate times and places, that strength will become a weakness, especially with the unforgiving opposite: the cool, composed, and critical Melancholy.

I was dating Pierre — a handsome, sophisticated Frenchman — who was the general manager at one of our local high-end hotels. He was a take-charge Choleric and a passionate, fastidious Melancholy. His hair was perfect! Pierre was attracted to my light, fun side, and we dated for six months, attending large community galas and elegant soirees. In our resort community, many of those in attendance included past US presidents, sports luminaries, and Hollywood stars. I know he felt confident with me as his date since I dressed beautifully and tastefully, had impeccable manners, and would look good on his arm. After all, he had his reputation with the hotel and the city leaders to maintain! We both knew how to be charming and were delighted to "work the room" together. As Cholerics, neither of us was a wall flower. We could hold forth in any conversation with anyone, and we moved in and out of couples and conversations with ease. It was fun!

One New Year's Eve, however, I blew it.

Looking fabulous in my expensive, sparkling St. John knit, feeling good about myself (and slightly intoxicated with the bubbly), I engaged with Pierre's two young boys, who were also present. In their little tuxedos, they were tucked away in a corner with me, away from most of the adults, and the boys were excitedly telling me all about the Teenage Mutant Ninja Turtles.

"I *know*! Michelangelo, Leonardo … right?"

And then in my high heels, I crouched down a bit, assumed a warrior pose with my arms and hands, and did a little karate sidekick, making sure I would not fall on my rear. I whooped,

"Kia!" (not *too* loudly) and then stood up, and we all laughed.

Pierre had just walked in and seen me. When I turned and saw him, he was throwing me a look of both horror and cold, steely, disgust. Gulp! I knew that was it. All those months of the elegant life would be gone. Had other adults seen me commit this mortal sin of being childishly charming with his kids? No, I had been careful. But I felt ashamed and not surprised that he was cool toward me for the rest of the night. And sure enough, within the week, he let me know it was over.

Melancholies are embarrassed when Sanguines get so silly, and they don't like it. What might be all right in private can never be permissible when all those other people might be looking. The introverted temperaments do not want any attention unless and until *they* decide when and how it will be. The out-of-control Sanguine can thus be a liability to the perfect Melancholy.

As I later reflected, I had done nothing wrong to damage his reputation, but I also understood he wanted a well-bred woman and not a wild card. After I cried a little, I was relieved that I was no longer in a relationship with such a highly critical man.

Other temperaments may not understand Sanguines, and some may be embarrassed by us, but they will still be drawn to our charming, light, sweet, and sparkly personality — at least at first. Let's look more closely at this extroverted type. What are some other traits of the Sanguine?

Sanguines are extroverts: A Sanguine's responses to life tend to be quick, but unlike the other extrovert (Choleric), those reactions are inclined to be short-lived rather than enduring. We are expressive, demonstrative, and open with our thoughts and feelings. We are quick to offer others an encouraging word, a compliment, or a cheerful smile. We're young at heart, love to laugh, and usually have something funny to say. Others admire us for being so sweet, upbeat, and fun.

Sanguines are born looking up and out to the world around them:

Like the Choleric, we have a big worldview, but we are more focused on relationships than ideas, concepts, and goals.

Sanguines are silly and fun: Roald Dahl's character Willy Wonka said, "A little nonsense, now and then, is relished by the wisest men!" Everyone can be fun when they have time and are relaxed, feeling creative, or up on stage and expected to be entertaining and interesting. Joy, silliness, humor, and excitement are universal, but Sanguines are blessed with an abundance of these characteristics. We excel at lightness, laughter, and entertainment. My Sanguine friend Patty had a twinkle in her eye when she shared this about herself: "I snort laugh, both frequently and loudly. You're welcome. I love show tunes and musicals, and probably know all the words by heart. I can fit my fist in my mouth."

Sanguines are optimistic: Born with the sunniest of dispositions, Sanguines quickly see the bright side of life and of others. Worries come, but not for long and not too much. If we need help, we will charm someone into assistance. We need to be careful, though; there *are* real problems in the world, and we shouldn't laugh them off.

Sanguines are cheerful and refreshing: We don't hesitate to openly offer kindness, love, and a sweet vivacity even when things are not going well. We move in quickly to touch, assure, encourage, and bring a rosy optimism to those who are feeling blue. When things are stale, we refresh them. We're naturally quick with a riddle, a joke, or a word of cheer.

Sanguines love everyone and are affectionate: We *love* people! We'll go to the death for our forever best friends — even though we only met them five minutes ago. We see the best in everyone, even those who would use, hurt, or betray us. We don't think twice about waving first at a stranger, smiling first at the store clerk, and forming friendships. We thrive on others' love, affection, and attention and don't get ruffled when others call us

"Honey." If someone moves into our space and gives us an unexpected pat or a hug, we don't feel violated or offended. In fact, we love it and lean right into it.

Sanguines are quick to recover, quick to forgive: When we're unhappy, we Sanguines will quickly fall to pieces and maybe into self-pity, but it won't last too long. It may have seemed like the end of the world, but before you know it, we'll bounce right back up — faster than anyone else — ready to find love, joy, and fun again.

When I worked with my mostly Choleric (with some Melancholy) father in our family business, he abruptly fired me three times. We butted heads, I got angry, went home, and cried. The next morning, I washed my face, put on my lipstick, and showed back up at the office.

"I'm sorry, Dad," I said.

"I'm sorry, too, honey."

We hugged and got back to work.

Sanguines just want everyone to love each other, so we are quick to let go of even serious offenses and forgive. We must be careful, though, not to trade dignity for affection, or allow others to use and sin against us.

Sanguines are childlike and naïve: Sanguines have a natural trust in others that is genuine, appealing, innocent, and childlike. We feel safe in the cotton-candy world and hate to come out of it to face harsh realities. We share in the Phlegmatic's head-in-the-sand innocence and naivete. While the peaceful Phlegmatic wants to keep the status quo and avoid conflict, Sanguines want to preserve a sunny, romantic view of life, where everyone loves each other.

Sanguines are generous: We'll hand over our lunch, lend our last twenty bucks, and offer to help at the drop of a hat. We will also (maybe too quickly) write off big debts, cancel obligations, or otherwise free others from painful burdens. We're quick to make a grand gesture or a big promise but may not always follow through because of a failure to take time to calculate the cost in time or money. Thank God for the Cholerics and Melancholies who can help us with the big picture, the details, and the risk.

Sanguines are hot-blooded: They lean first toward the passions rather than the intellect. Not that Sanguines are unintelligent or incapable, but we'll first be drawn by the taste, touch, sight, smell, and sounds of life. Our passions are strong, but remember, they tend to be short-lived. So, signing up for piano lessons (likely at too high a price) probably won't last. Our opposite, the Melancholy, who is also sensuous and passionate, is the one who will become the virtuoso and earn our exceeding admiration.

Sanguines are playful: We're like big kids, and we love to kid, tease, flirt, excite, and arouse, all in a good spirit, but in our naivete we may offend or confuse others about our motives.

Sanguines have a wild streak: Sanguines like to shock; it's usually an immature response to the high expectations of the Melancholy. It's a way of saying, "You're no fun, and I'll never be like you!" Some Sanguines can be crude when reacting to a prude, but we don't need to go to the other extreme to make our point. Rightly ordered and properly directed, our wildness is a fiery, beautiful thing.

Sanguines are high energy: We are easily and quickly excited about things and can seem tireless, but the truth is, even Sanguines can and do burn out. When we crash, we may get stuck in self-pity, especially if no one loved us enough to help or take care of us in childhood. After a period of whining, crying, or "thumb-sucking," we get tired of that, eat a cookie or buy a blouse (or a house!), and then pop right back up — away we go again! But we must be careful about signing escrow papers.

Sanguines are adept at charming others: Others can be stuck in doubt, fear, or distrust, but Sanguines have a gift for charming them right out of it. By sweetly and persistently pointing out the positive, the possibilities, the rewards, and the fun, we can sell sawdust to a lumber mill! We must be careful to use such power only for good.

Sanguines gather people in: A Sanguine's door is always open to others. But if people are too lethargic, depressed, or critical — or if no one seems to notice or care about us — they can drain and deflate us. We are also just fine by ourselves, able to amuse ourselves when alone. We don't just need to be with people, we need to be having *fun* with people who love us.

What's Wrong with Sanguines?

Nothing that grace, wisdom, and experience can't fix. Our weaknesses are our strengths carried to extremes — and everyone has them. Usually pride and fear are at the heart of our sinfulness. Our deep desires are to have fun and for everyone to love us. Those desires, and the fear of not having them met, may move us into bad behaviors.

We can be too quick, impulsive, and foolish. We need to slowwwww dowwwwwn. We can be *too* charming, especially while trying to persuade others who never asked for our opinion or our help. We can be too ready to forgive, ignoring common sense and the warnings of others, only to be used and abused again. We can be too upbeat, not seeing the fear, hurts, or struggles of others who just don't need our cheerful words as much as they need some quiet understanding. We can be too loud, flirtatious, whiny, wild, and silly.

But take heart; Sanguines are adorable and beautifully made in the image and likeness of God. Our big hearts and grand gestures are a sharing in the heart and merciful works of God. He will stay with us and perfect us — if we will only keep our eye on him, and not the mirror.

Do you think you are a Sanguine but are not quite sure? Sanguines are not common. Everyone can be cheerful, upbeat, sunny, silly, sweet, forgiving, and fun, but all for different reasons and at various times, places, and circumstances. But the Sanguine is blessed with these virtues and strengths in abundance and is naturally and effortlessly predisposed to them. Remember, every Sanguine also has another temperament, either Choleric or Phlegmatic.

A Sanguine-Choleric is better able to maintain focus and (somewhat) orderliness. Careful, though; with that double dose of adrenaline running through their veins, some Sanguine-Cholerics may still be a bit too loud, too fast, or just too much for others to handle.

Sanguines who are also Phlegmatics will be so pleasant and easygoing that they'll be the most enjoyable, fun people around. But they'll also need structure and deadlines to get things done, and someone to make them clean out their closet every few years.

• • •

Reflections

If you are Sanguine, what do you like most about having this temperament?

If you are not Sanguine, what do you value most in them?

What can you say to or do for a Sanguine in your life to make him or her feel more cherished?

What is one Sanguine temperament trait that you think helps them grow in holiness?

• St. Andrew the Apostle (d. c. 60 or 62) •

One of the Twelve Apostles, Saint Andrew was Saint Peter's brother, with some calling him the rock behind the Rock. "Solid as a rock" is one of the phrases most used to describe the strength of a Phlegmatic. Andrew was the first disciple Jesus called.

What do we know about his temperament?
Scripture tells us Andrew didn't hesitate to follow Jesus (see Mt 4:18–20). Phlegmatics are known to be good followers and strong supporters, especially when they see and believe that a leader is worth following. We don't have any indication that Andrew was as zesty as his Choleric-Sanguine sibling, but we know that he was also a good observer and could speak up. At the feeding of the five thousand, it was Andrew who offered a possible solution to the hungry crowd: "One of his disciples, Andrew, Simon Peter's brother, said to [Jesus], 'There is a lad here who has five barley loaves and two fish; but what are they among so many?'" (Jn 6:8–9). There's his other type, the doubtful, worried Melancholy: What good are a few measly fish?

What can we learn from him?
Don't hesitate to follow the Lord. And when you can't see a solution, still speak up about the possibilities. Even though Jesus knew what he was about to do, he built his solution on the courageous introvert who cared enough to offer his observations. Every leader needs a good wingman.

Saint Andrew, pray for us.

• 17 •

Respecting the Phlegmatic

The heart of her husband trusts in her, and he will have no lack of gain. She does him good, and not harm, all the days of her life.

— Proverbs 31:11–12

The North Wind and the Sun had a quarrel about which of them was the stronger. While they were disputing with much heat and bluster, a traveler passed along the road wrapped in a cloak.

"Let us agree," said the Sun, "that he is the stronger who can strip that Traveler of his cloak."

"Very well," growled the blustery North Wind, and at once sent a cold, howling blast against the Traveler.

With the first noisy gust, the ends of the cloak whipped about the Traveler's body. But he immediately wrapped it closely around himself, and the harder the Wind blew, the tighter he held it to himself. The North Wind tore angrily at the cloak, but all his fierce efforts were in vain.

Then the Sun began to shine. At first his beams were gentle, and in the pleasant warmth after the bitter cold of the North

Wind, the Traveler unfastened his cloak and let it hang loosely from his shoulders. The Sun's quiet rays grew warmer and warmer. The man took off his cap and mopped his brow. At last, he became so heated that he pulled off his cloak, and, to escape the blazing sunshine, threw himself down in the welcome shade of a tree by the roadside.

Gentleness and kind persuasion win where force and bluster fail, Aesop reminds us.

When studying the four temperaments, the even-keeled Phlegmatic is sometimes woefully under-appreciated. So let's take a look at some of the ways the peaceful Phlegmatic really does shine.

Phlegmatics are introverts: "Quiet" does not mean "timid." A Phlegmatic's strength is sometimes kept carefully hidden until the right time and place. Gifted with an impeccable sense of occasion, their responses to life tend to be thoughtful and careful; initial hesitation to reveal themselves, in certain situations, comes from a desire to avoid conflict.

They can be expressive, demonstrative, and open — but only after first checking out the situation and assessing both the need and the appropriateness. Because they possess a generally positive outlook and tend not to get too emotional, others admire them for being loving, kind, calm, steady, and loyal. They can be smart, outgoing, and in charge — but only when they so choose.

Phlegmatics are careful observers: Phlegmatics are watchers, and while they might miss the million other things going on in the room, they are good at focusing on what is right in front of them. Because they are sitting there quietly and saying nothing (yet), some may think they've checked out, but no — they're checking things out. They're observing and listening and musing on the many possibilities. Others may react more quickly, but Phlegmatics know the wisdom of waiting, taking note, and contemplating *before* responding.

Phlegmatics are unwavering: "Someone just honked to get me out of my parking space, so now I have to sit here until both of us are dead" (Unknown). After sufficiently careful thought or research, when Phlegmatics have made up their minds, no one can move them. Feet planted firmly in the soil, they stand their ground. Even when others may be crying, whining, or screaming for them to change, move, or get out of the way, they remain fixed. I often say the Choleric strength is *bullish* — she snorts and grunts and loudly bashes her head against the wall and then gives up and moves on. But Phlegmatic strength is *mulish.* He just quietly and stubbornly plops down, and no force on earth can make him move. Who is stronger? You decide.

Phlegmatics are no pushovers! Sometimes they are so nice, so accommodating, and so adaptable that others misread Phlegmatics as weak. This is a mistake. They will give in to others because it's easier than arguing, but most of the time Phlegmatics really are OK with "whatever." However, they're not prepared to be pushed by others into strange or uncomfortable situations without adequate time and space to get familiar with things. They have minds of their own and know their worth. The trouble is, it can often seem as though few give them the respect Phlegmatics know they deserve.

Phlegmatics are good leaders: They have a lot to offer and sincerely want to give it; they won't push but will welcome being able to take charge when needed. My Phlegmatic-Melancholy friend Connie shares: "I like to sit in front, and I like to be at the mic, even when I'm nervous. I want people to notice and appreciate what I do, and I long to be remembered. I feel like I'm overlooked and don't like it."

Phlegmatics are consistent: Phlegmatics are not weak, dull, or stupid but, sadly, a quick, careless study of the temperaments will plop them into the couch-potato category. While those who lack maturity and virtue can indeed settle into the sofa, the easygoing Phlegmatics are not dimwits. They just take more time (and care) to pick up external clues or to process information. Once they do, they can be firm, steady, consistent (even persistent), reliable, and like a rock.

But they are also the gentle river that cuts through rock over a thousand years — the tender green shoot that breaks through concrete. Phlegmatics simply plant one foot in front of the other, block out all distractions, and plow forward. They must be careful, though, not to do the same things over and over and over — and over. It's easier to stay on that railroad track and silently scoff at the others who jumped off long ago, but sometimes Phlegmatics can hit the dead end that the others already saw.

Phlegmatics are loyal: Once they pick a favorite restaurant, they're happy with going there again and again. After the agonizing process of choosing from the menu (so many choices!), they will not look back and think about what they could have had. Who needs change? A Phlegmatic's favorite sweater may be thirty years old, and if he does like to shop, it may not be as frequently as others.

My Melancholy-Phlegmatic husband lines up all his shirts by color in his closet (Melancholy!), and he washes, dries, and hangs them very gently so they can last another three decades (Phlegmatic). Phlegmatics are like that with their most comfortable friends, too: They never want to give them up and are careful to be kind and gentle with them.

Phlegmatics are focused: They work hard at the task at hand and can even seem like "workaholics" when they grind away at the familiar. Sometimes work not only helps them feel productive but also buffered from difficult demands. When Phlegmatics have too much on their plate, it's usually because they've had trouble saying no to others. They can get overwhelmed with too many choices and possibilities, but Phlegmatic focus brings with it a natural ability to block out all distractions, focusing on the one thing, person, or goal that matters. The other temperaments could benefit from this gift!

Phlegmatics are adaptable: For all their single-mindedness, Phlegmatics are also the most adaptable temperament. Like a chameleon, they can "change color" and function as the other temperaments on a temporary basis. If there is no Sanguine in the group, Phlegmatics know how they do it, and they can bring in excitement and humor. If there is no in-charge Choleric or perfect Melancholy at the party, the Phlegmatic will make the lists, check the details, and make sure there is enough food and drink for all.

Don't be fooled into thinking that they *are* all temperaments, though. Phlegmatics are quite content to sit back, watch, and let the Choleric drive the bus, the Sanguine be the entertainment, or the Melancholy act as the event manager — as long as things are going smoothly. But if the Choleric leader has had a heart attack and dropped dead on the spot, and the Sanguine's started crying and screaming, and the Melancholic's slipped into a dark depression, the Phlegmatic will quietly step up and take the wheel, never needing to be the leader, but perfectly able to when necessary. As long as they don't cave to the pressure or opinions of others, they'll hold the reins steady and get everyone to safety while handing the Sanguine a candy bar and drying her tears and assuring the Melancholy that the end of the world has not arrived.

They don't mind not being the center of attention, and most of the time prefer it that way. As with most of us, however, they're hurt when they feel altogether ignored. They want to be seen and loved, but only when they are ready.

Phlegmatics are peaceful: Possessing a quiet spirit, Phlegmatics are not mute, but they radiate calm. With friends or in a familiar, comfortable environment, they may have quite a lot to say. Their walk, talk, voice, facial expressions, and mannerisms are usually warm, loving, kind, gentle, and assuring. Some might say they can look blank, but I say Phlegmatics exude serenity.

Phlegmatics avoid conflict: Diplomatic Phlegmatics do not like conflict and tend to avoid it at any cost, holding the tongue and biting the lip when necessary, but they also have a hard time asking for what they want for fear of making waves, or worse. Sometimes they wonder why people can't just anticipate their needs — a trait that comes so easily to them!

Phlegmatics are procrastinators: Part of avoiding conflict is procrastination, and that hesitation to address things tends to build until they blow up. Kristin shared a story with me about her Phlegmatic mother: "My mom didn't like conflict at all. Growing up, I liked that because she didn't seem to get very upset about things. Mom set boundaries but she didn't like the effort or conflict that came with enforcing them. She also had that Melancholy idealism that expected a perfect family life with no conflict. She gave warnings but didn't back them up much.

"I remember when she put the Oreos in the cookie jar and told us not to eat them, but we did anyway. Instead of getting upset, she just moved the cookie jar higher and higher. But we kept getting into them.

"One day I saw the jar was at the very top of the kitchen cupboards. I started climbing up. She was at the table reading, saw me, and said quietly, 'Kristin, get down.'

"I hesitated and then, when she wasn't looking, I kept climbing. She said it again, '*Kristin, get down.*'

"I just waited, and she kept reading.

"It was a contest of wills. She said 'get down' again and again. I wasn't afraid of her. I climbed again and was taking the lid off the jar when she screamed so loudly, I swear it blew out her vocal cords: '*GET DOWWWWWWN!*'

"She stood up, flipped the table over, and came AT me, still screaming, and she spanked me as hard as she could. It was horrible for both of us."

Understanding the temperaments, Kristin knew what had happened: "My mom procrastinated; she didn't take the time to deal with our disobedience the first time and instead let it build. She thought she could avoid conflict by ignoring it, but it only made it worse."

Phlegmatics are stress-handlers: Most nurses, police officers, EMTs, and firefighters — those who work in high-stress situations — have a Phlegmatic side. They are peacemakers, peacekeepers, and mediators. Stable, steady, focused, balanced, and adaptable, they remain calm when the blood is oozing, the house is burning, and people are threatening to kill each other. They, and often they alone, can bring the boiling moment down to a slow simmer.

Phlegmatics are balanced: Phlegmatics are not usually prone to emotional outbursts. They have the same desires, fears, and feelings as others, but they tend to keep them in check. They work hard at the things that interest them, but they know when to stop and take it easy, too. They worry, but not to excess. They plan, but also stay open to spontaneity as long as it doesn't come too swiftly and knock them off their feet. They open up and talk, but not incessantly. They love, but not obsessively.

Phlegmatics find the easy way: Our Phlegmatics not only love peace but ease. They like to keep things simple (*Why do all the rest of these people make things so complicated?*). They also tend to be inventors; they have all the best ideas for how to make life easier. They find the life hacks and shortcuts that really work. Anything to keep the peace and allow more time for relaxation!

Phlegmatics are caretakers: That natural gift for quietly watching and looking out for others is innate and powerful. I have two very special Phlegmatic girlfriends; if ever I want to curl up in a ball and suck my thumb and need someone to bring me tea, pull a blanket up over me, stroke my forehead and coo, "There, there,

Rosie ..." I will call one of them. They are a beautiful balm to the over-excited, stressed out, depressed people in the world. Even if some people won't respect them, they'll still need them!

Phlegmatics are a much-needed tranquilizer: Sometimes when my Choleric side has been burning the candle at both ends, I will have a mini breakdown. That's when I book lunch with one of my warm, loving, and supportive Phlegmatic girlfriends. I need their quiet calm and their consistent availability. They laugh at my jokes and affirm me in their love. Sometimes we know the problems are not really solved over lunch, and that things will not just "be all right," but for the day, it can be enough.

Phlegmatics are comforting and comfortable: Phlegmatics are like warm, cozy comforters that wrap us up into their hearts. Sometimes they don't need to say a word — their kind smile or caring look says all that the rest of us need to hear. Unless there is work to do, they will take advantage of the time to rest. An example which the charged-up rest of us should copy!

Phlegmatics are the best when life is the worst: With catastrophe, the Sanguine has departed for la-la land, never to be seen again; the Melancholy has jumped off the bridge into the dark, gloomy waters of despair; and the Choleric has imploded, leaving carnage everywhere. The Phlegmatic, meanwhile, is the keel on the boat of life, keeping us all from emotionally capsizing. They calm us, listen to us, support us, and love us — softening life's rough edges, stilling the turbulent waters, smoothing the rocky road, and cooling the fiery shame. They hold the world together even while shaking their heads and quietly wondering, "*What's* wrong *with all these people?*"

Archbishop Fulton Sheen said, "Meekness is not cowardice; meekness is not an easygoing temperament, sluggish and hard to arouse; meekness is not a spineless passivity that allows everyone to walk over us. No! Meekness is self-possession. That is why the reward of meekness is possession [of the earth]."

What's Wrong with Phlegmatics?

Nothing that grace, wisdom, and experience can't fix. Their weaknesses are their strengths carried to extremes — and everyone has them. Again, it is usually pride and fear at the heart of our sinfulness. The Phlegmatic's deepest desires are to have peace and for everyone to respect them. Those desires, and the fear that they won't be fulfilled, may lead them into bad behaviors.

Phlegmatics can be too focused on what is in front of them, failing to see the big picture or even pick up clues from others in the room. They can be too accommodating, allowing others to walk all over and hurt them. They can be too easygoing, not getting involved or being concerned when things go wrong. Sometimes they are too laid-back, dismissing or procrastinating until things pile up and everyone gets angry with them (including them). They can be too patient, allowing others to hurt themselves or others because the Phlegmatics are afraid to look bad, lose affection, or stand up to others. At times they are too quiet, timid, hesitant, disinterested, disengaged, or lazy.

If you are Phlegmatic, take heart: Phlegmatics are tenderly and beautifully made in the image and likeness of God. They share in his stable, unchanging nature, gently and patiently persisting, enduring, and loving to the end. He will walk quietly alongside you and perfect you — if you will keep the steady course to eventually win the race.

Do you think you are a Phlegmatic but are not quite sure? Everyone can be careful, prudent, stable, adaptable, kind, and gentle, and everyone desires peace — but for different reasons and at various times, places, and circumstances. The Phlegmatic is blessed with these virtues and strengths in abundance and is naturally and effortlessly predisposed to them. Remember, you're not just Phlegmatic; you have another temperament: Sanguine or Melancholy. Phlegmatic-Sanguines have an energy boost when needed that helps them to keep things moving. With a Sanguine side, Phlegmatics are doubly easygoing, light, and fun. Phlegmatic-Melancholies are doubly compassionate and sensitive. This person is the best friend who is most reliable, always there, and rich in kindness.

• • •

Reflections

If you are Phlegmatic, what do you like most about having this temperament?

If you are not Phlegmatic, what do you value most in them?

What can you say to or do for a Phlegmatic in your life to make him or her feel more valued?

What Phlegmatic traits do you think are helpful for attaining holiness?

• St. John of the Cross (1542–1591) •

St. John of the Cross was a Spanish priest, mystic, and Carmelite friar, and was a major figure of the Counter-Reformation. A Doctor of the Church, he's known as the "Mystical Doctor." He was mentored by, and worked with, the older Carmelite (also a Doctor of the Church), St. Teresa of Ávila.

What do we know about his temperament?

John is known for his impassioned writings, his poetry, and his studies on the human soul, particularly his *Dark Night of the Soul*. These are considered the summit of mystical Spanish literature. He once had a vision of Christ crucified and drew a picture of it. This art later influenced Salvador Dali's work *Christ of Saint John of the Cross*. Clearly a Melancholy-Phlegmatic, John was naturally drawn to solitary and silent contemplation. But when he met the Choleric Teresa of Ávila, she had other ideas and convinced him to follow her in reforming the Carmelite order, which had fallen into physical and spiritual laxity.

Amid political tensions and resistance to the reform, some Carmelite friars unjustly threw John in prison, where he patiently endured brutality, public lashings, and severe isolation in a tiny, stifling cell. That is where he wrote some of his most profound works, using paper passed to him by a guard. He was eventually rescued, nursed back to health, and continued to work with Teresa in reform until his death.

What can we learn from him?

John turned his intense suffering into magnificent, mystical poetry that still inspires millions today. May God help us all to bring something beautiful from our own sufferings.

St. John of the Cross, pray for us.

• 18 •

Understanding the Melancholy

She opens her hand to the poor,
and reaches out her hands to the needy.
She is not afraid of snow for her household,
for all her household are clothed in scarlet.
She makes herself coverings;
her clothing is fine linen and purple.

— Proverbs 31:20–22

It had been a long, difficult day of writing.

At six o'clock I turned off my computer and trotted into Bob's office where he was leaning back in his comfortable, padded chair and announced, "Well, the Choleric, Sanguine, and Phlegmatic summaries in this book are complete!"

He just looked at me blankly.

"Now I must do the Melancholy," I added.

Nothing.

I admit, I was fishing for a compliment. I wished he would have said, "Wow, that was a LOT! And you have been working so HARD! I could NEVER write as much as you. You're such an AMAZING Choleric!"

But no. He slowly and dramatically assumed the crouching posture of a mad scientist (because Melancholies love an audience, too). "Heh-heh-heh ..." he slyly grinned with a low, slow, drawn-out chuckle, wringing his hands in dastardly delight. "The Melancholy is going to take pages and pages and pages and PAGES! Mua-ha-ha-ha!"

Oh, brother. I rolled my eyes.

"The others are easy!" he said with a smug smile. "The Melancholy is so-o-o-o-o complex."

Yes, Bob. As if I didn't know.

My husband and all three of my stepsons are part Melancholy. My parents and seven of my siblings are all part Melancholy. Trust me; I've come to love, respect, and appreciate the Melancholy temperament. Some Melancholies I even hold in genuine awe. But sometimes they can weigh me down, and sometimes — when they are comfortable and feeling creative — they might compete with me for the limelight, gently elbowing me off the stage, and getting *my* round of applause.

But when a Melancholy loves you? No one is as deeply romantic and tender.

Let's focus on some of the qualities and characteristics that make up this temperament.

Melancholies are introverts: Their responses to life are carefully guarded at first, and so Melancholies tend to be thoughtful and careful, without rashness or overreacting. Their initial hesitation to reveal themselves in certain situations comes from a place of not fully trusting, until trust is appropriate. Once that natural suspicion is cleared, they can be extremely expressive, demonstrative, clever, wryly entertaining — even comedic — and open with thoughts and feelings. People admire them for being loving, compassionate, tender, sensitive, creative, and clever. And

Melancholies can be humorous, outgoing, and in charge — but only when *they* choose to be. No pushing.

Like the other introvert (Phlegmatic), Melancholies are not shy, but self-protective until they are sure that others can be trusted to *understand* them. Personal space is kept safe from intruders until they open the door, so to speak, and let others in on their terms. In-your-face extroverts (Cholerics and Sanguines) often don't understand this and can find Melancholies to be aloof. They're not! They just don't throw friendship, love, and loyalty around like candy to trick-or-treaters. They are not weak; their strengths are intense, however, and most people really don't understand that.

Melancholies are deep and complex: Melancholies are some of the world's greatest academics and intellectuals. They may find themselves contemplating the mysteries of the universe, even while changing a diaper or doing the dishes. They love knowledge! While their desk may look a mess to others, they know exactly where every little thing is. A Melancholic memory is like a computer, with tons of files stored there — you never know when you may trigger an access to some of that important data. They love complexities and intricacies so much that they may get lost in them and discover they've overcomplicated things altogether.

Melancholies are idealistic perfectionists: An idealist is someone who envisions a world where everything is as it should be: perfect! Some people consider them to be naïve, impractical, and out of touch with reality. But I think idealistic Melancholies may just be a little more naturally in touch with the divine than the rest of us; they want to bring heaven to earth. Melancholies crave order, like the Choleric — but if it isn't productive or cost-effective, the Choleric won't pursue absolute perfection to the level Melancholies (who are often aghast that others settle for such sloppiness, priding themselves on perfection in even the littlest things) quite naturally will.

Melancholies are critics: Because they strive for excellence in themselves, Melancholies expect it in others. That's valuable because they hold all of us to a high standard. But they can also be highly critical of others and — if carrying their own unresolved hurt or anger — can be sharp, arrogant, and even cruel. They can crush a person into dust, or slice their emotional throat, with words or even by just a look. They would never dare openly punch someone in the face but can manage the same effect with the softest of words, when they want.

Melancholies are compassionate: They push for noble causes and dedicate many hours to what they believe is worthwhile. Their hearts go out to the hungry, poor, and mistreated. They are passionate about righting the wrongs, healing the broken-hearted, and binding up the world's wounds. Their love, when released, is genuine and deep.

Melancholies are detail-oriented: They love detail since that is a necessary path to perfection. Melancholies can get delightedly lost in the mystery of minutia, and it shows. I love my Melancholy family members and friends. Although I have learned to slow down and pay more attention, I am often rushing around and can seem haphazard by comparison to them.

For Melancholies, there are two realms of detail: one in the proximate and physical, and the other in the great beyond and otherworldly. Some can live in both realms. The Melancholy who cares more for the here and now usually finds purpose, pleasure, and even security in mastering his immediate physical environment: his hair, clothing, shoes, house, desk, files, work product, car, and closet (you get the picture) are perfect. He is happy when everything is lined up, organized, categorized, alphabetized, and sanitized. (These Melancholies tend to be the germophobes and hypochondriacs.) I call this Melancholy "Perfect Patrick."

But the other Melancholy I call "Mad Max." It's not that he can't be orderly and neat in the exterior, but he tends to care far less about it. He leaves aside attention to his desk, house, car, and on most days even his hair, to venture deeper into the worlds of philosophy, math, music, science, nature, mechanics, politics, religion — any deep, meaningful subject which draws him in. He is often lost there, but when he emerges, he may just change the world. Do you know someone like Mad Max? As a child, I remember learning about Madame Marie Curie, a French-Polish scientist who discovered two of the chemical elements. She worked on radioactivity, developed X-rays, significantly furthered medical research, and was the first woman to win a Nobel prize. In her photographs, it's clear she had no interest in, or time for, a hairbrush. And speaking of Melancholy geniuses, Albert Einstein could have used a comb occasionally, too. With his rumpled clothes and messy desk, he gives us an accurate picture of this type. But these Melancholies take their love of detail to another place, hearing and answering the call of the deep unknown.

Melancholies are pessimists: Melancholies are "masters of suspicion" in that they can default to distrust — especially when a situation or person is unknown to them. While they may sometimes go overboard in this, they should not be too self-critical about it; they worry so much because they *care* so much. After all, distrust is the mother of safety.

In social groups, they may be labeled the "negative Nelly," but much of the time their worries are valid. The world *is* a dangerous place, bad things *do* happen, and people *can't* always be trusted. Others of us can be so busy with our important work, playing our games, and taking life easy that we don't realize how much we need Melancholy's pessimism. Debbie Downer? Maybe, but not always, and many of us will thank them in the end.

Yes, Melancholies tend to get depressed more easily than

others. They sometimes seem happy being miserable. The good news is that some forms of depression are necessary; they help us slow down, process, grieve, and heal. But other forms can indulge in powerlessness, self-pity, and bitterness. Melancholies shouldn't feel like they must listen to others who say, "Don't get depressed," but they should listen when asked, "What year may you be leaving your cave to join the rest of the world?" A good rule of thumb for Melancholies comes from St. John Vianney: "God commands you to pray, but he forbids you to worry."

Melancholies are fiercely dedicated: In important matters, Melancholies do not let go easily or quickly. They'd rather die than abandon or surrender, and that is the root of their willingness to sacrifice and even be martyred. But it also means they struggle with letting go of worries, fears, and offenses. Melancholies are especially prone to living with a repressed bitterness that can suck the air right out of the room.

Melancholies never forget: No detail from the past ever seems to escape the cataloged cabinets in their minds. Melancholies need to remember what needs to be remembered and let go of the rest.

Melancholies are creative: Melancholies excel at using words to paint pictures, conveying their intellect, deep passions, and imagination in the details of even a simple story. Once again, distinguished intellectual writers, painters, and poets all have some Melancholy. One of the things I love most about my husband's Melancholy side is the artistry in his voice. Like a fine wine, it's got the rich complexity of Melancholy and the smoothness of the easy Phlegmatic. Bob was a professional voice actor for many years, and he's able to speak with eloquence and charm. As a child he greatly admired, and was influenced by, Mel Blanc, the "man of a thousand voices" and the voice behind Bugs Bunny, Porky Pig, and Daffy Duck. Bob loves to talk, as do most Melancholies when they know and trust their audience. When Bob tells a story, sometimes he will interject his own voice characters: a professor, a pirate, or an old prospector.

One of his friends told me, "I love Bob's voice. I could listen to it for hours."

Colorful, fanciful, and meaningful details are lovely but, like everything else, they have their place. Some Melancholies can tell a story with such abundant side-features and added particulars that listeners get hopelessly lost or fall asleep. With a gift of gab and a love for detail, the Melancholy must watch for those who have nodded off.

Melancholies are curious: No one loves to go down rabbit holes like Melancholies. Sometimes it is suspicion that drives them; other times it is a natural interest or wonder at details. When they're truly interested, they love research. Those Melancholies who are also Phlegmatic will have the patience to stick with the painstakingly dull to get the answer or reward. When they are also Choleric, that part will help to keep them from getting completely lost in the weeds.

Melancholies are quietly intense: Like the extroverted Choleric, Melancholies feel things with the greatest intensity, but their emotions tend to remain inside. When they fall in love, it is forever, and they love as if it is the greatest love ever known. Loyal to a fault, they'll stick with something until the hurts have them bleeding out and their suffering is equal to that of any holy martyr. True or not, they feel it to that degree. Everything is intense. Everything is quietly dramatic. Everything is deep. Everything is meaningful.

Melancholies possess an inner sanctum: Their heart is a sacred place, reserved only for those who have earned trust and to whom they have given their fierce love and undying loyalty. At their center pulses a sensitive, tender, beating heart. It takes time and testing for a special few to really prove they want to know, understand and (importantly) respect the Melancholy. Only then will these be allowed into those deep hearts — into the holy of holies.

Melancholies are delighted when people reach this inner sanctum, finding themselves lighter, more loving, and even frolicking with joy. But! Should anyone betray that delighted trust, well, it would be better for them had they never been born (see Mt 26:24). The Melancholy's doors will slam shut, and the betrayer will not only be permanently blocked but may even be dead to them. Of course, Melancholies who are serious Christians will make every effort to genuinely forgive and to pray for the offender. But even with forgiveness, they'll never trust the person who betrayed them again. If they come crawling back pleading for mercy, Melancholies may give it, because their heart is big. But the penitent will never enter through those interior golden doors again, because the Melancholy will never forget.

What's Wrong with Melancholies?

Nothing that grace, wisdom, and experience can't fix. Their weaknesses are their strengths carried to extremes — and everyone has them. It is usually pride and fear at the heart of our sinfulness. Melancholies deeply desire to be truly understood, and to be honored for their depths. Those desires, and the fear that they won't be fulfilled, may move them into bad behaviors.

Melancholies can be too deep, getting lost in the process and forgetting the people. They can be too critical, not loving others in their imperfect state. They can be too sensitive, becoming a bleeding heart and an enabler. While attention to detail is good, Melancholies can be too detail-oriented, never relenting to themselves or others until everyone is distressed. And they can be too reserved, arrogant, and unforgiving.

Take heart, though, Melancholies: beautiful and complex, made in the image and likeness of God, you share in his deep, mysterious beauty, and that depth is worthy of awe. He will meet you in the complexity and perfect you — if you will not fall off into the darkness along the way.

Do you think you are a Melancholy but are not quite sure? Everyone can be creative, complex, sensitive, passionate, self-sacrificing, and striving for perfection, but all for different reasons and at various times, places, and circumstances. The Melancholy is blessed with these virtues and strengths in abundance and is naturally and effortlessly predisposed to them. Remember, Melancholies also have another temperament, either Choleric or Phlegmatic. Melancholies who are also Choleric are less likely to sink too deeply into the dark, which helps them to accomplish remarkable things. Melancholies who are also Phlegmatic are better able to let go of the angst that sometimes cripples them.

• • •

Reflections

If you are Melancholy, what do you like most about having this temperament?

If you are not Melancholy, what do you value most in people you know who are?

What can you say to or do for a Melancholy in your life to make him or her feel more understood?

What is a natural Melancholy gift that can help lead them to sainthood?

Part 4

Looking to Sainthood

Do not forget that holiness consists not in extraordinary actions, but in performing your duties toward God, yourself, and others well.

— St. Maximillian Kolbe, text for the Assumption, 1940

• St. Raymond Nonnatus (1204–1240) •

After his mother died in childbirth, Saint Raymond (Ramon) was delivered by the dagger of the Viscount of Cardona, who took the child out of his mother's womb; thus, he acquired the nickname Nonnatus (not born). As a young man, he joined the Order of Mercy (Mercedarians), which was founded to ransom Christian captives from the Muslims in North Africa.

What do we know about his temperament?
The Mercedarians raised redemption funds and ventured deep into the Muslim camps in Algeria to ransom Christian prisoners. Imagine the saint sitting in smoke-filled enemy tents bargaining for people's lives! When he ran out of money, Raymond offered himself in exchange and remained in captivity for years before he was also ransomed.

Most orders take vows of poverty, chastity, and obedience; the Mercedarian "fourth vow" is *my life for your freedom*. Raymond was reported to have been very pious and zealous, and this, coupled with the literal self-sacrifice of his life, makes it likely that he was a passionate Melancholy.

In captivity, to keep him from preaching, his captors bored a hole in his lips with a hot iron and padlocked them. Even unable to speak, his heroic example converted several Muslims.

What can we learn from him?
Melancholies, when they love you, are the first to willingly suffer for you. If you have a Melancholy in your life, thank God. May we *all* learn to give our lives so willingly for others' freedom.

St. Raymond Nonnatus, pray for us.

• 19 •

Perfecting Your Temperament

If we are calm and persevering, we shall find not only ourselves, but our souls, and with that, God himself.

— *Padre Pio,* Spiritual Maxims

Who can forget the delightful ballroom scene in Rodgers and Hammerstein's *My Fair Lady*? Linguistics professor Henry Higgins has bet his colleague he can pass off an unkempt, uneducated flower girl — Eliza Doolittle — as a member of the upper-class nobility at the Embassy Ball. After months of rigorous training, the night of the ball arrives, and a tuxedoed Higgins introduces a magnificently transformed Eliza. As she glides across the floor in a shimmering gown and sparkling tiara, heads turn, gasps are heard, and everyone is dazzled by her stunning grace and exquisite beauty.

This once raggedy young woman, whose grating Cockney accent Professor Higgins found "depressing and disgusting," was not transformed into someone else. Instead, she learned to shed her lower thinking and habits to allow her unique, natural grace and dignity to emerge and shine.

What God created as good — no, *very* good — has been burdened by the street-smudge of sin. When, by grace, you can lift away the sin, you can reveal the bright and glowing divine nature in which all of us are called to partake (see 2 Pt:1–5). Let's remember, though, that nothing unclean will enter heaven (Rv 21:27). We need to be rid of our inordinate attachments and anything that still stands in the way of our total purification. Like Eliza, if we continually submit to God's loving and careful "training," he will perfect everything about us — including our temperament. So let's talk about what it means to perfect our temperament. St. Thomas Aquinas addresses man's ultimate perfection in heaven in his *Summa*: "This disposition of newness will be neither natural nor contrary to nature, but above nature (just as grace and glory are above the nature of the soul): and it will proceed from an everlasting agent which will preserve it forever" (q. 91, a. 1, obj. 4).

Let's look at four truths about the soul's perfection:

1. *Perfection is ultimately not our work, but God's*: God will lead. Our job is to pay attention and follow. Yes, of course, we get to prayerfully chime in, but we can trust that the Creator already fully knows us and our temperaments and will help us discover what works for us as we strive for perfection. He promises that when we take up his yoke, our burdens will be light, and we will find rest for our souls (see Mt 11:29–30).
2. *Perfection is a trusting surrender to God*: A Choleric, for instance, can work toward developing balanced, quiet virtues that come naturally to the Phlegmatic and can even share in them, and yet remain Choleric. A Choleric who orders all of himself to God

will find his Choleric nature perfected. And we can surmise he will retain his perfected Choleric nature for eternity.

We do not need to become something or someone else to be perfected. We do not need to diminish or downplay our own God-given bent. But we *do* need to ask God to help us remove our impurities of mind, memory, imagination, thoughts, and habits. A good, bottom-line definition of perfection is "total abandonment and surrender to God." A good working definition of perfection of one's temperament is "the unburdening of all inordinate attachments, wrong beliefs, fears, and anxieties to make way for the grace-infused, natural strengths to emerge, operate, and shine."

3. *Perfection is the ultimate self-care*: The world would tell us that perfecting ourselves is the goal of self-care, by healthy eating and exercising, cutting out of our lives the toxic people who irritate us, making time to breathe, getting in touch with some higher power, and spending whatever time or monies are necessary for soothing pleasures.

   Some of these are good and necessary at the right time and place because we do have a responsibility to take care of our mind, heart, body, and soul, especially in ways that direct us toward God and are pleasing to him. We must take the time, and make the effort, to properly nurture ourselves while also feeding on the truth, rooting out vice, and developing virtue. We do need to protect ourselves from those who would promote lies and encourage us in our sins. We should be in touch, always, with the God who loves us and draws us to himself.

In fact, self-care properly understood is part of our perfection. As part of our path to perfection, consider these three things: 1) Proper self-love is a grateful acceptance of who we are both in our littleness and nothingness compared to Almighty God and also in our goodness, having been loved into being by God and made in his image. 2) Appropriate self-care, then, is attending to the legitimate needs of mind, heart, body, and soul at times and in ways that are directed to God, be it properly enjoying or making a sacrifice of what God has given us. 3) Perfection is defined as the complete detachment from everything and everyone except God — not in rejecting lower goods or even the people we love as bad, but in desiring first and foremost the absolute goodness of God.

Yes, we can still enjoy and love our family and friends. Yes, we can savor a glass of wine, a good meal, and maybe a fine cigar. But properly defined, self-love, self-care, and perfection mean that while we appreciate those things, we don't need them. As St. Teresa of Ávila said in the prayer she kept in her breviary, God alone is enough.

4. *Perfection is replacing fear with love*: I've addressed the effects of fear throughout this book because, being at the root of our imperfection, they can't be stressed enough. Fear and love are like bus drivers: One will drive your natural desires to virtue, the other to vice. Love perfects our temperamental desires; fear corrupts them. Love moves us into our temperament's strengths; fear into its weaknesses. If we can find the fear and the wrong thinking behind our mistakes and replace them with truth and love,

we will be saints.

The key is making enough space for God to fill us to the brim with his love so that it will overflow and spill out to others. Let's look at how love or fear can move us in different directions, to either virtues or vices. Overly attached and fearful of not getting what they want, the types will be disconnected, anxious, or angry and function in their weaknesses:

- Phlegmatics will be avoidant, isolated, cowardly, lazy, timid, and indecisive.
- Melancholies will be suspicious, critical, moody, dark, and depressed.
- Sanguines will be clingy, loud, undisciplined, self-centered, and permissive.
- Cholerics will be domineering, impatient, intolerant, cold, and unsympathetic.

But filled with God's love, the types will be appropriately detached, at peace, joyful, and able to function in their strengths:

- Phlegmatics will be kind, patient, calm, respectful, consistent, stable, and supportive.
- Melancholies will be noble, attentive, sensitive, self-sacrificing, analytical, and creative.
- Sanguines will be cheerful, optimistic, light, affectionate, compassionate, and playful.
- Cholerics will be productive, decisive, protective, hard-working, and courageous.

The reality is everyone can become a saint. None of the four temperaments is more suited to holiness than the others. You can and should be inspired by the other temperaments, seeking to understand their loveliness and advantages, but not rejecting your own wonderful temperament in the process. Work with God to smooth the rough edges of your own temperament. God will call each of us according to our nature, and he is the one who will perfect us. We must trust and cooperate with him.

Did Jesus Have All Four Temperaments?

Perhaps not wanting to be preferential or exclusive, some say that Jesus either did not have a temperament or that he had all four. Why might someone assume that?

They may believe that a specific temperament combination is incomplete or imperfect because it lacks the natural strengths of the other two. They might think that since we are all meant to be Christ-like, Our Lord must possess all four temperaments, so none are left out. Perhaps they think that if Jesus only had a natural combination of two, then the other two would be lesser temperaments. What a sad state that would be; the two supposedly inferior temperaments would somehow be doomed to work harder for perfection.

Isn't all that just us projecting our worries and fears upon the Lord and thus creating him in our own image?

The temperaments are complementary. Pope St. John Paul II tells us that man and woman are different but equal in value and dignity. Temperaments, too, in their original purity can thus be considered different but equal, possessing distinctly different, and sometimes opposite, natural tendencies and orientations. Saint Paul reminds us that the Spirit has endowed each of us with different and specific gifts (see 1 Cor 12) so that, together, we can form a holy communion; so that no none of the temperaments can say to the others, "I have no need of you," and, conversely, so that none of us can reject our own goodness or cry in self-pity, "They have no need of my Sanguine lightheartedness, my Choleric desire to lead, my Melancholy gift of seeing the problems, or my calm, steady Phlegmatic support."

It's important to remember that Jesus was fully human. Scripture reminds us that he was like us in all things except sin (see Heb 4:15). If you're still not convinced that Jesus had a specific temperament as we do, then here are some other points to think about:

- *He wasn't both man and woman*: Jesus wasn't an angel who could take on human form but had no sex. He wasn't an unnatural combination of male and female. He was a man. He had a biological sex, and it was male. He did not need to be or become female to be perfect or to complete his mission on earth.
- *He didn't have all four blood types*: Every one of the verified Eucharistic miracles (where the Blessed Sacrament turns into human cardiac tissue), as well as the Shroud of Turin, all confirm the same blood type: AB+. For those of us who believe, does that make the other blood types less desirable? Would Jesus have to have had all four to be perfect? Of course not.
- *He was like us in all things except sin*: He grew in wisdom (see Lk 2:52), so we know his natural temperament was shaped by his parents, education, understanding, and his maturing. Did he already have an adaptable, gentle temperament, or did Mary help shape him that way? How much of his speak-out-and-take-charge side was from his temperament? Was it learned from his father or other extroverted Jewish men? We may never know this side of heaven. But I like to believe that Our Lord, like us, had a specific temperament that — unaffected by fear, anxiety, or vices that would lead him to sin — was pleasing and perfected.

Not all of us are the same sex as Jesus, or the same ethnicity, or possess the same physiological makeup. Since that is true, then we can also be content with having been gifted by the Spirit with a different temperament than Jesus. It's not what you have but what you do with it that pleases God.

Our Humanity Can Become Perfected

As I watch myself, friends, and family grow in maturity, I see the rough edges of all the temperaments begin to soften. This happens when the soul begins to let go of what it had been grasping for so long — when it surrenders its heart to God and begins to see eternity everywhere. Saint Irenaeus tells us that "the glory of God is man fully alive," so we do not have to reject or diminish anything about our humanity. Rather, we allow God to purify it and infuse it with his divine nature. With maturity, we become more fully alive as humans, which ultimately is more Christ-like.

This is true for all of us, regardless of temperament. The angry, bossy Choleric mellows and becomes kinder, gentler, and more patient. The flighty Sanguine is still sweet and a bit sassy but has grown calm and grounded in God's love. The brooding Melancholy no longer worries excessively and has centered in trusting God. The peaceful Phlegmatic finally speaks up, no longer afraid to stir the proverbial pot.

God wants to give you the power to perfect your gifts of temperament. You do not need to kill yourself trying to gain all the strengths and avoid all the weaknesses of all four. Just bringing your own natural dispositions back into right order is work enough. And don't wait until your golden years to begin!

To return to *My Fair Lady*: like Eliza, each of us can hold the world captive as we grow into the person God made us to be. At the glamorous Embassy Ball, the sleazy Hungarian language expert Zoltan Karpathy was astonished at Eliza's perfect poise and punctuation. He was dying to find out who this glorious creature really was, suspecting some secret to her identity. So, he took her out onto the dance floor and put her to the test, "oozing charm from every pore," and with "every trick that he could play, he used to strip her mask away."

But in his arms, Eliza floated flawlessly across the room, and he was utterly captivated. In the end, Karpathy was convinced she *had* been keeping a secret: that she was indeed so stunning that she was not just nobility — she could be nothing less than royalty!

The more God tenderly and deftly shapes my own smudge-faced ways, the more I long to dazzle him with my temperamental beauty. This is the hope of the soul for whom fear is cast out and sin stripped away, until God's love in us and through us radiates to such a degree that it holds him, and the world, captive. Let us be unburdened of our fearful, sinful tendencies so that our true humanity — be it Sanguine, Phlegmatic, Melancholy, or Choleric — can give glory to him whom we reflect.

• • •

Reflections

What does "perfection" mean to you?

What are your thoughts on the term *surrender*?

Are there any old ways of thinking you have been able to wash away as you have matured? If yes, what are they?

What is one area of your life where you would like to be more pleasing to God?

• St. Teresa of Ávila (1515–1582) •

Saint Teresa was a Carmelite nun, Spanish mystic, religious reformer, author, and theologian of the contemplative life and of mental prayer. Most people know her by her seminal work, *The Interior Castle*. She was the first woman to be named a Doctor of the Church.

What do we know about her temperament?
Teresa had an outgoing and even fiery personality, described as vibrant, affectionate, and buoyant. She loved clothes, boys, and flirting. When she was sixteen, her father sent her to the convent, thinking she was out of control; initially she thought it no fun but, aware of her own temperament, she decided it was the best place for her. Eventually her take-no-prisoners Choleric side took over and reformed the entire order.

As a Sanguine, she often wrote in colorful and humorous analogies that added wit and sparkle to her writings, including those about chess, bullfights, butterflies, and precious jewels. She often grappled with deep contemplation, unlike the more naturally pious Melancholies. Struggling with this even to her death, she eventually surrendered her Choleric-Sanguine heart and learned to let her beloved Spouse lead her.

What can we learn from her?
As her passion was steadily directed to Our Lord, she was horrified by the terror of sin (particularly hers) and her powerlessness in confronting it, and recognized the need to be obedient to the Lord. The double-extroverts often find it difficult to slow down and follow God, but his grace is sufficient for them, too!

St. Teresa of Ávila, pray for us.

• 20 •

Assessing Your Situation

Self-knowledge leads us by the hand,
as it were, to humility.

— *St. Josemaría Escrivá,* The Way

"It's demo day!" is a familiar cry on the popular TV show *Fixer Upper*. Hosts Chip and Joanna Gaines buy old houses, and we viewers watch them magically transform dilapidated dumps into stunning showcase homes. I admit it, I'm a home makeover TV series nut. I suspect it's part of my Choleric nature to get excited about bringing beautiful order out of messy chaos.

Before making a plan to build something new in our lives, we must first assess the current situation. Do you want to grow in virtue? Do you want to put God more centrally in your day-to-day life? Do you want your life to be, as St. Teresa of Calcutta advised, "something beautiful for God"?

Well, first we might need a demolition of some of the walls in our hearts that need to come down, the shoring up of unstable foundations, and the rewiring of old ways of thinking. Be patient; none of this will happen in one day, like it does on TV.

With my coaching clients, I ask four questions to help them

get started in surveying the situation so that they can create a plan to get them where they want to be:

1. Where do you want to go?
2. What steps will you take?
3. What's in your way?
4. What does God have to say?

As you embark on your path to perfection, remember that we are mind (intellect), heart (emotions), body (physical), and soul (spiritual). The way of perfection for our temperaments must not be limited to religious practices, but must also aim at an integration of the whole person. What affects our moral life will also affect our intellectual, emotional, physical, financial, social, familial, and marital life, and vice versa.

I'm sharing my life inventory list to help you get specific in your assessment. It includes six general categories that you will rate on a scale of 1:10, with 10 as the ideal and 1 as in you need a complete overhaul. If you can, set aside a day where there are no distractions or time constraints and prayerfully make your own life assessment. There's no rule against having a close friend, therapist, coach, or spiritual director work with you on this.

Because we all can get easily confused or overwhelmed by all that we want to do or change, just focus on one or more at a time, depending on what is most appealing, necessary, or urgent for you:

1. *Career*: How is your job or homemaker vocation doing? Are you at or close to a 10? What does it need to improve? Do you get along with others or is there something that is chronically exhausting or irritating? Is it all-consuming or the center of your life? Is there room for time with God there? Are you free to

express your faith? What would be an ideal or better situation for you? What must you start or stop doing to be where you want to be? If you're in ministry or retired, are you using your time wisely?

2. *Finances*: Are you financially secure, or living with constant anxiety? Do you live on a budget? Are you appropriately generous with almsgiving? What must you start or stop doing to get it to a 10?
3. *Relationships*: Do you even remember your family? Just kidding, but are you loving them as God loves you? Can you sit and listen as well as direct and teach? Are you tolerating family members who treat you with disobedience or disrespect? Do you need counseling or other help with relationship skills? Are you struggling with loneliness, being single, or fear of missing out? Are you aware of your family members' temperaments and do you know how to best meet their emotional needs? Are you stuck in a difficult marriage and don't know what to do? Are you dating someone who is not good for you? Do you have a good support system of friends? Why or why not? What must you start or stop doing to get it to a 10?
4. *Spiritual*: What would this part of your life look like if it were a 10? Would you like to go to daily Mass? Would you like to make a habit of monthly confession? What would you like to add or eliminate from your days to make more time for God? What preconceived notions or beliefs do you hold on to that may be in the way of doing this?
5. *Health*: Are you taking appropriate care of your body? Do you seek comfort or solace in too much food, drink, work, play, shopping, gambling, or

screen time? What about your mental and emotional health? Why or why not, and how? Are you neglecting yourself because of work? Maybe spending too much time at the gym? Are you exhausted, depressed, or anxious? What needs to change? Follow your favorite advice to others: Just do it.

6. *Space*: Is your physical space (environment) of home, yard, office, and car clean, orderly, safe, and efficient? Even if it is, does it also have heart? Is it warm, inviting, and beautiful? Are there visible signs of your faith such as art prints, statues, and crucifixes? What would it take to bring reminders of God (and his angels and saints) into your environs?

It's a lot, I know. I suspect that's part of why God gives us all these years on earth.

Sanguines love to think of new projects and will get excited about making the whole thing fun. Of course, they will start with what's easy (they and the Phlegmatics are a lot alike in that regard) and go buy some new diet cookies or hang an image of Jesus their office. Is that necessarily a bad thing? Not at all. Many studies have shown that starting with the easiest task will help get you going, instead of being stuck at "overwhelmed." But when the Sanguines encounter the dry times or difficulties, they will struggle to stick with the plan. A secondary temperament of Choleric will give them a boost. If their other type is Phlegmatic, however, well forget it … for now.

Melancholies will have several responses to the assessment. Part of them will recognize and appreciate the depth of what needs to be plumbed. They may even be excited to expand the list to include more areas, but another part may feel lost in the endless possibilities and become stuck or discouraged. Self-criticism or criticism of the list might follow. If they are also a Choleric type, that part will help energize them and keep them on track. If they are part Phlegmatic, they will have the wisdom to take a break in between their difficult labors.

Phlegmatics will definitely be overwhelmed at first. But that doesn't mean they'll take flight or freeze. They are as dedicated and capable of working with God toward their perfection as the rest. It just means they might need more time to consider the list, sort it, think about it, or pray about it. They know enough to set a deadline to begin but might wait until the very last minute. If they have a Sanguine part, it will help to lift them from inertia and look for the rewards that will come. If their companion temperament is Melancholy, that side will remind them of God's love and how good and beneficial it will be to be on the path to perfection.

Cholerics, as we know, thrive on accomplishment and jump excitedly at the thought of a to-do list. However, they may get distracted and derailed by several other worthy and important tasks in life that they will add to their plate. Thinking there will be no problems doing it all, the Choleric forgets (or denies) that there are only twenty-four hours in a day and can get sidetracked from the path to perfection.

None of us should be discouraged. Recall that the Temple of Jerusalem was the center of religious and national life in Israel and took forty-six years to build! You are a temple of the Holy Spirit, so don't be discouraged if you can't reach perfection in a short time. God also gives us the Church as the builder's guild and his master craftsmen in the saints to help us design, build, and rebuild as needed.

And lest you get discouraged again along the way, take heart. The good work he has begun in you will be completed (see Phil 1:6). Jesus regularly visited the temple and on more than one occasion cleared the temple of those who would defile it. What he has built in you, he will also protect and purify. That's you!

• • •

Reflections

Can you describe in detail what kind of person you want to be?

Which area of your life (from the six listed in this chapter) seems to need the most help right now?

How is your temperament responding to the assessment questions?

Can you recall a time when God came into your life and did some cleanup? What happened?

• St. Catherine of Siena (1347–1380) •

St. Catherine Benincasa was a lay member of the Dominican Order, living a prayerful but active life outside any convent. She was a mystic, activist, and author who had a major influence on Italian literature, politics, and the Catholic Church, and she is a Doctor of the Church.

What do we know about her temperament?
She preferred a withdrawn life, but Jesus told her to go out into the world, so she began with helping the poor and sick. She traveled throughout Italy preaching, writing, and patiently and persistently advocating for the reform of the clergy and the people. Pope Gregory XI had run away from Rome to hide out in Avignon, France, during political turmoil, so Catherine went to tell him to get back where he belonged! He listened to her and named her an ambassador, widening her audience to include figures in authority as she negotiated for peace between the republics and principalities.

The Great Schism of the West later led Catherine to go to Rome with the new pope. She wrote to princes and cardinals to promote obedience to Pope Urban VI. You might assume Catherine was Choleric, but Phlegmatics are better natural ambassadors. A quiet, introverted woman can have courage and enough Phlegmatic stubbornness to address national dignitaries and hold her ground.

What can we learn from her?
It takes heart, conviction, and courage to stand up and speak out, especially to those in authority. With God's grace, both extroverts and introverts can handle the job, but the introverts would be better at avoiding a war.

St. Catherine of Siena, pray for us.

• 21 •

Rooting Out Your Sins

The soul who loves virtuously, places the root of her tree in the valley of true humility.

— *St. Catherine of Siena,* Dialogue

I hate spurge! It's an ugly, pesky weed that can take over a gorgeous lawn quite rapidly, here in our warm-weather desert. When I first discovered it in my yard, I went to my peaceful Phlegmatic mother, who had a green thumb.

"Mom, I sprayed these weeds, but the little suckers keep coming back! What the heck?"

"You can't just treat the surface of the plant, Rosie. You must carefully pull out the entire root."

Dang, I knew that. I just hoped the easy way would work.

This applies well to our spiritual life because we all have roots. We are told to be firmly rooted in Christ so that we can partake in his nature and bear rich fruit (see Col 2:7). But we can also attach ourselves to and take in what is not good for us. Too often we are tending to the surface of sins that just keep coming back. We find ourselves confessing the same old things, over and over again. Be patient, keep going, but start getting to the taproot, the true origin, of those sins.

Each of the temperaments has root sins. If we don't cut out the heart of our sins, we will be caught within that endless cycle of sin and confession. This is part of the work of perfection: taking the time, risking the shame, and identifying and changing the thinking behind the action.

For instance, if we tell lies to keep from being judged, or excessively people-please to gain their affection and approval, or we violate our own conscience to keep them happy, then we are struggling with the root sin of *vanity*. What? You thought vanity was someone gazing upon their loveliness in the mirror? Actually, that one is *pride*.

All root sins are present in all of us, but one or two may dominate — usually (unsurprisingly) according to temperament:

- *Pride (SELF)*: Excessive love of one's own power, skill, beauty, or excellence. It's seeking our security and self-worth in our own abilities, strengths, and even temperamental traits. Sadly, it also comes with thinking that others are (eyeroll) dull, stupid, uneducated, pathetic, or idiotic. Note: Pride is a sin, and where many like to use the term "healthy pride," as in "getting that A+ after studying those long hours," I like to use the word *pleased* instead: *Son, we're so pleased for you! I'm pleased with the way I stood up to that bully! She should be pleased with herself for her success.*
- *Vanity (OTHERS)*: Excessive attachment to and seeking our security in how we are perceived by others. Do they see me, like me, approve of me? This is classic codependency, where we set others up as little gods whose approval becomes the food that feeds us. We give them the power to control

us. Sadly, I find people-pleasing has become a cultural epidemic, especially since so many have defined being a good Christian as always being nice, accommodating, and tolerant even of disrespect, disobedience, and abuse. Read the gospels where Jesus was not always "nice" to others; he often privately and sometimes publicly called people out and told them to stop their bad behavior, and even called them names (see Mt 23:4–24). Sometimes he was calm, other times he made a whip and turned tables. We must be like Jesus: detached enough to refuse to tolerate sinful behavior in and from others.

- *Sensuality (THINGS)*: Seeking our self-worth in or excessive attachment to possessions, pleasure, or comfort. This also comes with excessive avoidance of discomfort and is not limited to the pursuit of sexual pleasure only.

Desire for Happiness Lies at the Root of Root Sins

The desire for happiness drives every decision and fuels our temperamental responses. Peace, approval, affection, understanding, and respect from others are, in themselves, good things, and there is nothing wrong with desiring them. But in addition to darkening our intellect and weakening our will, original sin *disordered our desires.*

In a book I wrote on happiness, I addressed another ancient Greek teaching on the "four levels of happiness," which are listed here with the lowest level of good first:

1. THINGS: Things we enjoy in the created world
2. SELF: Enjoying our abilities and reaching personal goals

3. OTHERS: Happiness in giving up things and self for the good of others
4. GOD: Finding the ultimate happiness in our relationship with God

The Lord allows us to first experience lower securities, pleasures, and joys so that they will eventually lead us to him. Sadly, we can all get stuck pursuing the lower levels of happiness and never look up to see God as the Perfection of all of them.

With the hierarchy of human desires turned upside down, it's not a coincidence that these three lower levels of happiness are also what we call the three root sins. Our inordinate attachments to *things, self,* and *others* will block us from God, who is the highest level of happiness.

In the paragraphs below, the temperaments are listed in the general order of which types usually struggle with that particular root sin the most. Which do you recognize in yourself?

PRIDE

Temperament	**When They Struggle**
Choleric	Pretty much all the time because, let's face it, they are highly productive, natural leaders and almost always right. At least they think so. They can be demanding, impatient, cold, harsh, and quick to anger.

Melancholy	They are critical by nature and even though we might not hear it from their lips, they can judge others harshly. They are so deep and complex (or such martyrs) that no one ever really understands them. They can be as angry and arrogant as the Choleric.
Sanguine	They like to think they are smart, cute, adorable, funny, and entertaining and can't understand why anyone wouldn't like them. Preoccupied with themselves, they will overlook and hurt others and then giggle. They don't think they need to be perfected.
Phlegmatic	Although usually submissive by nature, they can resent being told what to do and will quietly refuse to submit, or they'll procrastinate. They are passively prideful and will dig in their heels to show that they have the real power and won't be cowed.

VANITY

Temperament	**When They Struggle**
Phlegmatic	As natural people-pleasers, they can go too far. Fearful of standing up and being exposed, of making waves or worse, they dread what others might say, do, or think about them. They can sacrifice their principles, beg for acceptance, and allow others' opinions to overinfluence them.
Sanguine	They can place too much importance on others' seeing and loving them. They can excessively primp and perform and thus "prostitute" themselves in the process. They can lie, cheat, and gossip to gain the attention and affection of others.
Melancholy	While not as obvious as the Sanguine, they can also worry excessively about appearance and performance. They want to be the best and will do anything to win the Oscar. Without praise, they can get very depressed.
Choleric	Least likely of the four to care about what others think, they still want our appreciation for all their hard work. They want us to be loyal followers and in return will look out for us. But if we don't praise them for this, they will be quick to anger and will walk away.

SENSUALITY

Temperament	When They Struggle
Sanguine	Naturally childlike, they can whine and complain about the smallest discomforts. With a clear conscience, they can put in the least effort and only do what they enjoy. They can be fickle and are the most easily distracted by the next distraction or pleasure.
Melancholy	Like the opposite Sanguine, they can also demand their own comforts, be picky eaters, or be too fussy about their things and their clothes. They let their moods and feelings dictate their actions and expect others to serve them.
Phlegmatic	They can be excessively passive and put in only the minimal effort. They can be too content with the basics: food, sleep, and entertainment devices. They can lack a moral backbone, won't communicate or follow through, and will happily wait for others to do it.
Choleric	Cholerics can pride themselves on being minimalists. They can feel so independent and self-sufficient that they don't need comfort or pleasure if they are being productive. When they finally crash and burn, their other side (either Melancholy or Sanguine) will run for the comforting pleasures.

Temperaments Need a Green Thumb

Getting back to my story, I went home intending to do what mom had told me — "Pull out the whole root" — but in my Choleric rush I was not slow and careful in the process. How could I know that each tiny leaf of the plant carries a seed, and my willy-nilly Sanguine methods were scattering hundreds of seeds all around?

Identifying and addressing our root sin is one thing. But we must also keep our lawn (mind, heart, and soul) clean, trimmed, and watered to prevent weeds. Some gardeners will recommend that you also regularly spray a pre-emergent barricade to prevent seeds from taking root. This applies analogously to the spiritual life: A frequent reception of God's special graces in the sacraments can be a most effective defense against pesky habits of sin.

• • •

Reflections

What do you think is your primary root sin?

Do you struggle with a secondary root sin? If yes, what is it?

How does your temperament struggle with a particular root sin?

What can you do to avoid feeling discouraged by your sins?

• St. Frances de Sales (1567—1622) •

St. Francis de Sales was born in France into a noble family and was educated in the humanities in Paris. He received his doctorate in both civil and canon law and was ordained a priest.

What do we know about his temperament?

He was intelligent and a prolific writer, best known for two spiritual classics: *Introduction to the Devout Life* and *Treatise on the Love of God*. For Francis, romantic love was an icon of our love for God, lived out with deep devotion and sweet, tender longings. His writings are sensitive, fervent, even poetic, and reflective of the Melancholy heart.

As a Phlegmatic, he was reported to have been gentle, kind, and remarkably patient. He was also known as "The Gentleman Saint." During the Protestant Reformation, he decided to bring Calvinists back to the Catholic Church. For three years, he trudged through the countryside, had doors slammed in his face, and even had rocks thrown at him. In the bitter winters, his feet froze so badly they bled as he tramped through the snow. Quiet, steady, Phlegmatic persistence!

But because of his non-offensive manner and gentleness, he continued to reach out by slipping little tracts under people's doors and engaging kindly with their children. When the parents began to open up and talk with him, it is believed he brought some 40,000 back to the Church.

What can we learn from him?

Francis shows how the Melancholy can order his poetic, creative nature to the good. He also shows us the saintly strength and power of patience, persistence, and gentleness. All Phlegmatic strengths.

St. Francs de Sales, pray for us.

• 22 •

Creating a Rule of Life

There is no arrival unless there is a definite plan to go.

— *St. John Cassian,* Conferences

The first act of creation was God bringing order out of chaos. He wants us to share in that divine action by bringing or restoring order to our own world. A rule of life is a carefully crafted set of commitments, guidelines, disciplines, and schedules that will direct us in detachment and creating space for God each day.

Here are some important points to remember about an ordered rule of life.

A rule of life requires structure: As we've seen, not all temperaments respond the same to the thought of rules, regulations, instructions, constraints, and discipline. Sanguines, who like to join programs, appreciate structure but will be tempted not to stick with it when it gets too difficult, or when they no longer feel inspired. Phlegmatics, who love to be fluid and adaptable, tend to resist structure because they can feel boxed in and controlled. Melancholies, who need room to be creative, also tend to feel restricted by structure but will love it when it applies to their passion. Cholerics, who crave order, will thrive within structure, as it allows them to see the big picture and be highly productive.

An ordered rule of life should bring you peace: In the late 1970s, my brother Joe went to hear Fr. John Hampsch, CMF (1925–2020), who was teaching in Palm Springs, California, where we lived. That night, a miracle occurred.

Father was known for his Healing of the Family Tree ministries, and he called himself an "itinerant preacher-teacher," with special emphasis on teaching and charismatic healing services. His talk that night was on peace, and my brother clearly recalls Father's core message and what happened at the event.

"There are two kinds of peace," said Father. "Peace *with* God and peace *of* God. Peace *with* God is what Jesus won for us on the cross, and now mankind is reconciled with the Father. We all have this peace by reason of our baptism. But not all of us have the peace *of* God."

Father went on to explain that when we let unnecessary fears, worries, and anxieties burden us, they rob us of the peace that God wants for us. When we know and trust God sufficiently, nothing can disturb us or deprive us of true peace.

The talk was being held at St. Theresa's Catholic Church, and at the break Father left the meeting room and went hunting for some coffee. Down the hall was another room with the lights off, but he could see it was a kitchen and that there was a small red light glowing up against the back counter. A coffee percolator! Father fumbled in the dark to grab a cup he hoped was clean and pressed the spigot for the coffee. He took a big gulp but then gasped in shock and pain. The cleaning crew had left a lye solution in the coffee pot to deep-clean it and Father had just drunk it down.

He was rushed to the local hospital where he heard the doctor say, *His vocal cords are fried; this man will never speak again.*

Panic gripped Father as he lay sweating on the hospital

gurney. Speaking was his whole mission! Speaking was how he spread the word of God. Speaking was his identity, his life! Speaking was also how he ministered and made money to sustain his ministry and order. What about all those souls he would never reach? And then suddenly he was aware of his growing panic and utter lack of peace.

He took a deep breath, remembered his own message on peace, and turned his mind and heart to God, thinking, *It doesn't matter, it doesn't matter, it doesn't matter. Thy will be done. Thy will be done. Dear God, I trust you. I love you.*

Father later reported that at that moment, he felt a warm tingling begin at the top of his head and move down through his entire body. He sat up and was beginning to put on his shoes to leave when the doctor stopped him.

"What do you think you're doing?"

In a clear and audible voice, Father said, "I'm fine now. I'm leaving."

The doctor immediately examined him and confirmed that there was absolutely no sign of any physical trauma to the inside of Father's mouth or throat where just minutes before there had been. Can you believe it? All kinds of miracles, big and small, can happen when we surrender our stress and worries to God.

What unnecessary worries might you be carrying? God wants to give you his peace. One of the ways we can experience the peace of God is to fix our minds and hearts on him and structure our days so that he is at the center. We can create a God-centered "rule of life."

A rule of life should not be too burdensome: A rule of life is typically followed by priests and religious but is something that can benefit us all. At its heart it brings love and intimacy into our relationship with God. It should be neither too easy nor too difficult, lest we puff up with pride or collapse into discouragement. It should be able to be kept without strain, with only occasional challenges. Life in general has enough of those! It should be both fixed and flexible according to the demands of our changing life and vocation. I'm reminded of Jesus' words about taking his yoke upon ourselves (see Mt 11:29–30), because with him the yoke will be easy (fit just to the way we are wired) and our burdens will be light. Our rule of life should fit so that our soul can grow into it.

St. Francis de Sales recognized that when lay people try to imitate saints who were priests or religious, there is tremendous frustration. In his writings, the saint gives us some consoling tips:

- *Be patient*: To attain perfection we must patiently endure our imperfection. This is the essence of healthy humility.
- *Be at peace*: We must labor at our perfection without uneasiness. Stress and anxiety about not being holy enough, or not being holy enough *fast* enough, will hinder and hurt us.
- *Be detached*: We must hold a balanced indifference about our advancement in virtue. This means caring about our holiness as God does but relaxing more and intentionally trusting him and letting him take care of us.

Also, St. John Henry Newman offers us an example of a simple path that includes the following:

- Getting up out of bed immediately upon rising
- Making a good visit to the Blessed Sacrament
- Saying the Angelus devoutly
- Praying the Rosary well
- Making a good evening meditation

The founder of Opus Dei, St. Josemaría Escrivá, first coined the term for getting out of bed immediately upon waking as "the heroic moment." It is the time fixed for getting up without hesitation, languishing, or hitting the snooze button. This is a good and simple discipline to start every day.

An effective rule of life should be developed over time: Your personal rule of life should be created with prayer and discernment and be open to change as might be required in the future. After reading this, I recommend you set aside some time to write out your rule of life. Keep it available or consider posting it in your home or office. You can use this list of components of a rule of life to begin:

- Prayer and practicing the presence of God
- Reception of the sacraments
- Fasting and abstinence
- Vocational duties
- Charity
- Examination of conscience
- Community involvement
- Spiritual reading, radio, podcasts, movies, and music
- Incorporating sacred and beautiful art into your living and working spaces
- Daily disciplines (rise, hang up clothes, make bed, do dishes, put things away)

A rule of life is about developing lifelong habits: It should be training you in virtue and instilling holy habits, so they become second nature. Good habits produce good character. How and where do we begin to develop holy habits? Right at home, in the here and now and the day-to-day. In the exterior as well as the interior. In the physical as well as the spiritual.

Remember that we are not spirits trapped in a body. We are

not spiritual beings as are the angels, but we are human beings. We are an integration of visible and invisible, the physical and the spiritual. What affects one part of us will affect the other.

I've mentioned that as a child, I got mostly A's but also consistent checkmarks on my report card about having a messy desk. It was just not in my often-scattered Sanguine nature to be tidy. So, Mom taught me to make my bed every single morning upon rising. She regularly had me organize and clean out my closet and under the bed. While my Sanguine side at first resisted, my orderly Choleric side was thrilled. These physical acts of discipline and order paved the way for me to know how to also clear the clutter from my mind and emotions. She consistently had all of us children go through our things and throw out or donate what we did not need or use. We learned to let go of some of the things onto which we were holding too tightly. This is at the very heart of the spiritual life: to let go of all inordinate attachments (physical, financial, social, relational, and more) to make room for God.

So, to prepare one for the rigors of spiritual order, I suggest beginning with something physical: cleaning out the "junk drawers" we all have. To throw out an old deck of cards that's missing an ace or thin out the rubber band ball is to face our habit of holding on to what has become unnecessary while learning the virtue of detachment. When that's done, hit the clothes closets and the garage. Hoarding is a horrible dependency, and it begins with small behaviors of over-attachment and neglect. Extroverts will love this; introverts will resist.

Some other habits you can cultivate include:

Acts of self-discipline

- Make the bed immediately upon rising
- Make a daily to-do list, with the most difficult or unpleasant thing first

- Take the extra minute to fold or hang up clothing
- Do the dishes promptly
- Keep the workspace clean and orderly
- Limit screen time
- Return all calls and emails before beginning the next project
- Leave fifteen minutes early so as not to ever be late again
- Leave work on time, so as not to neglect family or other important things
- Delete weekend activities that are too much or not necessary
- Get to bed at a decent hour
- Don't watch TV in bed

Acts of self-denial (mortification)

- Abstinence from meat on Fridays, with the Church
- Fast one day a week
- Limit snacks between meals
- Forgo small pleasures
- Give away that which you may be holding onto too tightly
- Quietly leave the biggest and the best for someone else
- Be more generous with your time and resources

Note: Because some temperaments are prone to skip the necessary deeper understandings, or fall into worry and anxiety, greater acts of mortification should be undertaken only with the guidance of a wise spiritual director.

A good rule of life always begins with time for prayer where you can be inspired, enlightened, and strengthened in all areas of your life. Let's explore more about prayer and the temperaments in the next chapter.

• • •

Reflections

Do you already have a rule of life? Is it written down?

In what areas of your life does structure help you succeed?

Can you recall a time when you were filled with the peace of God?

What is one daily discipline that you have already mastered?

• St. Teresa of Calcutta (1910–1997) •

Anjezë Gonxhe Bojaxhiu, known to the world as Mother Teresa, devoted herself to helping others and opening homes around the world for the sick, abandoned, and dying. Foundress of the Missionaries of Charity, she was an inspiration around the world, to both religious and non-religious people alike.

What do we know about her temperament?

Mother Teresa was driven by a deep Melancholy passion for humanity; her Phlegmatic side was expressed by her love and promotion of peace, harmony, and compassionate care for all. Winner of the global Nobel Peace Prize, she was a gentle, steady, and authoritative force in the world.

Phlegmatics naturally have a determined and unwavering sense of dedication and loyalty, starting with "doing small things with great love." When it comes to becoming a saint, Mother Teresa said that everyone can do *something*. She shared with Bradley, a friend of mine who worked with her, that one thing every person can and should do is answer their mail. She saw it as a small but important act of acknowledging others. Once, after a long and tiring sixteen-hour day of work, prayer, and meetings, Bradley observed that Mother did not head for bed, but continued to stay up almost all night, hand-writing responses to the letters she had received that day.

What can we learn from her?

Mother Teresa is a model for us all that simplicity and true power are synonymous. May we all begin by "doing small things with great love."

St. Teresa of Calcutta, pray for us.

• 23 •

Making Time for Prayer

Prayer is the raising of the mind to God. We must always remember this. The actual words matter less.

—Pope St. John XXIII, letter to niece Giuseppina, October 3, 1948

I first experienced the power of prayer when Mom tucked me in each night and taught me to say, "Good night, dear Jesus, God bless us all." It brought me a sense of being safe and loved and at peace. Every once in a while, all these decades later, I still say it.

In the second grade, I learned the Rosary. I recall being mesmerized by the rhythmic chant of the eighth-grade girls all praying the Hail Holy Queen in unison, and striking their breasts saying together, "O, clement, O loving, O sweet Virgin Mary." Our teacher taught us that Our Blessed Mother would grant favors to those who fervently prayed the Rosary, so one night at home, I decided to pray the whole Rosary by myself. Praying at the end of a long day is difficult at any age, and for a seven-year-old it was torture staying awake, but I had a mission: The school raffle was being held the next day, and the prize was an exquisite nun doll dressed in a hand-made, detailed habit. She even had a little rosary hanging from her waist and a golden wedding ring on her plastic finger. I had to have her!

The following morning, I waited anxiously with four hundred other students to hear who had won. When the principal drew the winning ticket and called, "Rosie Sweet, Room 2!" I was so thrilled. I do believe it was Mary who graced me. Sadly, as I grew into adolescence, I was lured away from a good prayer life by my immature desires and the cultural distractions that draw all of us to them.

But Mary did not forget me.

I love Our Blessed Mother and all the prayers of the Rosary, but as an adult and a double-extrovert, I used to dread sitting still for twenty minutes, repeating the same prayers over and over. My Choleric side didn't think it was as productive as reading about apologetics; my Sanguine side was just too restless. When I heard other Catholics pray and promote the Rosary, I would feel ashamed, wondering why I didn't feel their fervor.

What I did have, however, was a sincere desire to love God and know more about him. So, I prayed in ways my temperaments could both tolerate and delight in. That's enough for God to work with. Pope St. John Paul II tells us that we are each "unique and unrepeatable" in the world. If no other has ever been like you or me, and no other ever will be, then no one will have a one-size-fits-all plan for perfection that we must follow.

As you follow God's lead, you may find over time (and in different seasons of life) that your plan for spiritual growth will change. Our lives change; times change; *we* change. How we grow into deeper union with God is also bound to evolve. Don't worry: God is still in control. For myself, I found that as the Lord worked in me over the years to unburden me of fears, anxieties, and attachments, I began to embrace a slower-paced life and attitude. I was drawn by Scripture, music, history, and others' teaching and testimonies into understanding how much God loves me. As I would reflect on what he had done for me, given me, and offered me, my heart could not resist swelling with greater love for him.

And then one morning I arose, made the bed, put on my slippers, poured myself a hot cup of coffee, and sat in a comfy chair in my bedroom to pray the Rosary.

Surprise! It was delightful! Yes, I had *lots* of important things to do, emails to answer, and clients to see. But — like a mother — I gently told those parts of me clamoring to get going to sit still and pray with me first.

I once heard Venerable Archbishop Fulton Sheen talking about the life-changing power of making a holy hour every day. A whole hour of prayer? Yikes! At the very idea, my poor Sanguine wanted to run away and join the circus. My Choleric side, who never wastes an hour of the day, was skeptical about the value of it all: *Why? You're not a nun, you know*. But that part of me growing in love for God deeply desired to increase my time with him each day. It was my Choleric who finally bought into it because it would be a challenge: *YES! I'm going to expand fifteen minutes to a WHOLE HOUR!* My Sanguine part still just wanted to skip off to the cupboard for some chocolate cookies. Still, I made the commitment to get up a little earlier every morning and try to make a holy hour at home. Cholerics like to take huge bites out of anything in life and sometimes they can choke. But I was learning — with eager support from my Sanguine side — to consider slowing down and allowing my ongoing perfection to happen more easily in segments.

Being content with a slower and more natural pace, over time I added the Morning Offering and eventually expanded that, too. I made a list of everyone I wanted to pray for, and that keeps growing. I began to pray to my Guardian Angel and added the prayer to St. Michael the Archangel. Eventually, I included a list of inspiring saints I've come to call my spiritual posse. All of this led to embracing mental prayer — those intimate questions, chats, and tears before the Lord. I — Sanguine and Choleric — had learned to pause and to sit quietly and try to listen to God.

Even when I travel or am in circumstances beyond my control, I try to give the Lord the first fruits of my day. This has changed my outlook and my life, bringing deep inner peace. Do I still struggle, have problems, and fall into sin? Yes, of course I do, but nothing is as serious as it once was — and I have far less worry or anxiety.

Let's talk about prayer from the perspective of the four temperaments: Some temperaments are naturally wired for quiet and contemplation. Others are not. But we all need it, and we can all find methods of prayer that are suitable and even enjoyable for our temperament types. There are no cookie-cutter formulas. Fr. Jordan Aumann, a respected Dominican theologian, recognized temperament as being a part of our individual uniqueness that offers an individual way of holiness: "It is a truism in psychology that no two persons are absolutely identical. The same thing is true in the spiritual life: no two souls will follow the same path to perfection, identical in every respect." So let's be inspired by others on the path, taking on what we like at first, and pushing ourselves a little further each day to follow God's lead.

When it comes to making more time for prayer, especially first thing in the morning:

Cholerics tend to put too much on their plate and take pride in managing it all. They are pretty sure God, also a hard-working Creator of the Universe, will understand their minimal prayer life. After all, they are doing amazing, good works. Besides, who else will take care of all the underachievers out there?

Phlegmatics, who often see life as a series of fast balls aimed right at them, can get easily overwhelmed. They love God and hope he understands that they can only do *this one thing* right now. They will try to get to it when they can, they really will. Maybe tonight after dinner they can sit down with the Lord. Or over the weekend!

Sanguines similarly put difficult things off or try to take an easy way out. Or they will start with great fervor and get distracted by something more pleasing to the senses: listening to music (hey, that's prayer, too!) or walking in nature (contemplating God's creation, that's prayer!). They might try to charm the Lord: *OK, I said my Morning Offering; that makes the whole day a prayer, right?*

Melancholies are especially wired for meditation and contemplation, and love to pray, but they have another temperament (Choleric or Phlegmatic) that will have a say here as well. If the Melancholy thinks there is too much to pray for, the task may seem daunting and even depressing. Overall, though, anyone who is part Melancholy is ahead of the game when it comes to prayer.

Prayer Helps to Combat Pride

Each of the four temperaments has a lengthy list of natural strengths and gifts. It's easy to be pleased with ourselves — and rightly so, as one of God's magnificent creations — but humility is vital to perfection. Each temperament will struggle with some form of pride, but with God's grace and a clear plan, we can advance in humility. A sometimes painful but productive exercise I heartily recommend for everyone is a weekly reading (at least!) of Cardinal Merry del Val's Litany of Humility (included in the appendix).

Everyone is called to be a saint. Although the Melancholy temperament is more naturally disposed to prayer, recollection, and the inner life, it can be just as difficult for them to achieve holiness as the rest. That's because, as we have seen, the strengths and weaknesses inherent in our temperaments come into play everywhere, including in the spiritual life. Thus, the Melancholy can be a powerful prayer warrior but struggle with letting go of hurt and unforgiveness, while the opposite Sanguine may never sit still or go deep into prayer but will usually be the quickest to let go, forgive, and restore friendship. The Phlegmatic may struggle with motivation, but once he is convicted, no one will move him off the track to sainthood. The opposite Choleric tends to rely too much on herself, but when she embraces humility, she will swiftly direct her energies heavenward.

The Goal of Prayer Is Love

Prayer should help us to discover the reality and depth of God's love for us so that we can move our mind, heart, and will into his. This is where most of us get stuck; parts of us still worry, still fear, still struggle with belief, surrender, and trust. Therefore, we do not fully desire God as we should. The desire to know God is actually a gift and an invitation from our Creator to draw near. Pray for the grace to desire God above all else; don't get stuck in some level of presentation for him. Remember:

- *Don't just perform*: As children we learn that our actions can please or displease our parents or teachers. Obedience pleases God, even (perhaps especially) when our hearts and emotions may not be into it. But don't stay stuck in trying to use "good behavior" to earn a place in heaven, tap-dancing to earn God's favor. We do well to surrender to the Lord as fully and sincerely as we can without getting discouraged. We should pray for the parts of us that are still fearful or resistant and aim for a whole-person surrender to his love. This begins with offering up our will.
- *Be transformed*: Saint Paul tells us to "be trans-

formed by the renewal of your mind" (Rom 12:2). Lasting change begins with the way we perceive, believe, and think about things, not necessarily the way we feel. Emotions are normal and natural but also fleeting and fickle, so let us lead with the intellect. Let us pray that our disordered thoughts and beliefs be revealed and healed. We must give up our old ways of thinking and behaving, and that begins within our will. It's easy to say but difficult to do: Move away from sin and toward virtue.

- *Be content with progression rather than perfection*: While perfection is the end goal, perfection is not simply being or doing good and avoiding evil. Rather, holiness is conformity with Christ and union with God — a surrendered mind, heart, and will, and a loving friendship with him. Prayer is the way to be with him, know him, share ourselves with him, listen to him, laugh and cry with him, and grow in our trust in and love for him.
- *Pick a prayer style you like, but mix it up*: I won't name the temperaments, but some people think the more agonizingly slowly we pray or sing, the more sincere and reverent we are. This has driven some people mad. For Pete's sake, people, the *Gloria* is meant to be joyful — can you pick up the pace a little, please? Meanwhile, others are swaying and bouncing and have the music up so loud it's a wonder they can think at all. Sometimes one needs to put down the tambourine, enter into the calm, and consider whether they even know what they are praying.

Clearly, each of the temperaments has a preferred style of prayer, and that's as it should be. But we must all avoid focusing too much on how we are praying or feeling and instead ask God for the grace to truly come into prayer with a clear mind, a pure heart, and an appropriately tempered spirit.

Below are some choices for prayer time; if you have any questions or doubts, check with a reliable Catholic source (my go-to is www.spiritualdirection.com) for correct definitions or instructions:

Formal Prayer	Sung & musical prayer
Mental prayer	Meditation
Vocal prayer	Recollection
Written prayer	Liturgical prayer
Ignatian prayer	Scripture reading

You Can Pray Anytime, Anywhere

St. Thérèse of Lisieux said, "For me, prayer is a surge of the heart; it is a simple look turned toward heaven, it is a cry of recognition and of love, embracing both trial and joy" (CCC 2558). The moment your mind turns to God, you have entered prayer.

The Morning Offering is a quick way to offer God everything and turn your entire day into a prayer. It even covers all four temperaments. Did you ever notice? "O Jesus, through the Immaculate Heart of Mary, I offer you all my *Prayers* (Phlegmatics are naturally disposed to quiet, focused prayer), *Works* (Cholerics can gladly offer that long list of tasks to God), *Joys* (Sanguines can offer their light-hearted and silly moments as a gift), and *Sufferings* (Melancholies can unite their pain and sorrow with his) of this day ..."

We can pray anywhere and anytime: in our rooms, on a beach, at work, in the car, or in front of the tabernacle. While not all prayer forms (or places) work for everyone, if you're feeling stuck, try a less familiar style of prayer and see what happens. It's good to step out of a comfort zone and stretch our mental, emotional, and spiritual legs. And "rejoice always, pray constantly, give thanks in all circumstances; for this is the will of God in Christ Jesus for you" (1 Thes 5:16–18). Maybe you can begin with making a daily commitment to one of these prayer forms:

Acts of prayer

- Morning prayer
- Daily Rosary
- Scripture reading
- Daily Mass (even one or two days a week in addition to Sunday)
- Pray the Angelus at noon
- Pray the Divine Mercy chaplet at 3:00 p.m.
- Pray all or part of the Liturgy of the Hours
- Family prayer
- Night prayer
- Evening examen

Here are some suggestions for all the temperaments to help build and sustain a rich and beautiful prayer life:

- *Commit to a schedule to make time for God first.* All four types can struggle with this. Cholerics will commit but get pulled away by work. Sanguines will commit and forget three minutes later. Melancholies will commit but may get discouraged if they miss a day and think, *I'm a failure*. Phlegmatics might feel too much pressure and have to think more about it first. Flexibility and fluidity are the Phlegmatic's great gifts, so sometimes timelines, deadlines, and schedules can feel far too restrictive and rigid for them. But, like the Sanguine, they especially *need* schedules and will thrive with them! Start small and then add some of the various prayer forms suggested earlier. Slow and steady wins the race.

- *Create a physical space for a daily prayer routine.* Keep it separate from workspaces or the office. Cholerics, prayer is important to you but so is your "to do" list, and you may be in a hurry to finish prayer time. If your prayers feel rushed because something urgent has come to mind, just take a second, write it down, and get to it later — after you're finished praying. Sanguines, you can be easily distracted by sounds and people. Is there a clean, comfortable, and *quiet* place at home? Melancholies, you need space and quiet to go to the depths of which you are capable. God is waiting there with knowledge and answers, but mostly with his affection for his creature. Prayer is important to you, too, Phlegmatics, but you can be prone to procrastination, so you must make the effort to prepare a clean, comfortable, and quiet place at home.
- *Engage the senses.* Pray before an icon or a beautiful image. Light a candle or burn incense, or both. Get creative with this space. Does soft music engage or distract from your prayers? If it enhances prayer, it needn't be elaborate, just enough to help silence the unwelcome brain chatter. Cholerics would do well to slow down and become aware of what they are hearing, seeing, and smelling. Sanguines can be too excitable and may go over the top on this, with music that might actually be too distracting, unless the volume is low. Use fun and colorful apps like iRosary. Get a handsome Bible jacket or tabs. Keep it

beautiful but simple. Anything that gets us excited for prayer time is good, but remember this is time for God, not for all the gewgaws. Keeping things simple is a beautiful part of being Phlegmatic. In visiting the Missionaries of Charity (St. Teresa of Calcutta's order) I'm always struck by the simplicity of their homes, rooms, and environment. It's so peaceful.

While others like to look at statues or images, listen to music, or smell incense to augment prayer, some Melancholies do not. One woman told me, "I love Mary, I love statues of Mary, but if I am trying to pray, I must go inside of *me*. Exterior things can distract me or even irritate me. *The paint is chipped on Mary's veil. Why don't they fix that? Is anyone in this church paying attention? I would have made her eyebrows thinner ...*" What engages the senses can open the door to prayer, but Melancholies sometimes prefer to go inside themselves for prayer and contemplation.

- *Be aware of your blind spots.* Cholerics should remember to pray for others. We tend to focus on the end goal and forget the people. No matter the work — in the home, outside the home, or at church — we can too easily slip into the pride of our accomplishments and forget the people for whom, and with whom, we work. Make a list of everyone for whom you want to pray and then pray for them by name, daily. It keeps us connected.

  Sanguines have as much resolve to be prayer warriors as the Choleric and Melancholy, but we don't stick with it as long as the others. Sanguines particularly need and thrive on structure: dates, lists, schedules, reminders, and alarms. Don't fight these needs. Get clever or fun calendars or apps to help. What is easier for the introverts may be a challenge for Sanguines, who are naturally revved up and ready to go at all times. While Cholerics are rushing through prayer to get to their other tasks, Sanguines are anxious for the next fun thing and must *slow down*. It's important for Sanguines to be still. They don't necessarily have ADHD — they're just naturally excitable and often in the habit of quickly responding to stimuli. Sanguines would do well to imagine being with Jesus, coming into his presence and realizing his great love. Share concerns. Sit with him. Be still with him. Look at him. Listen to him. This is a relationship; prayer time is being with God, not performing for him.

Melancholies tend to dwell a little too much on all that is imperfect and all that could go wrong. The world needs people who are appropriately critical, but not hyper-critical. Without also seeing the good, true, and beautiful (which comes most naturally to the Melancholy's opposite, the Sanguine), they can become quietly angry, moody, dark, and bitter. Saint Paul, a deep Melancholy, writes: "Finally, brethren, whatever is true, whatever is honorable, whatever is just, whatever is pure, whatever is lovely, whatever is gracious, if there is any excellence, if there is anything worthy of praise, think about these things" (Phil 4:8).

Melancholies, be open to love. No one better realizes how imperfect we all are than the Melancholy. And those who believe our *perfect* God will only love and desire his children when they are *per-*

fect may have a deep and even terrifying fear of not measuring up. Some of my coaching clients who struggle with scrupulosity have admitted to having a parent who did not engage with them or show warmth, or who grossly neglected or abused them. As a result, their "God image" is distorted, and while they are heroically seeking perfection, they are also inordinately terrified of going to hell. Dear, sweet Melancholies … step aside from being precise and exacting for just a while; be open to receiving God's understanding, compassionate gaze and his friendship.

Phlegmatics must try to go deeper. They usually have no trouble sitting quietly, and they're champs at "resting in the Lord." In fact, sitting and thinking are quite comfortable for them. Rather than letting random thoughts swirl, however, Phlegmatics should consider some structured and active way of going deeper into prayer, such as Lectio Divina, which involves reading (*lectio*), thinking about what the reading or prayer says (*meditatio*), dialogue with God (*oratio*), and contemplation and rest (*contemplatio*).

- *Consider journaling.* It's not for everyone, but it can be a way to explore and order our thoughts. Cholerics, if you end up with lists and bullet points, well, enjoy! Sanguines will decorate their pages, and both Sanguines and Phlegmatics are likely to lose their journal at some point. My Melancholy sister Barb told me she likes to write journals but doesn't actually do it: "A part of me worries someone will find my journals, publish them, and publicly ridicule them. Rose, those words are my deepest *heart.*" Again,

> journaling is not for everyone, but Melancholies tend to let a million ideas and emotions build, grow, and become tangled in themselves, and so journaling can be a way to express the very *depths* of a Melancholy's thoughts, feelings, and beautiful creativity. Writing can be an effective outlet, so consider going into the deep, the dark, the wild, the poetic, and wherever the Spirit leads. And remember, some of the world's greatest poets are part Melancholy!

Recommended prayers are located at the end of this book: the Litany of Humility, the Litany of Trust, the Litany of the Fearful Heart, and the Surrender Novena. Which one sounds most like it is calling to you?

You Can Do This!

"But Rose, I have five kids!"

One of the most common complaints I hear from those who come to me for coaching is that there are not enough hours in the day to do what they want to or should do. Overwhelmed with work, young children, and the daily demands of life, they can barely squeak out a "Thank you, God" each day.

I understand; as a homemaker I also once ran a real estate appraisal company. It was not easy, but I learned from my Phlegmatic mother how to make prayer a priority and carve out time for it. Mom had nine children, and each day she put us all in our rooms with a book, told us it was "quiet time," and forbade us to come out under any circumstance except to go to the bathroom or to bury the dead! So, the laundry got delayed another day — not the end of the world. Few of us kids ever got to join scouts or sports, or take extra lessons, but in the big scheme we had a good, full life, and Mom got her naps! Where there's a will, there's most often a way.

Whatever your temperament may be, remember: *Yes, you can talk to God throughout the day.* Yes, you can gaze upon nature's loveliness and praise God. Yes, you can listen to music or write in your journal. Yes, it can all be prayer. But put some structure and habit into what you're doing to help sustain it. And don't get overwhelmed. When you're really ill or weighed down with some unbearable emotional burden and can't find the energy to pray, then just say, *Thank you, Lord. I will pray tomorrow.* Then make a firm resolve (set an alarm, write it down) to do it.

Years ago, Mother Teresa was speaking to one of the bishops in India about the overwhelming amount of work they were doing. He complained, "I am so busy that I hardly have time to pray." Mother Teresa replied, "If you are too busy to pray, you are too busy!" On the other hand, there is a saying attributed to St. Francis de Sales: "Every one of us needs half an hour of prayer a day, except when we are busy — then we need an hour."

There are many good resources on prayer. Filling an hour is surprisingly doable if you have the desire. Ask God for that desire. Then be aware of, listen to, reassure, and calm any of your protesting parts.

• • •

Reflections

Do you recall the first prayers you learned by heart?

Do you have a favorite place to pray?

Which type of prayer form is difficult for you and why?

How do you think prayer has specifically affected your relationship with God?

• Bl. Carlo Acutis (1991–2006) •

Blessed Carlo was the only child of wealthy Italian parents. He was a computer designer best known for documenting Eucharistic miracles and approved Marian apparitions. He catalogued them on a website he created before his death from leukemia at age fifteen.

What do we know about his temperament?
His friends called him a computer "geek." He was a boy computer genius and so skilled with programming and the internet that he developed not only the aforementioned website, but a website for his parish. He also taught himself to play the saxophone, and liked films, comic editing, and playing video games. Genius? Creative? Detailed? Musical? These are traits of the Melancholy.

He was also part Phlegmatic as a peace-loving mediator. His Polish nanny wanted him to be more assertive with other children, but he replied, "Jesus would not be happy if I lost my temper." He was known to be cheerful, humble, kind, and caring toward others, supporting his friends whose parents were divorcing, or standing up for other kids who were bullied.

Carlo was a daily communicant and was deeply interested in the lives of the saints, especially Saint Francis. He asked to be buried in Assisi.

What can we learn from him?
We are called to be united with God right now, not just in eternity. Some of his last words were: "To be always united with Jesus, this is my plan of life."

Bl. Carlo Acutis, pray for us.

• 24 •

Managing the Media

Through the study of books one seeks God; by meditation one finds him.

— *Padre Pio,* Spiritual Maxims

You've heard it said, *You are what you eat.*

We know that if we eat healthy, we'll be healthy. But we also know there is much more to physical wellbeing, such as exercise, genetics, medication, disease, aging, and more. Regardless, what we consume is crucial to good health.

It's the same in the moral life. Good spiritual reading is one of St. Teresa of Ávila's recommendations to attain perfection, but she didn't have radio, television, cinema, podcasts, the internet, or social media. With her books, she had a bag lunch; today we have a large cafeteria. Thank God for the age in which we live!

As a child, I loved to watch old movies and would spend hours (after I did all my chores, of course) immersed in romance, war, comedy, drama, history, and mystery. When Mom decided we'd had too much screen time, she'd tell us to turn off the TV and have our quiet time. That was when I'd change my diet and start consuming some of the delicious books Mom made sure we had. Books were aways included as part of our birthday and Christmas presents — classics such as *Treasure Island*, *Robinson Crusoe*, *The Adventures of Tom Sawyer*, the *Tarzan* series, Grimm's fairy tales, Greek mythology, and children's fiction series such as *Nancy Drew* and *The Hardy Boys*. And at least once a month, we'd all pile in the station wagon and go to the library to get even *more* books.

Woven into the stories we loved were the human condition, love of mankind, the search for God, and the fight between good and evil. In my youth, most of what we watched or read was family-friendly and helped to form our love of brother, country, church, and God. We must be more careful today with the increase in harmful content, as any media we consume can form us from the inside out.

The most important book we had, second to the large and expensive Encyclopedia Britannica, was the Holy Bible. It sat on a beautiful stand in our living room and was open to anyone who wanted to read it. On Sundays, we all sat around the dining table where Dad would carefully turn the tissue-thin and gold-lined pages and read Scripture to us. When he was finished, he'd look up at us and ask, "Now, kids, do you know what that passage means?"

You could see our temperaments right away. The Melancholies didn't want to give the wrong answer, and the Phlegmatics felt put on the spot, so they all kept their mouths shut. My Sanguine brother and I might hastily throw out some juvenile guess and get quiet eye-rolls from the Melancholies. It was usually my sister Barb who would speak up and give a pretty good answer. I attribute it not only to her intelligence, but to her deep, mystery-solving Melancholy side that was spurred on by her competitive Choleric side to be the first to win (give Dad the correct answer).

I still have our family Bible, with illustrations by James Tissot. It includes Dad's handwritten entries of each of our baptismal dates and places.

So, what should the temperaments know about spiritual reading? Here are some tips for this part of your rule of life:

For All Temperament Types

Make consistently consuming good materials part of your rule of life. Depending on how fast you read and the rest of your life priorities and schedule, be realistic about how many books you can read in a month or year. Try not to over-perform or you will get overwhelmed. It's not a contest or a race; it's your personally tailored plan.

Start with the word of God and make studying Scripture a part of your life. Memorize verses in his word or, as the sisters taught us in elementary school, *learn it by heart*. If you're not used to reading the Bible, many spiritual directors recommend beginning with the four Gospels, which really are at the heart of God's word. When I've had a day full of reading for work and have very few brain cells left, I love to go to Proverbs for those short, pithy, enlightening, and even funny verses. We are blessed today to have countless good Catholic Bible studies in print, online, or even in audio format. Make the Bible available to everyone in your home in some format, and consider reading together as a family. Find what works for you.

Every Catholic home must have a copy of the *Catechism of the Catholic Church*. What an indispensable resource it is for our moral life and even our relationships with others! There's hardly a topic that doesn't directly affect how we see God, ourselves, and others, and it is a beautiful guide to moral living. It's arranged in short, numbered (yay!) sections for easy reference.

You will naturally admire, be uplifted by, and want to emulate all the great saints. Reading about the lives of the saints was a powerful formation for me, starting in elementary school when I learned how the boy Saint Tarcisius gave his life to protect Jesus in the Most Holy Eucharist. I suggest you find a few saints who interest and inspire you and read more on their lives. Watch some of the professionally produced movies available through various websites and apps. Add these saints to your morning prayer list as special intercessors. And don't limit saints to those whom you believe share your own temperament. I pray daily to the deeply Melancholy Saint Paul, Padre Pio, and others to help me ground my Sanguine side.

Can you start with reading one book a month? Try to savor it and not rush through it. If work involves a lot of reading all day — as it often does for me — try audio or movies instead. It helps to create a quiet physical place in your home and a quiet time where no one is likely to interrupt you. One of my girlfriends, Kelly, locks the bathroom door at night and reads in her bathtub.

That said, stop reading books or listening to podcasts that are too critical, judgmental, cultish, fear-based, or overly performance-oriented. One of my coaching clients loves her Catholic Faith and is open and eager to consume as much as she can, but often feels overwhelmed and inferior by some of the podcasts she hears: "They are all so perfect and they expect us all to be perfect. Where is the grace?" Another client is struggling with media that overfocuses on the doom-and-gloom of end times, and it is keeping her stuck in a place of fear. I told her to stop, knowing it would likely be a process. A part of her can't yet fully rest in God's merciful love and be at peace.

Isn't that all of us to some degree? Just because some media is Christian or Catholic does not mean the content is suitable for you. If you're feeling agitated, angry, frustrated, overwhelmed, or shamed by the material, then go read or listen to something else. Ask your trusted Catholic friends what they read or listen to.

There are so many fine Catholic books on the interior life and spirituality, it's not difficult to find many that speak to a particular temperament and learning style. There are also many that are appealing but contain errors and even heresy. Be discerning and check with trusted sources when you are reading a new author.

Venture outside specifically religious reading. God's truth and inspiration can often be found in all kinds of good books: the classics, biographies and autobiographies, poetry, and fiction. There are many popular and edifying modern Catholic as well as non-Catholic authors and content creators. Be discerning in your selections and check with others whom you trust.

You may need to break your reading up by listening to podcasts. Have you tried Our Sunday Visitor's extensive podcast network (see www.osvpodcasts.com)? I also love to watch some of the well-produced lives of the saints and other videos available from Ignatius Press or on FORMED. My favorite ever is the epic mini-series, *Teresa de Jesus*, a Spanish production starring Concha Velasco as St. Teresa of Ávila. It might be time for me to watch it again.

Share what you have experienced. One of the easiest and best ways to evangelize others is to show your enthusiasm and insights from what you just read, watched, or heard. Bl. Carlo Acutis shared his love for Jesus in the Blessed Sacrament with the world using the website he developed, www.carloacutis.com/en/association/presentazione. You may not have his Melancholy IT genius, but you can still be like Carlo and share what you love about our faith. While evangelism is the work of the Holy Spirit, it is a duty of the Christian to reach out, and we can partner with God when we share our books and materials.

Go deeper! I could recommend a million books, but at the very least get generally familiar with Reginald Garrigou-Lagrange's *The Three Ages of the Interior Life* (TAN Books, 1989), Pope St. John Paul II's Theology of the Body, and Saint Ignatius's spiritual exercises.

And now for some temperament-specific advice.

For the Choleric

The Choleric side wants it practical: We like short, well-ordered books so we can take the golden nuggets and immediately get to work on them. We enjoy a longer book too, as long as it is in logical order and not burdened with unnecessary or endless detail (unless we're feeding our Melancholy side). Cholerics don't need to be emotionally entertained or inspired, but we do want to quickly find and take on the heart of the book. Practical to-do lists are a plus!

Don't stay in the head while reading or taking in spiritual content. A Choleric's gift is to sift through information, order it, and analyze it for future use. That's good! But try to move past bullet-point lists and charts to spiritual content that includes more story or detail. Healthy and holy integration must engage heart as well as mind. In our task-oriented focus, we mustn't forget ourselves!

For the Sanguine

The Sanguine side wants it exciting: Sanguines like short, easy-to-read books or daily inspirations with dramatic, charming, or surprising stories that inspire us. We love Scripture in small and digestible doses. Sanguines are sincere in our desire to be encouraged by spiritual reading and will be colorful and creative with living it out, but we may get distracted and not follow through. Sanguines with a Choleric side will likely be able to wade through longer, more academic books.

But don't just stick with stories that are entertaining and inspiring. Weighty, scholarly tomes are not necessary, but Sanguines do need both (a) depth, and (b) structure. Avoid anything too dark or detailed, as you may become too discouraged. If you're going to tackle something deep, do it in regularly scheduled short periods. Memorize some prayers or Scripture and recite them for friends, family, or coworkers. I memorized G. K. Chesterton's *The*

Donkey in high school and loved all the attention I got reciting it. But with grace and maturity, it has become less a trick and more a prayer as I meditate on its subject: Jesus' entrance into Jerusalem. If you're not familiar with it, look it up and read it. For healthy and holy integration, Sanguines must engage their head as well as their vibrant heart.

For the Melancholy

The Melancholy side wants it deep: Sure, they like a good story or laugh here and there, but Melancholies tend to avoid the feel-good and the fluff. Give them the details and bring on the rich history. Throw in the mystery and mysticism of the spiritual life, even the unusual and unheard of — material that is challenging but also credible. Prove to their suspicious minds that it can be trusted, and show them the sources. They relish all the insights and nuances, and if they do not have a Choleric side telling them it's time to get to work, they can settle in with their slow-and-steady Phlegmatic side and get lost for weeks.

Melancholies love words, and through them love to travel into the heads and hearts of the spiritual masters and saints as they share how they untangled themselves. Don't let yourself be overly burdened by materials that focus mostly on how bad the world is. One Melancholy told me, "I get so encouraged with spiritual reading, but then sometimes I think I must pray and sacrifice more; the world is worse than I thought!" Can you try something light and fun occasionally? My Melancholy husband sometimes dismisses something Sanguine I recommend reading or watching but, after an argument where I win, he reads or watches it and agrees it was fabulous.

For the Phlegmatic

The Phlegmatic side wants it easy. "Easy" is not always a bad thing; whatever it takes to get a person to sit still and enter into the interior world is good. Phlegmatics also like short, easy-to-read books and audio, such as daily inspirations and Scripture verses. The lives of the saints are inspiring if they don't get bogged down with too many side stories or details. Phlegmatics do like the deep and academic works as well (which will be easier for them if they also have a Melancholy side).

If getting into spiritual reading seems daunting, just remember: How do you eat a whale? One bite at a time.

Short, daily readings are always a good start, but also try to move past this into something more. While Phlegmatics (like Sanguines) prefer not to dive into scholarly tomes, they do need some (a) depth, (b) structure, and (c) a plan of action. For healthy and holy integration, Phlegmatics must surrender and make that commitment to the structure and effort they sometimes fear will pin them down and lock them in. Start by increasing your reading/listening time a bit. Some Phlegmatics have the natural patience (like Melancholies) to journal. The good thing about the Phlegmatic is that when they finally decide on what to watch or read, they will get comfortable, settle in, and give it their undivided attention.

Now that we've discussed some of the things you might consume in good media, let's talk in the next chapters about consuming Our Lord in his most precious Body, Blood, Soul, and Divinity.

• • •

Reflections

What are some books from your youth that you think shaped you?

Do you have a favorite way of reading the Bible? What is it?

What is a book or movie that made a huge difference in your life?

Have you memorized any Scripture verses? What are they?

• St. Ignatius of Loyola (1491–1556) •

Saint Ignatius was a Spanish Basque Catholic priest and theologian who, with others, founded the religious order of the Society of Jesus (Jesuits), and was its first Superior General. The Jesuits were leaders in the Counter Reformation. He is well-known for his *Spiritual Exercises* from which comes Ignatian spirituality.

What do we know about his temperament?

He was the youngest of thirteen and of a Choleric (practical) and Melancholy (dreamy and lofty goals) temperament. As a young man, he took up dancing, gambling, and the pursuit of the young ladies, and enjoyed sword fighting and duels. Some biographers describe him as arrogant, cocky, and rough. He had a dramatic and showy flair, was driven by a desire for fame, and loved stories of adventure and romantic chivalry.

Ignatius had a major conversion while bedridden after surgery. He wanted to pass the long and dreary hours with romantic novels, but none were available so his sister-in-law brought him the lives of Christ and of the saints. Thus began his desire not for fame but for following the lives of the saints. His writings are practical, common-sense, orderly, and methodical and marked by lists, numbers, and points — strong hallmarks of a no-nonsense Choleric.

What can we learn from him?

Melancholy passions can be redirected by grace. And even rough, tough Cholerics can be converted to direct their energies into voluminous — even timeless — blessings for others.

St. Ignatius of Loyola, pray for us.

• 25 •

Finding a Spiritual Director

The devil sees there is no path that leads more quickly to the highest perfection than obedience.

— *St. Teresa of Ávila,* Foundations

Enjoying a juicy rib eye and a sumptuous cabernet, I was dining with my long-time friend, Fr. Kidder. Decades prior, when I was a teenaged counselor at our CYO mountain camp, Father was the newly ordained priest in charge of the campers.

I was confiding some of my spiritual journey to him and shared how difficult it had been for me to find a good spiritual director. "The first was too soft on me. The next wasn't completely faithful to the teachings of the Church. I want someone who is *smarter* than I am and *holier*," I told him.

"Well, 'holier' will be easy," he quipped drolly. (He's a Melancholy, so I took it well.)

That was the night, however, he gave me the name of a priest who lived about forty-five minutes away. I called him, and he said he might consider me as a spiritual directee once we met in person. At our first session the priest handed me the *Spiritual Exercises of St. Ignatius* and told me to go home and make a list of all my fears.

Fears? I'm a take-charge, confident Choleric. I don't have fears.

"Um, what do you mean, Father? What kind of fears?" I asked.

He just looked at me. He was not very expressive, but direct and to the point. And very, *very* patient. "Fears," he repeated. "Like, are you afraid of spiders?"

"Yes."

"Going to the dentist?"

"Well … yeah, kind of."

"Then make the list. Work on it a little every day."

He knew that once I began with black widows and root canals, it would open me up to going deeper — fear of heights, of losing my looks, and of not finding a husband; fear of failing, of being unloved, of being rejected, and of not having enough money.

I was shocked at how long my list grew. And how quickly.

Fears — and their intensity — can reveal the depth of our inordinate attachments, all the things and attitudes that may stand in the way of our more completely surrendering to the love of God. I'm so thankful to have been under the direction of this good priest for over twenty-five years.

Finding a good spiritual director is a blessing, but it's also usually a challenge. (*Yes, so-o-o hard*, says the Phlegmatic. *Not fun at all*, says the Sanguine.) Fr. John Bartunek, LC, SThD, is a wise, down-to-earth author and writer at www.spiritualdirection.com, my favorite site for helpful resources on the interior life. He shares three things to do when the search for a good fit takes some time:

1. *Don't panic*: Keep your antennae up, keep asking and looking around, and keep praying for a good match.
2. *Do your part*: Continue your life of prayer and the sacraments. Keep reading and consuming good content that's consistent with Church teachings.

3. *Ask questions*: Find anyone in your life who is wise and knowledgeable and take your questions and concerns to them for now. Stay calm and trust God.

It's also important to be patient. The desire to submit to a good spiritual director is evidence that God is continuing to draw you closer to himself. Be pleased and thankful for that.

What is something you can do when you don't yet have a spiritual director? Absent such a good guide, ask a trusted friend to be a monthly accountability partner. Don't dismiss the need for accountability in some form:

- *Cholerics*, far from being unnecessary, this is a good practice in humility and vulnerability with others. Don't run the risk of being a lone ranger and staying stuck in narrow self-will.
- *Sanguines*, don't assume submission to a spiritual director is unnecessary; it's a good practice in humility and obedience. Don't avoid going into the deep. That's where the real treasures are.
- *Melancholies*, while it may seem impossible to find the perfect spiritual director, don't let it stop you from trying. It's a good practice in perseverance, humility, and trust in others. Don't stay stuck in the depths of your own complex universe.
- *Phlegmatics*, while it may seem to be too much work, the search is a good practice in humility and obedience. Don't avoid the difficulties, and find someone who will help you with manageable steps.

I hope that with enough time, prayer, and patience everyone can find someone suited to them and their unique temperament. My spiritual director is not a hard-driving Choleric or a warm, fuzzy Sanguine *at all.* He's a deep Melancholy and a steady, even-keeled Phlegmatic. He doesn't laugh at all my cute jokes. When I cry, he doesn't soothe me. But he is striving to be holy himself. He submits himself to spiritual direction. He lives a full, Catholic life and never stops studying. He embraces all the teachings of the Church and loves them. He cares, he listens, he guides, he admonishes. He prays for me, and I know he loves me.

One time, my spiritual director really drove home a point about detachment that I will never forget. Decades earlier, I had gone through a divorce and had lost everything — house, money, jewelry, good credit standing, and more. The trauma spurred me on to grow closer to God, and as time went by, I was feeling great consolation in my renewed faith. One rainy night, I sat on my small sofa wrapped in a warm, fluffy robe that had just come out of the dryer and smelled wonderful. I was sipping a cup of hot, fragrant, orange-spice tea and suddenly — with the sound of rain outside, and feeling safe and cozy — my whole body became relaxed, and I was filled with the peace of God. I knew everything would be all right.

Then, as Sanguines do, I marveled at how holy I was becoming! After all, didn't Saint Paul say that we must be content in all circumstances (see Phil 4:11–13)? Here I was, having lost everything, feeling truly content with only a cotton robe and a small cup of tea.

Excited to share with Father at our next session, I recounted my story of growing in detachment and contentment, just like the saints. He listened with very little reaction, and when I was finished, I expected to see him smile gently and nod his head at my progress.

But no.

He said, "Rose, what would you do if you had no robe and no tea?"

I was stunned into silence. My eyes grew wide and almost filled with tears. I took a slow, deep breath. He was right. Complete detachment from everything (even small, good things) is the goal of perfection. I laugh at this story every now and then, and am reminded that his was the perfect response for a spiritual director suited to my temperament.

Let's look at some helpful insight and instruction for spiritual direction for each of the four temperament types.

For the Choleric

As natural leaders, it may be difficult for Cholerics to submit to anyone we think is less capable or advanced than ourselves — we *must* be able to respect them. That's true, but don't assume others don't have what it takes. It may take trying out several different spiritual directors, guides, or coaches to find a good fit. While some temperaments will submit too quickly to others, a Choleric's challenge will be to remain discriminating but also open and humble in letting the Lord lead.

Focus on virtue. Continue to master your natural strengths and order them to the good so they bloom as virtues, not vices. For those virtues contrary to your natural disposition, look to the Phlegmatic temperament (not to become one, but to learn from them). Choose to become gentler and more patient with others (and yourself). Remain meek in keeping strengths and powers under control. Focus on getting along, not just getting the job done. Cultivate humility by making room for others' opinions and letting them go first. Be more dependent on God and not so darn self-sufficient.

For the Sanguine

As a natural people-person, a Sanguine can easily submit to spiritual direction. But two cautions: First, we must be discerning enough to choose someone who understands us and can get past our charming ways. This is not "a new friendship." A spiritual director is someone meant to help carry one's bloody, splintery crosses.

Second, boredom may set in, or procrastination, both impacting the follow-through on commitments and assignments. Finding a good fit may require trying out several different spiritual directors, guides, or coaches. The challenge will be to remain discriminate but also open and humble in letting the Lord take the lead.

Take developing virtue seriously; continue to master your natural strengths and order them to the good so that they become virtues, not vices. For those virtues that are contrary to a Sanguine's natural disposition, look to the Melancholy as an example. Choose to become more sensitive to the needs and preferences of others, detached from material pleasures, contemplative in slowing down to carefully think things though, structured and disciplined in daily activities, and committed to excellence in every undertaking.

For the Melancholy

Because they value the truth and strive for perfection, Melancholies need someone they trust to take the time to really get to know them and, more importantly, come to understand them. One of my close Melancholy friends shared, "My main concern with spiritual directors is that I will not be understood, and I will be misled." She's right to be discerning! Melancholies must give candidates time to show that they are in it for the right reasons and for the long haul. Try several different spiritual directors, guides, or coaches to find a good fit. Remember, even spiritual directors are not perfect. Ultimately trust must be given to the Lord, working through them.

Keep perfecting your natural strengths and ordering them to the good so that they become virtues, not vices. For those virtues that are contrary to the Melancholy disposition, look to the Sanguine type as a model. Choose to become more joyful in disposition, letting go of fear and worry; courageous in letting go of unforgiveness and obsessions; hopeful in the promises of God for all of us; generous with appropriate visible affection and praise; and understanding and less critical of imperfections, even your own.

For the Phlegmatic

As naturally amenable people, Phlegmatics can easily embrace spiritual direction. But two cautions: 1) Don't rush! Take the time needed to discern, and choose someone who not only understands the temperament but can patiently help move a Phlegmatic out of their comfort zone. Perfection takes humility, listening, and, gulp, work! Phlegmatics need someone to help them not just to wait for Jesus to perfect them, but to get up, pick up their mat, and go follow him (see Jn 5:8). 2) Like the Sanguine, Phlegmatics may become bored after a while, or *forget*, or wait until the last minute, or otherwise not follow through with their commitment and assignments. They may need to try several different spiritual directors, guides, or coaches to find a good fit. The great challenge will be to remain discriminate but also open to the work necessary for perfection.

Keep mastering your natural strengths and order them to the good so that they become virtues, not vices. For those virtues that are contrary to the natural Phlegmatic disposition, look to the Choleric temperament for your guide. Choose to become more courageous in facing fears, bold in speaking out when necessary, zealous for the Faith and what it inspires, committed to taking action and following through, and structured in daily activities.

• • •

Reflections

What would you like in a spiritual director?

If you have a spiritual director, what do you like most about him or her?

Do you find it easy to submit to the direction of others? Why or why not?

Have you ever been an accountability partner for a friend? Did you like it?

• Saint Bonaventure (1221–1274) •

Saint Bonaventure (Franciscan bishop, cardinal, and Doctor of the Church) is considered one of the greatest philosophers of the Middle Ages. Because of his deep love for Christ and the ecstasy of that love in which he found himself, he is known as the "Seraphic Doctor."

What do we know about his temperament?

He was clearly a deep, Melancholy thinker. At the University of Paris, he became intimate friends with St. Thomas Aquinas, who relied on some of Bonaventure's extensive theological and philosophical works as resources for his own. When Bonaventure was chosen to be the general of the order, he restored a perfect calm where peace had been disturbed by internal discord. He was known to be prayerful and a good administrator, and he steered the Franciscans on a moderate and intellectual course. Prayer, peace, calm, moderation, and good administrative skills? Phlegmatics, take credit!

There is a noticeable poetry and warmth to his writings that appeal not only to the intellect but the heart. One cannot help but be moved by his eloquent and passionate Prayer After Holy Communion, which is included at the end of this book.

What can we learn from him?

It's said that St. Thomas Aquinas once asked Saint Bonaventure from which books he obtained his unparalleled knowledge. Bonaventure simply pointed to the crucifix as his library. May we never forget that knowledge is good, but love for God is everything.

Saint Bonaventure, pray for us.

• 26 •

Receiving the Sacraments

The more you give yourself, the more
God will give himself to you.

— St. Louis de Monfort

The sacraments are intimate encounters with the real person of Jesus Christ and are crucial to a healthy, holy life. But what hasn't already been written about how beautiful, powerful, life-giving, and necessary they are?

So, I invited a few of my Catholic family and friends to share their personal experiences with me through the eyes of the four temperaments. Having taught the temperaments for over thirty years, most everyone I know *knows* their type (whether they ever wanted to or not). They gave me permission to share their thoughts and their names with you.

The Sacrament of Reconciliation

From Darrin (Melancholy-Phlegmatic)

I was away from the Church and living sinfully for a long time, finally heard the message to "come home," and went to my first confession after thirty years. Did I feel free and happy afterward?

No. I fell into despair and scrupulosity.

Why? Because as a Melancholy, I realized that to stay in a state of grace, I needed a complete overhaul of my life, and that was going to take some doing and a helluva long time. A part of me was truly relieved and thankful for Jesus' mercy, but another part was overwhelmed with the sorrow for my sinful past and the work ahead of me. I just wish the Church would stop selling coming back to confession as a quick fix for your life. "Just come home," they say. "Everything will be fine," they say. There is still so much work to do. I have to remember that Jesus promises to be there every step of the way.

From Margaret (Phlegmatic-Melancholy)
I go to Mass, and everyone thinks I'm a good Catholic, which mostly I am, but they have no idea. I've had a lot of trauma in my life that still needs healing. My temperament type is the two introverts, and I don't like to talk about it or call attention to myself. I had an extremely difficult childhood, and my husband has been horribly abusive. I often feel stuck and powerless to change anything. In confession, Jesus forgives my sins, but he doesn't heal all the wounds. Those take time. It's hard.

From Kelly (Choleric-Sanguine)
When I think about confession, my Sanguine side gets a little knot in the stomach. I used to cry every time I went. And my Sanguine tears weren't sad little quiet tears. They were big, ugly tears of shame. I always felt like I was groveling like a worthless worm at the feet of the king. After crying in confession over and over to the same priest, he suggested counseling to get at the root of my shame and fear. It has helped!

Back in those days I tried to avoid the confessional as much as possible because it was such a painful experience for me. Now, I am much more attuned to God's love and mercy, and going to confession is not nearly as painful. In the past I probably only went two or three times a year. Now, I go every month. My Choleric side is glad to be getting it done, but my Sanguine side is still uncomfortable to say out loud the ways that I have hurt and disappointed God. However, I don't ugly cry anymore, and I am much more confident in God's loving mercy. And instead of going immediately to the bathroom to check my face and being embarrassed if anyone saw me coming out of the confessional ugly crying, I now just dab at a weepy eye and give a big sigh of relief when exiting the confessional. Sometimes I don't even need a tissue. LOL!

From Francie (Choleric-Sanguine)
Once a priest yelled at me in confession. My Choleric side wanted to yell back, *How dare you? You're supposed to be merciful with me.* But my most tender Sanguine part just burst into tears, sobbed out an Act of Contrition, got my absolution, and walked out. I think my Guardian Angel tapped me on the shoulder and reminded me that I just went to Jesus, the priest is not perfect, and to avoid feeling sorry for myself. So, I did. My Choleric side still remembers that day, and she's still mad. I guess I still need to go to confession for that.

From Diana (Melancholy-Phlegmatic)
I recently scheduled a longer, general confession since my last confession was five years ago when I first came into the Church. I did procrastinate a bit and spent weeks making a long list of my past sins, and parts of me felt very vulnerable, ashamed, and anxious. There was one big sin in particular that I was beside myself with, feeling it was the sin of all sins. But the priest showed me such compassion. I did not feel judged. I felt God's love. My Melancholy side was so glad he really understood my remorse. After that, I felt a sense of peace, relief, and renewed joy as I experienced

God's forgiveness and mercy.

But now when I go to confession, Melancholy parts of me still feel nervous and worried. I live a quiet life alone (which my Phlegmatic side loves) and do not engage much with people and have limited interactions. So, to uncover habitual sins, I'm having to dig deeper into my interior life and need to analyze my conscience much more closely. Thankfully, a dear friend gave me a detailed Catholic Examination of Conscience checklist, which has been very helpful. My Phlegmatic side appreciates the structure.

From Sarah (Phlegmatic-Sanguine)
My priest extends his hands and places them gently on my head as he grants me absolution. At first the introverted Phlegmatic part of me is a little taken aback, but my Sanguine side loves it, and I feel safe, loved, and light as a feather.

From Joe (Melancholy-Phlegmatic)
I appreciate it when the priest shows he is truly listening to every word and asks you a couple of questions. I don't mind it. It makes me feel like he really wants to understand me. Actually, I could talk to him for hours.

These heart-felt revelations remind me of the prodigal son who came home (see Lk 15:11–32). He, too, must have felt a mixture of excitement and hope but also fear and shame. The father forgave him on the spot, but the son still reeked of a filthy pig pen, needed a whole new set of clothes, and still had bad habits that needed breaking. He probably still owed money and amends to a lot of people. The new robe and rings on his fingers were just the beginning of a long journey to get his life back on track. The same may be true for many of us.

In confession, we may not always get overwhelmed with regret or shame, but we can forget Jesus and focus too much on the priest. The more naturally critical types (Choleric and Melancholy) are likely to critique him, and the Choleric may even write him a letter or confront him in the parking lot.

The softer types (Sanguine and Phlegmatic) will hope the priest will comfort them, look kindly upon them, speak comforting words, and maybe chuckle warmly at their comments. The four types never stop seeking to have their deepest emotional needs met — even in the confessional. Remember those needs?

Choleric: Please appreciate all my hard efforts.
Sanguine: Please love me.
Phlegmatic: Please be gentle with me.
Melancholy: Please understand me.

An honest examination of our lives can be discouraging, and confessing our sins out loud can be embarrassing even for the extroverted Choleric and Sanguine, who usually don't mind displaying their inner world. But even those emotional responses can lead us to humility, hope, and gratitude for the mercy we receive. What are some takeaways for the temperaments?

God still works, even when the priest isn't perfect.

God will reach out and touch you in ways that are particular to your needs.

God will look past your emotions to see your contrite heart and surrendered will.

God will continue to complete the good work he began in you (see Phil 1:6).

The Sacrament of the Eucharist

From Cherie (Phlegmatic-Melancholy)

I'm a convert and only learned about the Real Presence about twenty years ago. I know in my head that the Eucharist is Jesus'

Body, Blood, Soul, and Divinity, but a part of me still struggles with believing it. Sometimes when I gaze up at the elevated Host, I have to remind myself, *This is Jesus. This is Jesus. This is Jesus.* But I know a part of me does believe. You know why? It hits me hard when I can't receive. Maybe I broke my fast or I think I need to get to confession. Then I feel so sad that at Mass, yes, I can still be with him but can't receive him in that intimate way. That sadness kind of stays with me until the next time I can go to Communion.

From Marie (Sanguine-Phlegmatic)
All I remember about my first holy Communion was the excitement of getting dressed up all pretty in white and checking out all the other little girls' dresses and veils and the little boys in their Sunday best. I remember it being fun because I knew Mass was all about us on that day, and we were the center of attention. Lord, please forgive me! Now I know it is not about me at all.

From Diana (Melancholy-Phlegmatic)
When I receive holy Communion, I feel I am renewing and strengthening my vow/relationship with God. I reflect on Jesus' sacrifice for me, how he offered himself for me, and I offer myself to him in return. I'm aware that Jesus is in me, and I celebrate him in me. I'm humbled and feel a spiritual connection, strength, spiritual nourishment, protected, reflective, and hopeful. It's intimate, and I feel Jesus' love, grace, and mercy. That's all my Melancholy poetry coming out. Ha! My Phlegmatic is happy to say it much more succinctly: I'm at peace.

From Barb (Melancholy-Choleric)
At age seven, my first holy Communion was the happiest day of my life. I worked hard all year in school to prepare to receive Jesus, to (as the song we sang said) welcome our "Little White

Guest." Think about that; he's a guest. He doesn't impose himself or force us to receive him, but he waits patiently for us to invite him in. Now that I think of it, Mary received the original holy Communion when God asked her if she would receive him into her body as his mother. The God of all creation waited for her to welcome him in. He is so kind, so loving. I'm so thankful for this gift we have as Catholics.

From Kelly (Choleric-Sanguine)
I admit my Choleric side gets distracted by other people. I notice their clothing and their hair, and I want to fix them. I make judgments such as "I can't believe this guy is wearing short pants and Crocs to church. Wow, she looks great! I wish I were thin like her. I wonder if she knows her shirt tag is sticking out? Should I reach out and fix it for her? No, probably not." To solve my own problem, I now sit closer to the altar to eliminate the distractions. I've started veiling as well, and that has helped me with humility.

From Jeff (Phlegmatic-Melancholy)
The Eucharist has always been a difficult concept, but I've learned not to let my senses or emotions, especially doubts, drive the bus. I'm not a theologian but I believe because Jesus said it is so. Plain and simple.

From Darrin (Melancholy-Phlegmatic)
When I go up the aisle to receive holy Communion, I have parts that are both excited and anxious. My Phlegmatic side is relieved that Jesus is coming to me, but my worried Melancholy side (and all my parts that still carry shame) starts quickly examining my conscience once again. Before I even get to the priest, I have recounted all my venial sins, and I think how can anyone ever be truly worthy to receive GOD! Lord, I am not worthy! But then my Phlegmatic side kind of pushes the dramatic, worry-wart

part aside and simply cries out in my soul, *Lord, I believe. Please help my unbelief.*

We are all unworthy. Sanguine St. Teresa of Ávila saw her unworthy self as a worm, or at least "wormlike." In her colorful analogies, she teaches that one must first die to have life, and she differentiates between these two selves by attacking the "wormlike" self so that God can quicken the "butterfly" self.

Our doubts, fears, and feelings of unworthiness are normal, but they must be held in tension with the truth of what we know: In his great love for us, and to our utter joy and gratitude, God is pleased to make us worthy. From the song — and most tender profession of love — I learned by heart for my first holy Communion:

> O Lord, I am not worthy
> That thou should'st come to me;
> But speak thy words of comfort,
> My spirit healed shall be.
>
> And humbly I'll receive thee,
> The Bridegroom of my soul,
> No more by sin to grieve thee
> Nor fly thy sweet control.†

Striving for sainthood is so much easier for all the temperaments when we frequently avail ourselves of Jesus' presence in his holy sacraments. Go to confession at least once a month if you can.

Cholerics, make it more important than all your other duties.

Sanguines, don't rely on God's love to keep you away from him for too long.

---

† Lyrics attributed to Landshuter Gesangbuch, 1777; set to traditional melody, "Non Dignus."

Melancholies, ask for the grace to face any scrupulosity that keeps you away.

Phlegmatics, do not procrastinate. Write it down on a calendar.

Daily Mass is available and convenient for many and almost impossible for others. Make it a habit to receive Jesus in holy Communion at least weekly and as often as possible, but don't compare yourself to others or fall into performance to earn his approval or love. You already have it.

• • •

Reflections

What are your memories of your first confession and first holy Communion?

What thoughts come to you when you think of the Sacrament of Reconciliation?

How have you managed any doubts about Jesus' presence in the Eucharist?

Why do you think frequent reception of the sacraments gives you strength?

• Mary, the Mother of God •

Mary is our most precious saint, our Mother, "our life, our sweetness, and our hope." She is the Queen of Heaven and desires to bring all her children into the loving arms of her Son for all eternity. What a magnificent gift she is to us!

What do we know about her temperament?
Scripture records few of Mary's words, but we see in the Gospel of Luke that she is naturally humble, patient, and obedient. She questions the angel Gabriel without arrogance or demands. She considers herself not a worker in the vineyard or a fierce warrior for God, but a little handmaid of the Lord. In her Magnificat (see Lk 1:46–55) she is balanced in naming her great blessings and privileges but credits all to God's greatness. Mary defers to Jesus at Cana (see Jn 2:1–12) but uses her quiet authority to nudge him. These are virtues everyone can acquire, but they come most naturally to the stable, steady, peaceful Phlegmatic.

We also know she worried about her Son being lost for three days (see Lk 2:41–52), as would any parent of any temperament type. And we know she worries tremendously about us, urging us to pray, sacrifice, and not forget the pains of hell. She bore unbelievable pains throughout her life, witnessing Jesus' passion and standing by him at the cross. Among many other names, she is known as Our Lady of Sorrows. It seems she was also a beautiful Melancholy soul.

What can we learn from her?
Mary models for all temperaments how to have a spirit that rejoices: through total surrender to the will of God.

O Mary, conceived without sin, pray for us who have recourse to thee.

• 27 •

Setting Sights on Sainthood

The most beautiful and stirring adventure that can happen to you is the personal meeting with Jesus, who is the only one who gives real meaning to our life.

— Pope St. John Paul II

I admit it. The only things I can clearly recall about my first holy Communion are the gorgeous dress and veil I wore, and the bear claws we had afterward. I know. But Sanguines can — and do — have special encounters with God.

My first mystical experience was with my little sister Barb in our backyard swings. It was a beautiful morning, and the sun shone brightly through the clouds. Suddenly we both noticed brilliant, colorful rays shooting down to earth, and it looked just like the rays coming from Jesus on our Catholic holy cards. Both of us gasped, looked at each other, and scrambled up to the top of the swing set to get as high as we could.

"It's God," said Barb.

"I *know*!" I replied.

We stood perfectly still and quiet, and I distinctly remember feeling God's presence flood over us. I felt his overwhelming love, and my little heart wanted to love him back with all I had. It only lasted a short while, but my sister and I talk reverently about our shared experience to this day. We both were given a little moment of pure, blissful union with him.

Union with God — our immediate and eternal vocation — is not a theoretical religious state, but a true, body-and-soul, familial embrace with the Persons of the Trinity. While it will be perfectly fulfilled in heaven, we can begin to experience some of its joys right here and now. And while we are still being perfected, sometimes this experience of union with God on earth will entail some suffering for us, too, as we allow him to purify us. With each new morning, throughout the day, and before sleep, we can offer ourselves to him.

What about YOU?

If you've read this far, you've absorbed a ton of information on the temperaments. Before we wrap this book up, is there anything else you must learn? A word of wisdom ascribed to Saint Bonaventure expresses it better than I ever could: *If you learn everything except Christ, you learn nothing. If you learn nothing except Christ, you learn everything.*

Let God's Word Guide You

The topic of temperaments should always point to Jesus and his love for you. The word *temperament* may not be in the Bible, but there are countless descriptors of man's natural dispositions: slow Abraham, sneaky David, impulsive Peter, intense Paul. If we assume Jesus was like us and had a combination of two of the four temperaments, then the other two would not have come as naturally to him. But he would have been able to appreciate, learn from, and even model some of the strengths of the other two. And it is *our* hope that, with grace, we may do the same.

In Scripture, Jesus Christ is prefigured and presented to us with names of honor in which one may see each of the four temperaments. For those who have eyes to see, behold Our Lord:

Sanguine Light
Bright Morning Star — Revelation 22:16
Light of the World — John 8:12
Radiance of God's Glory — Hebrews 1:3
Rising Sun — Luke 1:78
Sun of Righteousness — Malachi 4:2
Dayspring — Luke 1:78
The Glory of the Lord — Isaiah 40:5
The Rose of Sharon — Song of Songs 2:1
Beloved — Matthew 12:18
Indescribable Gift — 2 Corinthians 9:15

Phlegmatic Peace
Prince of Peace — Isaiah 9:6
Mediator — 1 Timothy 2:5
Intercessor — Hebrews 7:25
Holy Servant — Acts 4:27
Wonderful Counselor — Isaiah 9:6
Advocate — 1 John 2:1
Consolation of Israel — Luke 2:25
Lamb of God — John 1:29
Good Shepherd — John 10:11, 14
The Servant of the Lord — Isaiah 52:13

Choleric Courage
Power and Wisdom of God — 1 Corinthians 1:24
Arm of the Lord — Isaiah 53:1
Lion of the Tribe of Judah — Revelation 5:5
King of Kings — Revelation 17:14, 19:16; 1 Timothy 6:15
The Almighty — Revelation 1:8
Pioneer of Our Salvation — Hebrews 2:10

Spiritual Rock — 1 Corinthians 10:4
Living Stone — 1 Peter 2:4
Chief Cornerstone — Ephesians 2:20; 1 Peter 2:6, 7
Deliverer — Romans 11:26

Melancholy Mystery
Master — Luke 5:5
High Priest — Hebrews 3:1, 4:14, 7:26
Ancient of Days — Daniel 7:22
Judge of the World — 2 Timothy 4:1; Acts 10:42
Man of Sorrows — Isaiah 53:3
Suffering Servant — Isaiah 42:1
Stone Rejected by the Builders — Matthew 21:42
Faithful and True Witness — Revelation 1:5, 3:14
Shepherd and Guardian of Our Souls — 1 Peter 2:25
The Way, the Truth, and the Life — John 14:6

Our Lord desires that you share in his own blessed life. He longs for deeper intimacy with you, and he draws close to you at every moment (CCC 1), guiding you deeper into his Sacred Heart.

Finally, in echo of the angels and the many saints, and of our Lord himself: *Do not be afraid.*

• • •

Reflections

Which particular saints "speak" to you and why?

Is there a Scripture verse describing Jesus that is particularly memorable? What stands out to you about it?

What would you like to ask of God right now?

What do you think God might be saying to you right now?

Part 5

Taking the Test

Search me, O God, and know my heart!
Try me and know my thoughts!

— Psalm 139:23

• 28 •

Uncovering the Truth

And we all, with unveiled face, beholding the glory of the Lord, are being changed into his likeness from one degree of glory to another.

— 2 Corinthians 3:18

I love murder mysteries. Especially when the detective team is in the coroner's lab during the autopsy. What clues will be revealed when the body is opened? Will they find a .45 caliber bullet lodged in the heart? Further toxicology tests must be ordered to get a full picture!

We are all a little bit like the victim on the autopsy table — each of us looking "normal" on the outside but emotionally wounded or carrying the residual effects of old verbal or emotional "gunshot" wounds on the inside. One can never underestimate the adverse effects on our persons — and our temperaments — of long-standing childhood trauma, neglect, or abuse in work and relationships, and even in bad marriages. You may have sustained psychic injuries that could only be seen with an emotional X-ray.

Solving the mystery of temperament may be quick and easy

for some. Perhaps the prior pages have already nailed it down for you. But for others the same pages may be confusing, frustrating, or stirring up bad memories. If you take this test and find yourself more confused than ever, it may require a careful sifting through all the clues, a rigorous and painful visit to the past, or even further "testing" with a qualified therapist or spiritual director. Whatever may arise that causes you any fear, doubt, or confusion, take it to the Lord.

Also bear in mind: Tests are only the beginning. Some will prefer the following test style; it's quick and easy, but it may also be missing the necessary nuance for those who want to consider their answers more carefully, and the short descriptions are somewhat exaggerated. Let this test give you some clarity, but don't be afraid to seek more information if you need it. You, indeed, are a mystery but knowing your temperament doesn't need to be. Have fun!

INSTRUCTIONS

On the following pages, you'll find forty sets of descriptive words. While certainly not an exhaustive list, it can assist in discovering or affirming your natural strengths and weaknesses.

Step One

- In each set of four words, place a check mark in front of the word that *most* often applies to you. You might think you are all four temperaments at different times and circumstances, and that's normal. But when you select the one that is dominant, you will be clearing away the circumstantial for the substantial.
- If you have trouble choosing between one or two words, check two, but no more than two.
- Don't simply check the reaction that you have

learned, what is expected of you, or what you want it to be. Choose instead *your most natural and quick reaction to things in general.*

- Go back to your childhood; which word would you have chosen as a youngster? Your original giftedness is still with you.
- If you still aren't sure about which word best applies, ask a sibling, spouse, or someone who knows you well. Ask, for example, "Do you think that most of the time I'm more *adaptable* or *action-oriented*?"
- Understand that, at times, everyone can be, for example, adaptable, but only one of the temperaments is most easily, quickly, and *naturally* adaptable most of the time and in most circumstances.

Step Two

Once you've finished, transfer all your check marks to the corresponding words on the *Scoring Charts* that follow. For example, if you checked "animated" on the profile, check "animated" on the scoring charts. (Note: the words are in different orders on the profile and scoring charts.)

Step Three

Once you've transferred your answers to the scoring charts, added up the totals in each of the four columns, and added the totals from both the strengths and weaknesses sections, you should see your two personality types by the two highest totals.

- Because no test is foolproof, it is normal to have a few check marks scattered in all four categories, but two temperaments should emerge as the strongest. Now you can celebrate; these are your God-given gifts!

- If you scored two opposite temperaments (Choleric *and* Phlegmatic or Sanguine *and* Melancholy), I suggest you ask your friends and family to help you with choosing your true characteristics.
- The two lowest scores will be those temperaments that are not natural to you.
- If you've scored evenly between all four, it's likely that you're part Phlegmatic, the most adaptable temperament, which can operate adequately in every type (when and if necessary).
- Another reason that your two types might not be clear is that you have been functioning in a type that is not natural for you because of childhood pressures; expectations from employers, spouses, and others; or a desire to be like someone you admire. The culture also pressures men (and even women) to be Choleric.
- Your two natural types may be balanced, or one will dominate. The natural combinations are:

    - *Sanguine and Choleric* (double-extrovert)
    - *Choleric and Melancholy* (extrovert-introvert)
    - *Melancholy and Phlegmatic* (double-introvert)
    - *Phlegmatic and Sanguine* (introvert-extrovert)

Step Four

For some, taking tests is traumatic, so here are a few last-minute words of encouragement:

If you are confused: Maybe the word definitions were unclear. Maybe you always thought you were something else because others told you so. Maybe you simply wanted to be something other than what the test results said you were. I really wanted to be sensitive, deeply caring, and laser-focused like my Melancholy parents. Grace — and a continual openness to this concept — helped me accept the opposite gifts that God chose to give me. I now love being Sanguine, so I can easily no longer *worry* about it! Don't fret too much. Prayerfully receive any insight you get from this process and let the rest go.

If you scored all over the place: No, you're not schizophrenic! The most likely explanation is that you are introverted and either have trouble making up your mind, or you want it to be perfect. Where others may have rushed through, you took your time. You may be a well-rounded, adaptable Phlegmatic who can roll with the punches, step up to any role when necessary, and be what the situation needs now. If you want more clarity, ask an honest friend or family member for his or her assessment.

If you feel ashamed: The soul who is seeking humility will likely focus on her natural weaknesses. Fear of being unworthy and unloved is usually what produces the burning shame about our shortcomings. Remember that weaknesses are our strengths carried to extremes by some fear. In time, grace can bring them back into balance.

True humility acknowledges both the bad and the good. Let Our Lord's gentle breath blow away the black clouds of humiliation. He created you in *his* image. He loves you so tenderly. You're his beautiful work, and he is not finished with you, my dear!

Place a check mark in front of (or otherwise select, circle, or mark) the word in each set of four that *most often* applies. Don't overthink it!

STRENGTHS

Don't worry about false humility! Take credit for the gifts that God has given you.

1

__ *Action-oriented.* Quickly assesses then moves to swift and decisive action.

__ *Adaptable.* Doesn't mind changing a stance when it would keep the peace.

__ *Animated.* Full of life, sparkle, and even silliness, with lively use of body movement.

__ *Analytical.* Likes to examine the details and is seeking perfection.

2

__ *Powerful.* Natural leader; not easily swayed from course.

__ *Playful.* Frequently and readily full of childlike fun, lightness, and silliness.

__ *Perfectionist.* Idealist who is delighted when things are exactly as they should be.

__ *Peaceful.* Seems undisturbed and tranquil most of the time.

3

__ *Stable.* Emotions neither high nor low; even-tempered.

__ *Self-sacrificing.* Willingly endures personal pain for the genuine needs of others.

__ *Sociable.* Quick to like, hug, touch, and entertain everyone.

__ *Strong.* Focused, engaged, and a rock for others to lean on.

4

__ *Careful.* Can't be pushed; doesn't rush in and takes extra time if necessary.

__ *Controlled.* Maintains a high level of self-composure.

__ *Challenging.* Quickly and easily moves others to go higher, to be their very best.

__ *Charming.* Wins others over with compliments, attention, and touch.

5

__ *Refreshing.* Quick to stimulate, uplift, and joyfully encourage others.

__ *Respectful.* Treats others kindly, with deference, honor, and esteem.

__ *Reserved.* Self-restrained and poised; deep passion under control.

__ *Resourceful.* Able to act quickly and effectively in virtually all situations.

6

__ *Satisfied.* Quietly accepting of whatever happens; no strong preferences.

__ *Sensitive.* Deeply cares, even worries, about others.

__ *Self-reliant.* Can count on own capabilities, judgment, and resources.

__ *Spirited.* Expressive; full of life and high-energy excitement.

7

__ *Planner.* Likes to create and design, and mull over all the little details.

__ *Patient.* Unmoved by delay or trouble, remaining unruffled and calm.

__ *Positive.* Knows things will turn out right if he or she is in charge.

__ *Promoter*. Through charm, urges/compels others to go along, join, or invest.

8

__ *Sure*. Problem solving, confident, and decisive; makes things doable and exciting.

__ *Silly*. Likes to be the center of attention to distract, entertain, and make others laugh.

__ *Sentient*. Most of the time feels or perceives things on a deep level.

__ *Serene*. Quiet, calm, and peaceful; no compulsion to talk, lead, or excite.

9

__ *Observant*. Noticing every little and important detail that others seem to miss.

__ *Obliging*. Accommodating; quick to keep peace and avoid conflict.

__ *Outspoken*. Speaks quickly, frankly, and, when necessary, without reserve.

__ *Optimistic*. Sunny disposition and rosy outlook even when there are problems.

10

__ *Friendly*. Responds gently and kindly to everyone.

__ *Faithful*. Loyal and devoted, even "to the death" for those they love.

__ *Fun*. Brings a light, carefree, or humorous touch even to difficult situations.

__ *Fearless*. Quickly responds or acts, unafraid of pushback or consequences.

11

__ *Dauntless.* Driven and not worried about obstacles.
__ *Delightful.* High energy, upbeat, entertaining, and fun to be with.
__ *Diplomatic.* Deals with people tactfully, sensitively, and patiently.
__ *Detailed.* Remembers and takes the time to attend to all the important details.

12

__ *Cheerful.* Usually in high spirits and actively promoting happiness in others.
__ *Consistent.* Likes the status quo and has no need for change.
__ *Ceaseless.* Persists, holds tightly, and does not let go easily.
__ *Confident.* Self-assured and certain of own ability and success.

13

__ *Idealistic.* Visualizes things in their perfect form and strives to measure up to that standard.
__ *Independent.* Self-sufficient and self-confident with little need of help.
__ *Inoffensive.* Tries to avoid saying or causing anything unpleasant or objectionable.
__ *Inspiring.* Encourages others to work or join by stressing the bright, happy side.

14

__ *Demonstrative.* Openly expresses emotion and affection, often physically touching others.
__ *Decisive.* Quick and conclusive judgment-making ability with no looking back.
__ *Dapper.* Perfect hair, perfect outfit; polished and poised.
__ *Demure.* Gentle, quiet, and modest; no need for flair, drama,

or excitement.

15

__ *Mediator.* Easily encourages others to resolve differences and get along.
__ *Meditative.* Values deep reflection and contemplation before taking the final action.
__ *Motivator.* Quickly takes the lead and moves others to action.
__ *Merry.* Quick to playful humor and a cheerful word or touch.

16

__ *Trusting.* Rarely suspicious; quick to see the sunny side.
__ *Take-charge.* Sees the big picture; natural problem solver, delegator, and manager.
__ *Trust-worthy.* Will stick it out to the bitter end for someone they love.
__ *Tolerant.* Easily accepts others without the need to criticize or correct them.

17

__ *Level-headed.* Avoids high drama; sees the big picture.
__ *Loyal.* Faithful to a person, ideal, or job, even if it requires sacrifice.
__ *Lenient.* Flexible and easygoing; does not generally hold a hard or fast rule.
__ *Lively.* Almost childlike in natural optimism, vigor, energy, and bounce.

18

__ *Contented.* Easily satisfied with what he or she has and not driven for more.
__ *Chief.* Takes leadership quickly and expects others to follow.
__ *Cautious.* Appropriately concerned about the possibility of

serious problems or risks.

__ *Childlike.* Sweet, open, and emotionally transparent.

19

__ *Purist.* Takes appropriate pride and pleasure in doing things properly.

__ *Pleasant.* Easy to be around; careful not to alienate or offend.

__ *Productive.* Hits the ground running with a high level of activity and production.

__ *Plucky.* Appropriately displays a little good-natured spunk and feistiness.

20

__ *Bouncy.* A sweet, bubbly, lively personality, full of sparkle.

__ *Bold.* Forward, daring, and unafraid of offending others.

__ *Behaved.* Desires to conduct self within the realm of what seems proper.

__ *Balanced.* Stable, balanced personality; not subject to sharp highs or lows.

WEAKNESSES

Be brave; ignore the shame for now and be as accurate as you can.

21

__ *Blank.* Won't show much expression or emotion; keeps it tightly under wraps.

__ *Bashful.* Self-conscious; not used to unwanted attention.

__ *Brassy.* Showy, flashy, and a little bit classless.

__ *Bossy.* Commanding, domineering, and sometimes overbearing.

22

__ *Unaware.* Not able to see or be sensitive to others' hurt feelings.

__ *Unsympathetic.* Irritated with the whiners — they need to get over it.
__ *Unavailable.* Checked out and avoiding problems, hard work, or others.
__ *Unforgiving.* Struggles to let go of hurt and injustice; may hold deep resentment/grudges.

23

__ *Reticent.* Unwilling to face things; stress builds for a long time and then blows.
__ *Revengeful.* Wishes "justice" on others because of real or imagined offenses.
__ *Raging.* Quickly uses anger and a loud voice to get others to comply.
__ *Reckless.* Hasty, careless, rash, and wild.

24

__ *Fussy.* Insistent — maybe even anxious — about petty matters or details.
__ *Fearful.* May often experience feelings of being overwhelmed or dominated.
__ *Forgetful.* Doesn't care about the details enough.
__ *Frank.* Straightforward, outspoken; too quick to say exactly what he or she thinks.

25

__ *Impatient.* Wishes everyone would move faster, work harder, and talk less.
__ *Indecisive.* Unsure, overwhelmed, faking it; lacking in confidence.
__ *Intolerant.* Highly judgmental of others' imperfections — large and small.
__ *Inappropriate.* Takes silliness, fun, and childishness to em-

barrassing, hurtful, or harmful extremes.

26

__ *Unpopular*. Too busy or too important to fit in with others.
__ *Uninvolved*. Too overwhelmed, or may have limited to no interest.
__ *Unpredictable*. Fun and friendly one day, fickle the next.
__ *Unaffectionate*. Deliberately withholds approval or affection to punish/control others.

27

__ *Headstrong*. Insists on being in charge and making the decisions.
__ *Haphazard*. Scattered, undisciplined, and chases after the next shiny thing.
__ *Hard to please*. Standards are set so high that it is difficult to ever be satisfied.
__ *Hesitant*. Slow to get moving and hard to get and stay involved.

28

__ *Plain*. A detached state without highs or lows and showing little, if any, emotion.
__ *Pessimistic*. Even in hoping for the best, often fearing the worst.
__ *Pompous*. Has excessive self-esteem; sees self as always right and best person for the job.
__ *Provocative*. Too quick to provoke, excite, flirt, touch, or stimulate.

29

__ *Angry*. Quick to irritation that is usually loudly or physically expressed.

__ *Aimless.* Desires and goals seem too unreachable and difficult so why try?
__ *Argumentative.* Inappropriately takes on authority to get one's own way.
__ *Alienated.* Easily feels estranged from others; *no one understands me.*

30

__ *Naive.* Overly optimistic perspective; sometimes too simple and unsophisticated.
__ *Negative.* Too quick to see only the down or dark side of people or situations.
__ *Nervy.* Too full of self-confidence, fortitude, and sheer guts.
__ *Nonchalant.* Unconcerned, indifferent … *whatever* …

31

__ *Worrier.* Often feels uncertain, troubled, or anxious.
__ *Withdrawn.* Can often pull back and feel overwhelmed or exhausted.
__ *Workaholic.* An aggressive goal-setter; prefers production over perfection and even people.
__ *Wild.* Will throw convention out primarily to win the attention and "applause" of others.

32

__ *Talkative.* Overly focused on endless details he or she wants everyone else to know.
__ *Tough.* Sometimes expresses self in an offensive and inconsiderate way.
__ *Timid.* Can often shrink from overwhelming situations.
__ *Teasing.* Uses unsuitable humor when the situation is serious.

33

__ *Doubtful.* Hesitant; unwilling to engage or see the possibilities.
__ *Deflective.* Uses charm, seduction, and "tap dancing" to change the subject/focus.
__ *Domineering.* Sometimes takes charge and commands others too strongly.
__ *Depressed.* Can a little too easily feel discouraged and down.

34

__ *Improper.* Inappropriate responses or behavior to get a laugh or attention.
__ *Indisposed.* Doesn't want to be bothered; *can't someone else do it?*
__ *Irritable.* Quickly triggered by others' real or perceived incompetence.
__ *Interfering.* Meddlesome; unable to stop managing and perfecting others.

35

__ *Mercurial.* All show and no go; makes lots of promises he or she can't keep.
__ *Moody.* Can go into a discouraged, dark, or sullen place.
__ *Mumbles.* Passive-aggressive reluctance or refusal to speak up or more clearly.
__ *Muscular.* Too rough by dragging, pushing, and forcing people along.

36

__ *Slow.* Doesn't always act/think quickly — too much of a bother/not interested.
__ *Scornful.* Looking down on all the idiots.
__ *Silly.* A juvenile need for attention; wants to be watched and admired.

__ *Skeptical.* Disbelieving; questioning the motive behind the words or action.

37

__ *Long-suffering.* Dramatic; emotional tendency to martyrdom.
__ *Lords over others.* Quickly lets others know that he or she is right or is in control.
__ *Lazy.* Puts bare-minimum energy and focus into activities and relationships.
__ *Loud.* Laugh or voice can be heard above others in the room.

38

__ *Sluggish.* Slow to get started; needs push to be motivated; tends to be late.
__ *Suspicious.* Tends to initially doubt or distrust others or their ideas.
__ *Short-tempered.* Anger and impatience are quick rather than building or slow-seething.
__ *Shallow.* Flighty, not grounded; makes light of or laughs things off too quickly.

39

__ *Ruthless.* Can be downright nasty with sharp words: sarcasm, criticism, or mockery.
__ *Riled.* Quick to irritation and bad temper.
__ *Reluctant.* Thinks it's just too much effort and not that important or interesting.
__ *Ridiculous.* Carries humor too far or says inane things at inappropriate times.

40

__ *Compromising.* To keep peace, will often relax his or her position, even when right.

__ *Critical.* Quick to make judgments; frequently seeing, thinking, or expressing the negative.

__ *Calloused.* Just done with inept, unreliable people and fine by him- or herself.

__ *Clownish.* Undignified acting out meant for attention and laughs.

TEMPERAMENT SCORING CHARTS

Next step! Go back to the *Profile* and transfer the checkmarks to this *Scoring Chart.* Then, total the number of checkmarks at the bottom of each column — first for strengths, then on the next page for weaknesses, and finally you'll add the totals for all four columns.

STRENGTHS - A

Playful Sanguine	**Productive Choleric**
1. __Animated	__Action-oriented
2. __Playful	__Powerful
3. __Sociable	__Strong
4. __Charming	__Challenging
5. __Refreshing	__Resourceful
6. __Spirited	__Self-reliant
7. __Promoter	__Positive
8. __Silly	__Sure
9. __Optimistic	__Outspoken
10. __Fun	__Fearless
11. __Delightful	__Dauntless
12. __Cheerful	__Confident
13. __Inspiring	__Independent
14. __Demonstrative	__Decisive
15. __Merry	__Motivator
16. __Trusting	__Take-charge
17. __Lively	__Level-headed
18. __Childlike	__Chief
19. __Plucky	__Productive
20. __Bouncy	__Bold
Total checks for each column	

STRENGTHS - B

Perfect Melancholy	**Peaceful Phlegmatic**
1. __Analytical	__Adaptable
2. __Perfectionist	__Peaceful
3. __Self-sacrificing	__Stable
4. __Controlled	__Careful
5. __Reserved	__Respectful
6. __Sensitive	__Satisfied
7. __Planner	__Patient
8. __Sentient	__Serene
9. __Observant	__Obliging
10. __Faithful	__Friendly
11. __Detailed	__Diplomatic
12. __Ceaseless	__Consistent
13. __Idealistic	__Inoffensive
14. __Dapper	__Demure
15. __Meditative	__Mediator
16. __Trustworthy	__Tolerant
17. __Loyal	__Lenient
18. __Cautious	__Contented
19. __Purist	__Pleasant
20. __Behaved	__Balanced
Total checks for each column	

WEAKNESSES - C

Playful Sanguine	Productive Choleric
1. __Brassy	__Bossy
2. __Unaware	__Unsympathetic
3. __Reckless	__Raging
4. __Forgetful	__Frank
5. __Inappropriate	__Impatient
6. __Unpredictable	__Unpopular
7. __Haphazard	__Headstrong
8. __Provocative	__Pompous
9.__ Angry	__Argumentative
10. __Naive	__Nervy
11. __Wild	__Workaholic
12. __Teasing	__Tough
13. __Deflective	__Domineering
14. __Improper	__Irritable
15. __Mercurial	__Muscular
16. __Silly	__Scornful
17. __Loud	__Lords over others
18. __Shallow	__Short-tempered
19. __Ridiculous	__Riled
20. __Clownish	__Calloused
Total checks for each column	

WEAKNESSES - D

Perfect Melancholy	Peaceful Phlegmatic
1. __Bashful	__Blank
2. __Unforgiving	__Unavailable
3. __Revengeful	__Reticent
4. __Fussy	__Fearful
5. __Intolerant	__Indecisive
6. __Unaffectionate	__Uninvolved
7. __Hard to please	__Hesitant
8. __Pessimistic	__Plain
9. __Alienated	__Aimless
10. __Negative	__Nonchalant
11. __Withdrawn	__Worrier
12. __Talkative	__Timid
13. __Depressed	__Doubtful
14. __Interfering	__Indisposed
15. __Moody	__Mumbles
16. __Skeptical	__Slow
17. __Long-suffering	__Lazy
18. __Suspicious	__Sluggish
19 __Ruthless	__Reluctant
20. __Critical	__Compromising
Total checks for each column	

GRAND TOTALS

Now transfer your totals from the prior charts:

	Playful Sanguine	Productive Choleric	Perfect Melancholy	Peaceful Phlegmatic
Strengths A	—	—		
Strengths B			—	—
Weaknesses C	—	—		
Weaknesses D			—	—
TOTALS				
	Sanguine	**Choleric**	**Melan-choly**	**Phleg-matic**

Appendix

LITANY OF HUMILITY

O Jesus, meek and humble of heart, *Hear me.*
From the desire of being esteemed, *deliver me, O Jesus.*
From the desire of being loved, *deliver me, O Jesus.*
From the desire of being extolled, *deliver me, O Jesus.*
From the desire of being honored, *deliver me, O Jesus.*
From the desire of being praised, *deliver me, O Jesus.*
From the desire of being preferred to others, *deliver me, O Jesus.*
From the desire of being consulted, *deliver me, O Jesus.*
From the desire of being approved, *deliver me, O Jesus.*
From the fear of being humiliated, *deliver me, O Jesus.*
From the fear of being despised, *deliver me, O Jesus.*
From the fear of suffering rebukes, *deliver me, O Jesus.*
From the fear of being calumniated, *deliver me, O Jesus.*
From the fear of being forgotten, *deliver me, O Jesus.*
From the fear of being ridiculed, *deliver me, O Jesus.*
From the fear of being wronged, *deliver me, O Jesus.*
From the fear of being suspected, *deliver me, O Jesus.*

That others may be loved more than I, *Jesus, grant me the grace to desire it.*
That others may be esteemed more than I, *Jesus, grant me the*

grace to desire it.

That, in the opinion of the world, others may increase, and I may decrease, *Jesus, grant me the grace to desire it.*

That others may be chosen, and I set aside, *Jesus, grant me the grace to desire it.*

That others may be praised, and I go unnoticed, *Jesus, grant me the grace to desire it.*

That others may be preferred to me in everything, *Jesus, grant me the grace to desire it.*

That others may become holier than I, provided that I may become as holy as I should, *Jesus, grant me the grace to desire it.*

— Rafael Cardinal Merry del Val y Zulueta
(Cardinal Merry del Val was the Secretary of State to Pope St. Pius X (1903–1914))

LITANY OF THE FEARFUL HEART

In the name of the Father, and of the Son, and of the Holy Spirit. Amen.

Lord Jesus, you created me in love and for love. Bring me to a place of vulnerability within the safety of your loving arms. Help me today by transforming my fearful heart into a heart that can love you, myself, and my neighbor as you intend.

Jesus, I offer you my heart with all its sufferings.

Jesus, I offer you my heart with all its doubts.

Jesus, I offer you my heart with all its hurts.

Jesus, I offer you my heart with all its fears.

Jesus, I offer you my heart with all its burdens.

Jesus, I offer you my heart with all its hope, and all its lack of hope.

Jesus, I offer you my heart with all its joy, and all its lack of joy.

Jesus, I offer you my heart with all its love, and all its lack of love.
Jesus, Son of God, have mercy on me.
When I feel afraid, *Lord, have mercy.*
When I don't know how to feel safe, *Lord …*
When life feels chaotic …
When I'm confused …
When I don't know how to trust …
When I feel hurt …
When I feel unloved …
When I feel disappointed …
When others fail me …
When I feel let down …
When I feel all alone …
When I feel rejected …
When I feel I don't belong …
When I feel hopeless …
When I'm afraid of being hurt …
Jesus, help me love others when it is difficult.
Jesus, help me pray for those who have hurt me.
Jesus, I know you love me in all my wounds.
Jesus, most compassionate, *Open my heart.*
Jesus, healer of my wounds, *Open …*
Jesus, my shepherd, …
Jesus, my protector, …
Jesus, unspeakable love, …
Jesus, you created me in love, *Hold me in your arms.*
Jesus, you created me for love, *Hold me …*
Jesus, you created me to be loved, …
Jesus, you created my heart, …
Jesus, you see my heart, …
Jesus, you know my true heart, …
Jesus, you comfort my heart, …

Jesus, you treasure my heart, …
Jesus, you encourage my heart, …
Jesus, you created me as your beloved, …
Jesus, you are present with me, *I trust in you.*
Jesus, you bring me close to you, *I trust …*
Jesus, you walk with me, …
Jesus, you accept me, …
Jesus, you calm all my fears, …
Jesus, you protect me from threats, …
Jesus, you delight in me, …
Jesus, help me trust you, …

Lord, you are the healer of my soul and my heart. I ask that through this prayer you would transform me more and more into the likeness of your precious and sacred heart. Let your kindness and compassion transform my heart and bring me always into the security of your loving embrace. Amen.

— Dr. Gerry Crete.

LITANY OF TRUST

From the belief that I must earn Your love, *Deliver me, Jesus.*
From the fear that I am unlovable, *Deliver me, Jesus.*
From the false security that I have what it takes, *Deliver me, Jesus.*
From the fear that trusting You will leave me more destitute, *Deliver me, Jesus.*
From all suspicion of Your words and promises, *Deliver me, Jesus.*
From the rebellion against childlike dependency on You, *Deliver me, Jesus.*
From refusals and reluctances in accepting Your will, *Deliver me, Jesus.*

From anxiety about the future, *Deliver me, Jesus.*
From resentment or excessive preoccupation with the past, *Deliver me, Jesus.*
From restless self-seeking in the present moment, *Deliver me, Jesus.*
From disbelief in Your love and presence, *Deliver me, Jesus.*
From the fear of being asked to give more than I have, *Deliver me, Jesus.*
From the belief that my life has no meaning or worth, *Deliver me, Jesus.*
From the fear of what love demands, *Deliver me, Jesus.*
From discouragement, *Deliver me, Jesus.*

That You are continually holding me, sustaining me, loving me, *Jesus, I trust in You.*
That Your love goes deeper than my sins and failings and transforms me, *Jesus, I trust in You.*
That not knowing what tomorrow brings is an invitation to lean on You, *Jesus, I trust in You.*
That You are with me in my suffering, *Jesus, I trust in You.*
That my suffering, united to Your own, will bear fruit in this life and the next, *Jesus, I trust in You.*
That You will not leave me orphan, that You are present in Your Church, *Jesus, I trust in You.*
That Your plan is better than anything else, *Jesus, I trust in You.*
That You always hear me and, in Your goodness, always respond to me, *Jesus, I trust in You.*
That You give me the grace to accept forgiveness and to forgive others, *Jesus, I trust in You.*
That You give me all the strength I need for what is asked, *Jesus, I trust in You.*
That my life is a gift, *Jesus, I trust in You.*
That You will teach me to trust You, *Jesus, I trust in You.*

That You are my Lord and my God, *Jesus, I trust in You.*
That I am Your beloved one, *Jesus, I trust in You.*

— Written by the Sisters of Life (www.sistersoflife.org)*Nihil Obstat*: Reverend Matthew S. Ernest, STD.
Used by Permission.
Censor Librorum
Imprimatur: Reverend Monsignor Joseph P. LaMorte, VG
Vicar General, Archdiocese of New York
May 1, 2023

SURRENDER NOVENA

Day 1

Why do you confuse yourselves by worrying? Leave the care of your affairs to me and everything will be peaceful. I say to you in truth that every act of true, blind, complete surrender to me produces the effect that you desire and resolves all difficult situations.

O Jesus, I surrender myself to you, take care of everything! (10 times)

Day 2

Surrender to me does not mean to fret, to be upset, or to lose hope, nor does it mean offering to me a worried prayer asking me to follow you and change your worry into prayer. It is against this surrender, deeply against it, to worry, to be nervous and to desire to think about the consequences of anything. It is like the confusion that children feel when they ask their mother to see to their needs, and then try to take care of those needs for themselves so that their childlike efforts get in their mother's way. Surrender means to placidly close the eyes of the soul, to turn away from thoughts of tribulation and to put yourself in my care, so that only I act, saying, "You take care of it."

O Jesus, I surrender myself to you, take care of everything! (10 times)

Day 3

How many things I do when the soul, in so much spiritual and material need, turns to me, looks at me and says to me, "You take care of it," then closes its eyes and rests. In pain you pray for me to act, but that I act in the way you want. You do not turn to me, instead, you want me to adapt to your ideas. You are not sick people who ask the doctor to cure you, but rather sick people who tell the doctor how to. So do not act this way but pray as I taught you in the Our Father: "Hallowed be thy Name," that is, be glorified in my need. "Thy kingdom come," that is, let all that is in us and in the world be in accord with your kingdom. "Thy will be done on Earth as it is in Heaven," that is, in our need, decide as you see fit for our temporal and eternal life. If you say to me truly: "Thy will be done," which is the same as saying: "You take care of it," I will intervene with all my omnipotence, and I will resolve the most difficult situations.

O Jesus, I surrender myself to you, take care of everything! (10 times)

Day 4

Do you see evil growing instead of weakening? Do not worry. Close your eyes and say to me with faith: "Thy will be done, you take care of it." I say to you that I will take care of it, and that I will intervene as does a doctor and I will accomplish miracles when they are needed. Do you see that the sick person is getting worse? Do not be upset, but close your eyes and say, "You take care of it." I say to you that I will take care of it, and that there is no medicine more powerful than my loving intervention. By my love, I promise this to you.

O Jesus, I surrender myself to you, take care of everything! (10 times)

Day 5

And when I must lead you on a path different from the one you see, I will prepare you; I will carry you in my arms; I will let you find yourself, like children who have fallen asleep in their mother's arms, on the other bank of the river. What troubles you and hurts you immensely are your reason, your thoughts and worry, and your desire at all costs to deal with what afflicts you.

O Jesus, I surrender myself to you, take care of everything! (10 times)

Day 6

You are sleepless; you want to judge everything, direct everything and see to everything and you surrender to human strength, or worse — to men themselves, trusting in their intervention — this is what hinders my words and my views. Oh, how much I wish from you this surrender, to help you; and how I suffer when I see you so agitated! Satan tries to do exactly this: to agitate you and to remove you from my protection and to throw you into the jaws of human initiative. So, trust only in me, rest in me, surrender to me in everything.

O Jesus, I surrender myself to you, take care of everything! (10 times)

Day 7

I perform miracles in proportion to your full surrender to me and to your not thinking of yourselves. I sow treasure troves of graces when you are in the deepest poverty. No person of reason, no thinker, has ever performed miracles, not even among the saints. He does divine works whosoever surrenders to God. So don't think about it anymore, because your mind is acute and for you it is very hard to see evil and to trust in me and to not think of yourself. Do this for all your needs, do this, all of you, and you will see great continual silent miracles. I will take care of things, I promise this to you.

O Jesus, I surrender myself to you, take care of everything! (10 times)

Day 8

Close your eyes and let yourself be carried away on the flowing current of my grace; close your eyes and do not think of the present, turning your thoughts away from the future just as you would from temptation. Repose in me, believing in my goodness, and I promise you by my love that if you say, "You take care of it," I will take care of it all; I will console you, liberate you, and guide you.

O Jesus, I surrender myself to you, take care of everything! (10 times)

Day 9

Pray always in readiness to surrender, and you will receive from it great peace and great rewards, even when I confer on you the grace of immolation, of repentance, and of love. Then what does suffering matter? It seems impossible to you? Close your eyes and say with all your soul, "Jesus, you take care of it." Do not be afraid, I will take care of things and you will bless my name by humbling yourself. A thousand prayers cannot equal one single act of surrender, remember this well. There is no novena more effective than this.

O Jesus, I surrender myself to you, take care of everything! (10 times)

Mother, I am yours now and forever.
Through you and with you
I always want to belong
completely to Jesus.

— Servant of God Don Dolindo Ruotolo, contemporary and friend of Padre Pio

PRAYER AFTER HOLY COMMUNION (Saint Bonaventure)

Pierce, O my sweet Lord Jesus, my inmost soul with the most joyous and healthful wound of your love, with true serene and most holy apostolic charity, that my soul may ever languish and melt with love and longing for you, that it may yearn for you and faint for your courts, and long to be dissolved and to be with you.

Grant that my soul may hunger after you, the bread of angels, the refreshment of holy souls, our daily and supernatural bread, having all sweetness and savor and every delight of taste;

let my heart hunger after and feed upon you, upon whom the angels desire to look, and may my inmost soul be filled with the sweetness of your savor;

may it ever thirst after you, the fountain of life, the fountain of wisdom and knowledge, the fountain of eternal light, the torrent of pleasure, the richness of the house of God;

may it ever compass you, seek you, find you, run to you, attain you, meditate upon you, speak of you and do all things to the praise and glory of your name, with humility and discretion, with love and delight, with ease and affection, and with perseverance unto the end;

may you alone be ever my hope, my entire assistance, my riches, my delight, my pleasure, my joy, my rest and tranquility, my peace, my sweetness, my fragrance, my sweet savor, my food, my refreshment, my refuge, my help, my wisdom, my portion, my possession and my treasure, in whom may my mind and my heart be fixed and firm and rooted immovably, henceforth and forever.

Amen.

Other Popular Personality Tests

Some personality tests can be misunderstood and manipulated. They can also be erroneous or even heretical. Others have become popular in our churches and workplaces. Each is rooted in the classic four temperaments — some loosely based, some watered down, and some so convoluted it would drive even a Melancholy mad. Over the years I've taken and tested most of them and have found that sticking to the basics is best.

Meyer-Briggs (MBTI): Are you INFJ? ESTP? In 1942 a mother and daughter (Katharine Briggs and Isabel Briggs Meyer) took Carl Jung's archetypes and created a system for sorting a possible combination of sixteen (and up to sixty-four) different "personality types." It essentially subdivides the four temperament traits into smaller segments and then tries to piece them together to make new, more specific combinations. Although a pretty solid model, it does not clearly distinguish between natural and learned behaviors, masking, and the effects of maturity and grace. Those of us who are *both* introvert and extrovert will have trouble fitting neatly into either of their "I" or their "E" categories.

Clifton Strength Finders: This popular method simply focuses on a person's natural strengths. It's helpful in that it offers thirty-four basic strengths (including responses and ways of thinking) that stem from the temperaments and helps people determine their top five. But we know that different temperaments can share strengths; for instance, both Choleric and Sanguine tend to be "Activators." We also must remember that strengths can also be natural, learned, or hidden behind a mask.

DISC Personality Testing: This is a secular business place testing model. It is not as nuanced as but is generally based on the four temperaments. It identifies four main personality types: Dominant (Choleric), Inspiring (Sanguine), Supportive (Phlegmatic), and Cautious (Melancholy).

The Big Five: The Big Five personality test consists of five general traits: extroversion, neuroticism, openness, agreeableness, and conscientiousness (John and Srivastava, 1999). You'll see the four temperaments all over this but, like other models, it does not go into the clarifications and nuances necessary for a fuller understanding of what makes us tick.

The Enneagram: This test cannot be reconciled to the four temperaments and has been condemned by the USCCB (2000).[‡] Still, it gains popularity every few decades. But it is based on numerology and the occult, not the early Desert Fathers as some claim. It was introduced to the modern world in 1915 by occultists and contains just enough truth to be seductive. In the pontifical document *Jesus Christ, the Bearer of the Water of Life: A Christian Reflection on the "New Age,"* we are cautioned that "when used as a means of spiritual growth [the Enneagram] introduces an ambiguity (half-truths) in the doctrine and the life of the Christian faith." We should avoid it.

There are many more such tests, but our original model, tempered and matured over the centuries, stands above them and has been validated by centuries of use by wise — even bril-

‡Draft from the U.S. bishops' Secretariat for Doctrine and Pastoral Practices, "A Brief Report on the Origins of the Enneagram." http://www.natcath.org/NCR_Online/documents/ennea2.htm.

liant — and holy saints and scientists.

One more important reason to stick with the classic four temperaments? They give us greater freedom. All personality models create "boxes" into which one may fit. It may sound like the more types or boxes, the more accurate the theory. But the opposite is true: Once we close the door to other types and squeeze ourselves into one of nine, sixteen, or even smaller boxes, we further restrict the fullness of who we are. Within the fewer, bigger boxes of the four temperaments, there is much more freedom and room for individuality and diversity. And let's face it: Four are much easier to remember.

Works Cited

"Are You a Heretic? Distorted God Images Catholics Hold." *Souls & Hearts*, September 14, 2022. https://www.soulsandhearts.com/blog/are-you-a-heretic-distorted-god-images-catholics-hold/.

Augustine of Hippo. *The Confessions of Saint Augustine*. Peter Pauper Press, 1940, 1949.

———. *Enchiridion.*

Aumann, Jordan. *Spiritual Theology*. Bloomsbury Continuum, 2019.

Catechism of the Catholic Church, 2nd ed. Libreria Editrice Vaticana, 1997.

Catherine of Genoa. *The Life and Doctrine of St. Catherine of Genoa*. Christian Press Association, 1907.

Chesterton, G. K. *The Dumb Ox*, 1933.

Conquer, Will. *Carlo Acutis: A Millennial in Paradise*. Sophia Institute Press, 2021.

Huguet, Rev. Pere. *Consoling Thoughts on Trials of an Interior Life*. TAN Books, 2013.

John Paul II, Pope. General Audience. January 9, 1980. vatican.va.

———. "Analogy of Spousal Love Indicates the Radical Character of Grace." General Audience. September 29, 1982.

———. "Dialogue with Young People at the Parc des Princes." Paris. June 1, 1980.

Kipling, Rudyard. "If," in *Rewards and Fairies*. Doubleday, Page & Company, 1910.

Matousek, Mark. "The Meeting Eyes of Love: How Empathy Is Born In Us." *Psychology Today*, April 8, 2011. https://www.psychologytoday.com/us/blog/ethical-wisdom/201104/the-meeting-eyes-love-how-empathy-is-born-in-us.

Pontifical Council for Culture, Pontifical Council for Interreligious Dialogue. *Jesus Christ, the Bearer of the Water of Life: A Christian Reflection on the "New Age."* Vatican.va.

Schuster, Sarah. "The 4 Trauma Responses: Fight, Flight, Freeze, and Fawn." *Health*, October 17, 2023. https://www.health.com/fight-flight-freeze-fawn-8348342.

Sheen, Bishop Fulton J. *The Cross and the Beatitudes*. Liguori Publications, 2000.

Stanford Blood Center. "Blood Types." https://stanfordbloodcenter.org/donate-blood/blood-donation-facts/blood-types/.

Sweet, Rose. *A Catholic Woman's Guide to Romance*. TAN Books, 2019.

———. *A Catholic Woman's Guide to Happiness*. TAN Books, 2018.

Teresa of Ávila. *Interior Castle*. Translated and edited by E. Allison Peers. Doubleday, 1961.

Thomas Aquinas, *Summa Theologiae.*

Zanolini, Ida. *Storia Meravigliosa: Santa Giuseppina Bakhita*, 1931.

About the Author

Rose Sweet is a certified (Fowler International Academy of Professional Coaching) life and relationship coach, who has studied, worked with, written about, and spoken on the classic Four Temperaments for over thirty years. Rose is all about relationships and has authored fourteen books on the healing and strengthening of relationships and coauthored *PERSONALITY PLUS at Work* with Florence Littauer. She has appeared as a popular guest on Catholic radio and television, been a keynote speaker at national and international Catholic conferences, and led parish missions, which included talks on the temperaments. She has created relationship video content for Catholic Match, developed parish video programs on healing after divorce, and served as a Catholic retreat leader across the country. Rose is married, has adult children, and lives in Palm Desert, CA, where she continues to provide personal coaching and retreats to Catholics. Her website is https://www.rosesweet.com.